RAZA STUDIES

Raza Studies
The Public Option for Educational Revolution

Edited by
JULIO CAMMAROTA AND
AUGUSTINE ROMERO

Foreword by
DAVID STOVALL

THE UNIVERSITY OF
ARIZONA PRESS

TUCSON

I would like to thank Mom, Dad, Raul Edgardo, Talisa Dian, and my wife Eydie for all the love.
   Augustine Romero

I would like to thank my family for their support throughout the creation of this book, especially my wife, Rebecca.
   Julio Cammarota

The University of Arizona Press
© 2014 The Arizona Board of Regents
All rights reserved

www.uapress.arizona.edu

Library of Congress Cataloging-in-Publication Data

Raza studies : the public option for educational revolution / edited by Julio Cammarota and Augustine Romero ; foreword by David Stovall.
   pages cm
   Includes bibliographical references and index.
   ISBN 978-0-8165-3079-3 (pbk. : alk. paper)
   1. Mexican American children—Education—Arizona—Tucson. 2. Mexican Americans—Study and teaching—Arizona—Tucson. 3. Tucson Unified School District (Pima County, Ariz.) 4. Critical pedagogy. I. Cammarota, Julio, editor of compilation. II. Romero, Augustine, editor of compilation.
   LC2688.T68 R39
   371.829'680791776—dc23
                                                                 2013034409

Publication of this book is made possible in part by the proceeds of a permanent endowment created with the assistance of a Challenge Grant from the National Endowment for the Humanities, a federal agency.

♻
   Manufactured in the United States of America on acid-free, archival-quality paper containing a minimum of 30% post-consumer waste and processed chlorine free.

19 18 17 16 15 14   6 5 4 3 2 1

Contents

List of Illustrations	vii
Foreword: Committing to Struggle in Troubling Times DAVID STOVALL	ix
Preface: Revolutionary Education in Tucson AUGUSTINE ROMERO	xiii
Introduction: Paulo Freire in Raza Studies JULIO CAMMAROTA AND AUGUSTINE ROMERO	3
1. Critically Compassionate Intellectualism: The Pedagogy of Barriorganic Intellectualism AUGUSTINE ROMERO	14
2. Lies, Damn Lies, and Statistics: The Impact of Mexican American Studies Classes NOLAN L. CABRERA	40
3. The Battle for Educational Sovereignty and the Right to Save the Lives of Our Children AUGUSTINE ROMERO	52
4. Self-Inflicted Reductio ad Absurdum: Pedagogies and Policies of the Absurd in the State of Arizona MARY CAROL COMBS	63
5. "When You Know Yourself You're More Confident": Resilience and Stress of Undergraduate Students in the Face of Anti–Ethnic Studies Bills ANDREA J. ROMERO AND ANNA OCHOA O'LEARY	91

Contents

6. The Social Justice Education Project:
   Youth Participatory Action Research in Schools ... 107
   JULIO CAMMAROTA

7. Encuentros with Families and Students: Cultivating Funds
   of Knowledge through Dialogue ... 122
   JULIO CAMMAROTA AND AUGUSTINE ROMERO

8. Researching the Institute for Transformative Education:
   Critical Multicultural Education in an Embattled State ... 135
   LARA DOS PASSOS COGGIN

9. Deconstructing the Doublethink Aimed at Dismantling
   Ethnic Studies in Tucson ... 159
   JEFF DUNCAN-ANDRADE

10. Expanding on Freire: Enriching Critical Pedagogy
    with Indigenous Theory toward a Pedagogy of Humanization ... 171
    CHIARA CANNELLA

    Contributors ... 193
    Index ... 197

Illustrations

Figures

2.1.	Improvement in AIMS passing rate, 2010 graduating cohort	45
4.1.	The Language Star: The Five Components of Arizona's English Language Development Program	69
4.2.	What English Language Development is NOT According to the Arizona Department of Education	70
4.3.	How to Accelerate English Language Learning	70
4.4.	How to Learn English in One Year	71
5.1.	Interaction of level of stress and engaged coping with SB 1108	103

Tables

1.1.	Critically Compassionate Intellectualism Model of Transformative Education	18
2.1.	Initial AIMS Passing Rates, 2010 Graduating Cohort	43
2.2.	Non-MAS AIMS Final Passing Rates, 2010 Graduating Cohort	44
2.3.	Final AIMS Passing Rates, 2010 Graduating Cohort	44
2.4.	Rates of AIMS Passing Improvement, 2010 Graduating Cohort	46
2.5.	Graduation Rate Differences, TUSD 2010 Graduating Cohort	46
2.6.	Graduation Rate Differences, TUSD 2010 Graduating Cohort by SES	47

2.7.	Tucson Magnet High School, MAS and AP Class Size	48
4.1.	Time Allocations for Elementary School Levels	73
4.2.	Time Allocations for Middle School and High School	74
4.3.	How English Is Taught through the Discrete Skills Inventory (An Example)	75
4.4.	Gray versus Brown Cultural Generation Gap	79
4.5.	Metropolitan Areas with the Largest Cultural Generation Gaps	80
4.6.	*Arizona Republic* Poll of Voter Support and Opposition to SB 2010	81
5.1.	Description of Demographic Sample	97
5.2.	Variables Used to Determine Engaged Coping and Disengagement	98
5.3.	*t*-Test Values for Ethnic Group Differences in Variables of Interest	99
5.4.	Pearson Product Moment Correlations between Variables of Interest by Ethnic Group	100
5.5.	Multiple Linear Regression Analyses for Responses to SB 1108 by Ethnic Group	102

Foreword

Committing to Struggle in Troubling Times

David Stovall

> *During the curriculum audit period, no observable evidence was present to suggest that any classroom within Tucson Unified School District is in direct violation of the law ARS 15-112C(A). Schools associated with Mexican American Studies Department courses promote a culture of excellence and support a safe and orderly environment conducive to learning. Teachers collectively are building nurturing relationships with students and work to improve student achievement and attendance. . . . A culture of respect exists and students receive additional assistance beyond the regular classroom instruction to support their academic learning.*
> CURRICULUM AUDIT OF MEXICAN AMERICAN STUDIES DEPARTMENT, TUCSON UNIFIED SCHOOL DISTRICT, MAY 2, 2011, 63

If you were unfamiliar with schools in the Tucson Unified School District (TUSD), the aforementioned epigraph would appear supportive and affirming. Nevertheless, despite the clear language of the independent audit performed by National Academic Learning Partners, which was commissioned by the Arizona Department of Education, the findings of the report have been dismissed by the department. Instead, members of the Arizona legislature, in support of the Department of Education, have engaged in subtle and overt warfare against a particular group of students, teachers, parents, and central office administrators in Tucson, Arizona. Whether it comes in the language of HB 2281, which is now Arizona law ARS 15-112(A) or HB 1070 (legalizing the profiling of suspected undocumented residents), it should be understood as an onslaught against Latinas/os in the state.

For the purposes of this foreword, I do not use the terms "warfare" or "onslaught" lightly. I move toward this terminology because the women and men of the Ethnic Studies Department in TUSD and the Social Justice Education Project (SJEP) are in a collective battle for their lives—not in terms of their individual employment as teachers in the district, but of a struggle for justice in education. As a collective body, they are under attack. Whether it comes from current governor Jan Brewer, former superintendent of public instruction Tom Horne, current superintendent of public instruction John Huppenthal, or certain members of the TUSD governing board, the Ethnic Studies Department has been positioned as a pariah in Arizona public education.

Accusations of separatism, dissemination of materials harmful to the US government, and anti-American sentiment are unfounded. Despite accusations in the local courts, state legislature, and in the court of public opinion, the Ethnic Studies Department of TUSD is not hell-bent on destroying the US government or killing white people. Instead, they are concerned with providing a holistic education for students within the district, focusing on their humanization by teaching them how to respect others. As the result of their efforts, many students, from myriad ethnic and socioeconomic backgrounds, have collectively decided to demand that the district guarantee a quality education for all students, particularly those who have experienced almost two centuries of disinvestment and marginalization.

Despite these realities, HB 2281 passed the Arizona legislature, effectively declaring TUSD's ethnic studies program illegal. The case is dubious at best, but reflects a process of white supremacy embedded in policy retrenchment and the politics of fear. The mere fact that students have made a conscious decision to stand for justice regarding their education through research and action sends chills through the veins of those in power. Instead of fleeing from this fact, Julio Cammarota and Augustine Romero challenge us to think deeply regarding the times we live in. As active participants in the ethnic studies program in TUSD and originators of SJEP, they dare to venture to another world: a world of possibility, hope, and struggle.

Through the foundational concepts of Tezcatlipoca (an indigenous word meaning reflection), Quetzalcoatl (precious knowledge), Huitzilopochtli (the will to act), and Xinachtli (nurturing the seeds of knowledge), students in ethnic studies courses are taken through a process that challenges them to look at themselves from an alternative perspective. Instead of the imposed false one-dimensional stereotypes that plague our young people (gang banger, drug dealer, hypersexed female, loud, ignorant, etc.), the foundational concepts allow students to ask questions regarding how these stereotypes become ingrained in our understanding and the steps needed to undo that type of thinking. Contrary to popular belief, this process does not include indoctrinating a cadre of students of color who hate white people. On the contrary, the focus is to develop a sense of self-worth and commitment to help others. The idea is that if young people see themselves as valuable, they are less likely to engage in behavior that jeopardizes the life of another. In addition to reflection, "In Lak'ech" translates to "you are my other me." To incorporate this into one's value system is to begin the process of transformation.

To my knowledge, no student, regardless of race, class, ethnicity, sexuality, or ability, has ever been denied entry to an ethnic studies course. In fact, ethnic studies teachers in TUSD go out of their way to demonstrate that all students are welcome. In schools where ethnic studies courses are taught, they have the highest demand of any course. More importantly, these schools record the highest achievement gains of students of color in the district. For these reasons, it has always been puzzling to me why the district would attempt to destroy a program that records some of the highest achievement gains in the state. Wouldn't it serve as a beacon of light for a district that has historically underserved students of color? Wouldn't they try to falsely take credit for the work of the Ethnic Studies Department and claim that they were doing something for low-income students of color? After my brief moment of puzzlement, I am reminded of a sordid history of white supremacy, containment, isolation, and marginalization of students of color in public education. To use an idiom passed on by elders in African American communities, it is "too much like right." Translated: because the proper thing to do is so simple, the powers that be will not let it happen because it would resemble justice too closely. It is quite right for certain groups (read descendants of white Western Europeans) to stand up for their rights. It becomes a problem when members of the "wrong" group (i.e., people of color) decide to stand for justice. Following in lockstep with the construct of colonialism, fear rises in the heart of the rulers at the threat of the colonized beginning to understand, critique, and oppose colonization.

In my own investigation and observation of the work of SJEP and ethnic studies in TUSD, I am continually impressed with the commitment of the teachers, students, families, and supportive administrators. Over the past ten years I have completed a program review of ethnic studies with my colleague Jeffrey Duncan-Andrade, highlighting areas that were strong and those in need of improvement. To their credit, the Ethnic Studies Department delivered in all of the areas marked for improvement. In our interviews with students, teachers, families, and administrators, all spoke of a clarity that the department brought to their understanding. Not because the teachers were some anointed group of education saviors, but due to their understanding of themselves as people committed to justice and improvement of their practice as teachers. Teachers from the Ethnic Studies Department understand that they are not missionaries with the duty to save the downtrodden. Instead, they understand their role as teachers to be members of the community they serve, through humility, reflection, and practice. In their practice, teaching is as much the process of facilitating engagement as it is the process of self-development. The teacher stands in solidarity with the student—not distant from their realities, but connected to their human condition because all are in the struggle for a better way. Not in the hokey sense of thinking a hug will wash all the pain away, but in the critical sense of coupling that hug with developing strategies to physically and materially address a troubling situation. If this was the foundational core of teacher training programs, I posit that we would have a different set of educational outcomes.

Simultaneously, I have also participated in the TUSD and the University of Arizona's Institute for Transformative Education as a keynote speaker and workshop presenter. Every summer I am encouraged to improve my practice as a secondary classroom teacher and a college professor by observing the practices of ethnic studies teachers and students in SJEP. Ranging from essays and poetry produced in ethnic studies classrooms to strategies designed to confront educational injustice, their work is a testament to the possibilities for the education of students of color in urban spaces. Instead of standardized test scores, the gains made in ethnic studies courses, beginning with self-worth, allow students to develop the necessary confidence to engage whatever assessment measures the state places in front of them. To their credit, students have met and exceeded goals set forth by the state. Yet again the state of Arizona wallows in absurdity and fear. Again, it is just too much like right.

In closing, I am beyond honored to write this foreword for my comrades in struggle. They are the shining examples for what is possible in education. As long as I am on this side of the soil, my heart, body, and soul are with them.

Preface

Revolutionary Education in Tucson

Augustine Romero

Classroom Visit: A Visit by an Unknown Brother

It was late April 2002, and I was getting ready to have my students go through an exercise wherein they evaluate the historical and modern-day impact of the Fourteenth Amendment, rewriting it in a way that creates greater equity for historically oppressed ethnic and social groups. As the students were rushing in, I saw the principal, Dr. Tom Scarborough, in the doorway. I immediately thought, "Oh shit, what did I do now?" In most cases, the only time Dr. Scarborough came around was for evaluations or when I said something or offered a lesson or exercise that someone, usually a conservative (anti-intellectual) teacher, complained about.

Dr. Scarborough immediately said that he had brought someone by to observe my class. This was not unusual. Even back then people would request to come by or Dr. Scarborough or someone from the central office or the college of education would request a class visit. However, the visit on this day would turn out to be most unusual. Dr. Scarborough introduced me to Dr. Julio Cammarota and said they wanted to observe my class. I of course obliged the request. As we had many times before, my students and I did our thing. We dialogued and we pushed each other to go beyond low-level or superficial thoughts. The students made numerous arguments regarding the white-black binary, and how they as Chicanos or Mexican Americans and their communities and ancestors have not experienced the same level of access and opportunity as the vast majority of whites and some blacks. I recall one student that I will call Santos Angelo stating, "I do not want to make this a competition or create problems with my black brothers, but when people think about racism they usually think about whites being racist toward blacks. Most of the time people do not realize the racism whites put Chicanas/os through." That was a pretty good explanation of the white-black binary.

After the class, Dr. Cammarota stated that he enjoyed the session, and that he would like to get together for coffee. I said that I would be happy to join him. For the next few minutes we talked about critical race theory. Dr. Cammarota said he had not thought about using it in a high school classroom. I told him that I had been using it the classroom for the past seven years, and the students drew genuinely strong connections between critical race theory and their own lives. We agreed to get together.

Café y Teoría Revolucionaria

A week or so later, we met at a café near the University of Arizona. The first part of our conversation focused on who we were and what we believed in. He discovered that the two of us were not necessarily the greatest high school students, which led both of us to the community college to start our academic careers. Also, we shared the same passion to find out how to better serve students like ourselves who had strong academic capacities but were intentionally let down by a system constructed to marginalize, exclude, or exploit us as a means of perpetuating America's racial and social order (Delgado 1999; Romero 2008).

This led to a conversation about our intellectual influences: Freire, Darder, Fanon, Said, Bell, Delgado, Spivak, Derrida, Foucault, Kuhn, Bell, Tollefson, hooks, funds of knowledge, critical pedagogy, and critical race theory. This conversation took us to our shared belief that we could create an educational setting wherein students became scientists studying their social conditions. We both recognized that students' intellectual capacities and knowledge construction capacities have been grossly underestimated, and in most cases intentionally ignored and subverted.

We talked about how the communities from which our marginalized students derive are fertile with intellectualism, blossoming with the capacity to engender intellectual ability, and ripe for intellectual pursuit. Unlike our larger society, we believed that the communities of the historically marginalized and exploited are filled with intellectualism. Julio and I left this meeting knowing that we wanted to work together. We agreed that we should get together soon.

An Opportunity to Transform and Revolutionize Education

In between meetings with Julio, I met with Dr. Becky Montaño, who at the time was TUSD's deputy superintendent. During our meeting, she asked if I would take over the district's Hispanic Studies Department (changed in 2002 to Mexican American/Raza Studies, and changed again in 2008 to Mexican American Studies). Dr. Montaño stated that given the mandates of No Child Left Behind, the district needed to close the achievement gap for Latino students. She had mentioned this in a previous meeting. She then said that as the program director it would be my responsibility to design a program that would close the achievement gap between Latinos and Anglos. I told Dr. Montaño, "I can do this."

This assignment gave me carte blanche in the design of this program; it opened the door for the creation of the Social Justice Education Project (SJEP); it gave me license to leave my own thumbprint on the curriculum and pedagogy; and it created the opportunity to rethink and re-create our continuing education opportunities for teachers (Redemptive Rememberings and the Institute for Transformative Education). To say the least, this was an incredibly exciting time.

Café Mocha y Revolución Educativa

I remember rushing to the second meeting with Julio in total excitement about the news I was going to share. We met again at the same café. It was warm in early summer, but unlike most days the heat did not bother me. All I wanted to do was get the work started.

Julio and I exchanged greetings, and I immediately stated, "I have good news." I told him about my meeting with Dr. Montaño. Right away he cracked a big smile, saying, "Do you know what this means?" I said, "We have our project." Right then we started to formalize our thoughts about what it was that we wanted to create. One of the things we immediately agreed upon was that we were not going to dumb down the curriculum. What many people have failed to understand, but what we both knew from past experience, is that if teachers want to maximize the cognitive demands (rigor) we place on students, they must be relevant—a deeper sense of relevance than is included in the standard educational literature (International Center of Leadership in Education). For us it was critical that we create pedagogical and curricular artifacts out of the lived condition of our students. This meant that we needed to problematize their lived condition (Freire 1994). This was also where we could construct rigor. Unlike the mainstream understanding of rigor, we construct rigor through the lens of being liberatory or revolutionary educators. It is this lens that helped us understand and respect the intellectualism of the students, and through this process we also recognized the importance of helping more students understand that the world does not have to be stagnant, rigid, or preordained. On the contrary, we hoped to help our students realize that our world is a space of transformation. More importantly, we hoped to help them recognize and understand that they are the agents of this transformation, which raises hope, which in turn continues to increase both transformation and hope.

We understood that the intellectualized (rigorous) process of problem posing (Yosso 2006) and cycle of critical praxis (Duncan-Andrade and Morrell 2008) empower students to create an educational opportunity that is both truly relevant and rigorous. Both of these processes require the highest levels of intellectual engagement (see Bloom et al. 1956) and the highest threshold of relevance. In short, both processes require a significant amount of evaluation, synthesis, and creativity, and our definition of relevance is how subjects are directly relevant to the lived condition of our students. Above and beyond the mainstream paradigm, we believed that these processes offer an elevated sense of empowerment for our students by giving them an opportunity to name, challenge, and begin the process of overcoming their lived structures of oppression.

This was the basis of our conversation during this meeting. We knew that our students would rise to this opportunity. We talked about how this project needed to be truly revolutionary and emancipatory, and stated then that we could not apologize for these pursuits, and that regardless of what happens we would never compromise the mission and calling. It may seem kind of silly, but we actually shook hands and promised each other that we would pursue this mission *con sangre*.

Bringing My *Camarada* into the Mix

As we started to construct this experience, we needed a place to house the project, and we needed to partner with the right teacher. I had one in mind, who I knew would be the perfect match, Lorenzo Lopez Jr. He was a graduate of the high school where we housed the project, and he had been a teacher there for three academic years. During the 1999–2000 school year, I was Lorenzo's cooperating teacher, and during our semester together I found him to be highly motivated, incredibly intelligent, and decidedly relevant. However, Lorenzo's primary asset was how easily the students connected to him. His authentic, caring, and nurturing nature drew students to him. They knew he was a real person who was interested in who they were, and they caught the sense that he truly cared about their well-being.

As time went on Lorenzo and I shared many lunchtime conversations, in which I grew to appreciate Lorenzo's decision to become an educator. I grew to appreciate him as a man with strong convictions, a strong sense of service, and a strong sense of community. It was easy to see, feel, and understand why Lorenzo had decided to become a teacher, and why he chose to teach at his alma mater.

For Lorenzo to return to Cholla was much like my return to Tucson High (my alma mater) five years earlier. It was a return home. We were not taking a job; we were coming back to invest in the future of our community, to return to the place that had let us down, the place that had historically failed our community, our parents, our *tíos* and *tías*, our *primos* and *primas*, our *vecinos*, and our children in the current condition. This return became our small battle to change things for as many students as possible.

Moving the Vision to Fruition

After the meetings with Julio and Larry, I met with Dr. Montaño to share the proposal that Julio and I put together. I gave a short description of our plan of the SJEP and she asked a few questions. I remember leaving that meeting not quite sure what to think. Dr. Montaño did not seem as excited as she had been during other meetings.

I called Julio and told him about our upcoming meeting with Dr. Montaño, also mentioning my concern about her demeanor. Julio agreed that we needed to be extremely sharp for the upcoming meeting. Over the next week Julio and I met twice.

About twenty minutes before our meeting Julio showed up at the office and I said, "There is no way she is not going to like this proposal." Nevertheless, we were nervous as we entered Dr. Montaño's office. As soon as we sat down, she said, "Tell me about this idea." She added, "I have read the proposal, but I want to hear your thoughts." Julio jumped right in with the idea that remedial education has failed because of its repressive and stereotypical (mis)understanding of children it has relegated to the margins and the bottom rungs of our society (Delgado 1995, 1999). I added that in a hypercapitalist society the very same people have been exploited for profit (Delgado 1995; Cass 2005). I went on to say that these (mis)understandings have constructed extremely low expectations of our historically underserved children. We intended to flip that paradigm on its head. We intended to elevate the curriculum, and we intended to make it relevant by superimposing it upon their social conditions and lived experiences. Julio brought up our ideas about youth participatory action research (see chapter 6; Cammarota and Romero 2006, 2011; Cammarota 2011) and how through this methodology we believed that we could drastically elevate the level of relevance; because of this relevance we could dramatically increase rigor; and, most importantly, because we believed that these children have the capacity to create knowledge (Delgado Bernal 2002; Romero 2008), we could give them the opportunity to represent themselves as intellectuals (Romero 2008).

We went on to talk about how we would incorporate elements of the funds of knowledge (Gonzalez, Moll, and Amanti 1994), Freirean methodologies (Freire 1994), our understanding of authentic caring (Valenzuela 1999), how critical race theory could be used to design curriculum (Yosso 2002), how we could help our students reframe and transform the praxis with regard to the status quo (Solórzano and Delgado Bernal 2001), and how this project could create the opportunity for our students to construct counterstories (Delgado 1989). We believed that it was critical that our students rewrite the hegemonic narrative that has been written about them. This project would give them the opportunity to tell their own stories, to insert themselves into the curriculum, and to construct learning around their understanding, their realities, and their needs.

In the end, Dr. Montaño's response was, "When could we get started?" We decided to start in the fall of 2002, and she agreed that Cholla high school would be a good place for the project. She asked us to set up a meeting with the Cholla administration as soon as possible. She concluded by saying, "If you have any trouble, come back and see me."

Overcoming and Educating the Naive Consciousness

Previously Julio and I had talked to Dr. Scarborough about the SJEP. He liked the idea and was prepared to implement it at Cholla. However, by the time we received the blessing of Dr. Montaño, Dr. Scarborough had retired and new leadership was in place. This meeting with Cholla leadership was rocky. None of these folks understood youth participatory action research, critical pedagogy, funds of knowledge, cultural studies, critical race theory, or any of the elements of truly transformative education. In fact, most of this leadership team operated from a deficit discourse orientation.

After many questions and a lot of explaining, one of the administrators expressed his primary perspective by saying, "Auggie, what are we going to do with twenty-five or thirty kids running around here pointing out problems? We can't have that type of thing going on." Beyond the issues of engagement and relevance shown by this scenario, at a minimum the expectation of the administration is to fix educational issues, especially those that have created barriers for students learning and the pathway to academic success. So my response to this administrator was, quite simply, "Fix the problems."

Needless to say, at this point the project did not have a home. As she instructed, I went directly to Dr. Montaño. Fortunately for our students, she was able to convince the administration to green-light the project. We started the SJEP with Lorenzo Lopez Jr. and seventeen of our students on the first day of school in August 2002. What a blessing.

La Creación de Critically Compassionate Intellectualism

We were blessed in that we were able to implement all of the theoretical and academic elements we talked about in those early meetings at the café. We had borrowed all these pieces from the theories and practices of others and we had many of our own theories and practices that we knew to be successful. But while these pieces as an aggregate created a new experience, we had not formally named or defined this experience.

On a warm day in early May I walked into our classroom when I was not scheduled to be there. I arrived before the students so that I could talk to Lopez about an idea I had. After a short conversation Lopez said, "Go for it."

As the kids walked in, many said things like, "Romero, what are doing here?" or "You are here on the wrong day, Romero." I remember one saying, "Romero, you are confused. You aren't supposed to be here until tomorrow." We laughed and I said, "I got it right because I am here with a huge purpose."

We got settled in and I stood and said, "I've got one question for you. Why are you still here?" At first the students looked confused. I threw it out again. "Why are you still here? Why do you still come to this class? We have been working all year, and we want to know why you come to this class." It took a few seconds, but the responses started flowing, and as they came I wrote them on the board.

The primary theme was "what you teach us," which I formally named SJEP curriculum. For this theme students responded with statements such as, "You guys teach us about us, about our culture, about our history. You guys teach us how we can change things, and you guys teach us how we can stand up for ourselves and our *gente*." The next theme was "how you teach us." I labeled these responses as SJEP pedagogy. The responses for this theme were, "You let us talk out things. We can talk with guys about the things we are learning. We can ask real questions, important questions. You guys really want us to think. You guys want us to find our answers. You let us connect things (academics and social realities) together, and you want us to find the root of the problem." The last theme that emerged from this dialogue was "how you guys treat us and our parents." I labeled this SJEP parent-student-teacher interactions. For this theme students said, "You guys understand us. You relate to us. There is respect in here. Man, all you guys care about us—we can tell. My dad likes you. He feels respected by you all. My mom feels respect too. It's like you guys appreciate us and our families. You guys don't trip on things. I think this is because you understand us and what we are going through. My parents don't feel down with you guys, and there is *cariño* with you guys."

It was this dialogue that became the framework of the critically compassionate intellectualism model and how we did things in raza studies. This understanding manifested itself in our redemptive rememberings, in the restructuring of our teacher institute (the Institute for Transformative Education), in our Ce Ollin Parent Encuentros, and most importantly in the everyday classroom experience of all the students we serve. It is important that we thank Adelita Grijalva and Kim Dominguez for their contribution in our struggle for academic excellence and equity.

References

Bloom, B. S., M. D. Engelhart, E. J. Furst, W. H. Hill, and D. R. Krathwohl. 1956. *Taxonomy of Educational Objectives: The Classification of Educational Goals.* New York: Longmans, Green.

Cammarota, J. 2011. "From Hopelessness to Hope: Social Justice Pedagogy in Urban Education and Youth Development." *Urban Education* 46(4): 828–844.

Cammarota, J. and A. Romero. 2006. "A Critically Compassionate Pedagogy for Latino Youth." *Latino Studies* 4(3): 305–12.

———. 2009. "A Social Justice Epistemology and Pedagogy for Latina/o Students: Transforming Public Education with Participatory Action Research." *New Directions for Youth Development* 9(123): 53–65.

———. 2011. "Participatory Action Research for High School Students: Transforming Policy, Practice, and the Personal with Social Justice Education." *Educational Policy* 25(3): 488–506.

Cass, J. 2005. "Dismantling the Cradle to Prison Pipeline Draft." *Children's Defense Fund* (April): xv.

Delgado, R. 1989. "Storytelling for Oppositionists and Others: A Plea for Narrative." *Michigan Law Review* 87: 2411–2441.

———. 1995. *The Rodrigo Chronicles: Conversations about America and Race.* New York: New York University Press.

———. 1999. *When Equality Ends.* Boulder, CO: Westview.

Delgado Bernal, D. 2002. "Critical Race Theory, Latino Critical Theory, and Critical Raced-Gendered Epistemologies: Recognizing Students of Color as Holders and Creators of Knowledge." *Qualitative Inquiry* 8(1): 105–126.

Duncan-Andrade, J., and E. Morrell. 2008. *The Art of Critical Pedagogy: Possibilities for Moving from Theory to Practice in Urban Schools.* New York: Peter Lang.

Freire, P. 1994. *Pedagogy of the Oppressed.* New York: Continuum.

Gonzalez, N., L. Moll, and C. Amanti. 2005. *Funds of Knowledge: Theorizing Practices in the Households, Communities and Classrooms.* Mahwah, NJ: Lawrence Erlbaum Associates.

Gonzalez, N., L. Moll, F. Tenery, A. Rivera, P. Rendon, R. Gonzales, and C. Amanti. 1995. "Funds of Knowledge for Teaching in Latino Households." *Urban Education* 29: 443–470.

Moll, L. C., C. Amanti, D. Neff, and N. González. 1992. "Funds of Knowledge for Teaching: Using a Qualitative Approach to Connect Homes and Classrooms." *Theory into Practice* 31(2): 132–41.

Romero, A. 2008. "Towards a Critically Compassionate Intellectualism Model of Transformative Education: Love, Hope, Identity, and Organic Intellectualism through the Convergence of Critical Race Theory, Critical Pedagogy, and Authentic Caring." Unpublished PhD diss., University of Arizona.

Solórzano, D., and D. Delgado Bernal. 2001. "Examining Transformational Resistance through a Critical Race Theory and LatCrit Theory Framework: Chicana and Chicano Students in an Urban Context." *Urban Education* 36(3): 308–342.

Valenzuela, A. 1999. *Subtractive Schooling: U.S.-Mexican Youth and the Politics of Caring.* Albany: State University of New York Press.

Yosso, T. 2002. "Toward a Critical Race Curriculum." *Equity and Excellence in Education* 35(2): 93–107.

———. 2006. *Critical Race Counterstories along the Chicana/Chicano Educational Pipeline.* New York: Routledge.

RAZA STUDIES

Introduction

Paulo Freire in Raza Studies

Julio Cammarota and Augustine Romero

In 2009, the Arizona State Senate held hearings on whether to pass a law, SB 1108, that would ban ethnic studies from public schools. Although SB 1108 was slated to wipe out ethnic studies across the state, the real target was Tucson Unified School District's Mexican American studies (MAS) department. The hearings included the questioning of some of the program's creators, namely, former MAS director Dr. Augustine Romero. State Senator John Huppenthal had specific questions for Dr. Romero on the use of Paulo Freire's *Pedagogy of the Oppressed* as a core textbook in the program. He was concerned that Freire was a Marxist and referenced other Marxists in the text, including Che Guevara, Fidel Castro, and, of course, Karl Marx. Romero responded by saying that while those individuals are indeed referenced in the text, the person from whom Paulo Freire drew most of his inspiration was Jesus Christ. Romero stated, "I am sure all of you are aware of the humanistic qualities of Jesus. Well, Paulo Freire wrote *Pedagogy of the Oppressed* with the same framework of humanism as Jesus." The senators did not know how to respond to Dr. Romero's statement.

Indeed, the story of *Pedagogy of the Oppressed* is one of humanism. Similarly, the story of Mexican American studies is based in humanism and the educational process of assisting students to fully realize their human goodness. *Raza Studies: The Public Option for Educational Revolution* follows in the tradition of critical pedagogies that educate for the benefit of humanity. It reports on young people's transformation from followers to leaders—a revolution, so to speak, of emergent intellectuals who now see their place in the world and strategies to achieve greater justice within their communities and school districts.

To achieve this transformation, students use *Pedagogy of the Oppressed* as a theoretical map to find new locations in which to challenge oppressive forces that prevent them from determining how they can contribute to improving the living conditions that the oppressor group has constructed for them. In the context of the MAS program, social and educational transformation is unlikely to happen without the map of liberation that Freire delineates for students and educators. The use of *Pedagogy of the Oppressed*, therefore, renders raza studies more than a program to teach young people academic skills. Certainly, students acquire advanced skills in reading, writing, and analysis, but they also learn to address the social, educational, and economic problems that hold people in oppressive and subordinated conditions and spaces. Raza studies is therefore a story not only of learning but also of critically progressive transformation, whereby students comprehend their roles as historical agents to promote, restore, and sustain generosity and compassion among humankind. Duncan-Andrade (2007) reaffirms our belief that to be effective pedagogues, to be caring humans, to be true teachers, we must connect rigorous academic content to the lives of our students. These connections of rigorous content, social conditions, and lived realities not only promote intellectualism but most importantly foster a sense of hope (Duncan-Andrade 2009; Romero 2008). We invite you to follow us in a journey through an educational process that leads to an engagement and embracing of humanity for the sake of improving life conditions for all.

About Paulo Freire

Educators and students alike find the work of Paulo Freire (1993, 1994, 1998a, 1998b) compelling because of his message of bettering ourselves by removing the ideological restraints that might suppress our creative spirit. According to Freire and other humanists, our true vocation as humans is to create and contribute to the positive development of our world. Freire (1998a, 75) states, "Education as the practice of freedom . . . denies that man is abstract, isolated, independent and unattached to the world; it also denies that the world exists as reality apart from people." Economic, educational, and political systems, however, prevent people from realizing their creative potential to engage the world by imposing oppressive forces that mask the true knowledge of their intellectual and human capacities. Thus, Freire thought that the primary emphasis of education should be to liberate people from oppression in order to attain a true sense of themselves as creative and intellectual beings who realize and engage the significance of their cultural agency in the world. Someone who enters into a liberating educational process "would begin to effect change in his or her former attitudes, by discovering himself or herself to be a maker of the world of culture, by discovering that he or she ... has a creative and re-creative impulse" (Freire 1998a, 85). It is in this creative capacity that students and teachers become creators and redeemers of humanity. This is the role and these are the true words wherein teachers and students fulfill their full humanity. They quite simply become the chance to save the lives of all students whose teachers engage in the creation of hope as an intellectual and liberatory project (Duncan-Andrade 2007, 2009).

Freire completed this work of redemption and liberation, like Jesus, among the most disenfranchised and marginalized—illiterate rural peasants. Working with this population, Freire clearly established himself as a humanitarian who hoped to better the conditions for people suffering from an oppressor group's exploitation. Those that see the value and purpose in helping the poor, oppressed, or downtrodden connect with the humanitarian aspects of Freire's work. He developed a fundamental educational philosophy that helps subordinate individuals reframe their subjectivities in a manner that fosters an understanding of the reality behind their subordination.

Freire called this approach "critical literacy," which establishes a process for reading educational, social, and economic circumstances to identify the problems that lead to limited possibilities and potential while maintaining the status quo within the social and economic order. He notably asserted that "reading" should not be limited to the word but also expanded to include a literacy of social and economic pressures that might prevent one from reaching one's full human and creative potential: "the literacy process must relate speaking the word to transforming reality, and to man's role in this transformation. Perceiving the significance of that relationship is indispensible for those learning to read and write if we are really committed to liberation. Such a perception will lead the learners to recognize a much greater right than that of being literate. They will ultimately recognize that, as men, they have a right to have a voice" (Freire 1998b, 486–487).

Reading and transforming the world require a change in consciousness, whereby we remove the ideological blinders through which our vision and understanding of the world are limited to the constructions of the oppressor group. This limited vision and understanding construct a reality without hope and without a sense of empowerment and emancipation.

Critical literacy elevates our consciousness to become aware of all the humanly produced inequalities and inequities that permit some of us to advance socially, politically, and economically while others remain deprived of opportunities and resources. The primary purpose of critical literacy is therefore to develop a critical understanding of how deprivation—in any way, shape, or form—sabotages our human potential to become creators of our world. This knowledge of deprivation leads to an awareness of how to articulate and demonstrate new ways of living with the greatest amount of peace, justice, and equity. "Learning to read and write has meaning in that, by requiring men and women to reflect about themselves and about the world they are in and with, it makes them discover that the world is also theirs, that their work is not the price they pay for being citizens but rather a way of loving—and of helping the world to be a better place" (Freire 1998a, 106).

The method to attain critical literacy is what Freire would call "praxis—critical reflection and action." This two-step method is a necessary couplet because critically reflecting on an object in one's social and economic context requires taking action to determine the conditions in which the object will undergo some type of change. Seeing how change occurs in one's reality awakens the possibility of critical consciousness. Freire (1998b, 515) argues that achieving critical consciousness happens not "through an intellectual effort alone, but through praxis—through the authentic union of action and reflection." The two-step method, according to Freire (1998b, 500), serves as the basic process for liberation: "Only beings who can reflect upon the fact that they are determined are capable of freeing themselves. Their reflectiveness results not just in a vague and uncommitted awareness, but in the exercise of a profoundly transforming action upon the determining reality."

Praxis to produce greater equity in educational experiences within a particular school would require not only thinking about how to establish equity but also real efforts to address the problems and structures fomenting inequities. In this way, engaging the inequities produces knowledge of how possibilities and conditions might change. This knowledge informs thinking and guides actions that construct possibilities and conditions of a new world. The outcome of praxis is an understanding that the transformation of content and context of the environments we inhabit is contingent upon human agency, and that all of us, when we attain critical consciousness, possess the agency to construct and transform the conditions of our lives.

Ultimately, praxis is achieved through dialogue. The role of education and the educator, therefore, is to generate dialogue so that teaching is not only a technical process of learning but also one of engaging people in conversation about their social realities and conditions. Freire (1998a, 89) asserts that instruction on the technical aspects of knowledge "is not difficult; the difficulty lies rather in the creation of a new attitude—that of dialogue, so absent in our own upbringing and education." Liberatory education is, on one hand, an interaction between teacher and students and, on the other, the action of spreading dialogue throughout multiple levels of society. Thus, dialogue should happen among the oppressed, between the oppressor and oppressed, and most importantly between the subject and object of one's social, political, and economic context.

In terms of the last dialogue, the subject is oneself, and the object includes the circumstances that shape human experience. When the self engages these circumstances, there is communication—a metaphorical talking to and speaking back—with the institutional and systematic forces that bear down on one's existence. This communication builds knowledge steeped in a social justice epistemology, which leads to a greater awareness of how to end the oppression causing human suffering, and, equally important, how to construct the conditions for social transformation (Romero 2008). Freire (1998b, 490) comments on how dialogue builds knowledge for transformation: "For dialogue to be a method for true knowledge, the knowing subjects must approach reality scientifically in order to seek the dialectic connections that explain the form of reality. Thus to know is not to remember something previously known and now forgotten. No[r] can doxa be overcome by logos apart from the dialectic relationship of man with his world, apart from men's reflective action upon the world." Dialogical praxis moves people beyond suffering to a place in which they become connected to their human potential to create, produce, and act upon their world.

Dialogue becomes revolutionary when it blossoms and strives toward inclusiveness so that interlocutors continuously address situations that prevent people from self-determination. Revolution is change, and therefore it is not a static process but a dynamic one. A dynamic dialogue parallels the natural process of change and ensures that the discussion follows the evolution of society. Revolutionary dialogue should move societal evolution in directions that allow people to determine who they want to be and how they want to contribute. An evolved society is not one in which people are told about themselves and what they should offer but one in which people maintain some control over determining their identities and potential.

Freire's hope was that education could be the stage for a revolutionary dialogue. Through learning in a critical way, we would achieve the knowledge to rearrange unequal social relationships while removing the possibility of domination. A world with domination foments exploitation and social and economic conditions that render survival difficult for some. An education based in revolutionary dialogue would address these conditions, helping people to go beyond survival and thrive with the potential to control their own destinies. This plan for revolution would happen with education and without losing a drop of blood.

A Revolution of Intellectualism

Raza studies students engage in critical literacy to understand the systematic and institutional forces that generate roadblocks preventing their progress. Through their newfound skill of critical literacy, students discover that the reasons for their failures, and in many cases the historical failures that have plagued their families and communities for generations, are much more complex than the simplistic explanations of apathy, cultural deficit, or genetic deficiencies. The students' elevated consciousness and heightened intellectualism expose the social, political, and economic structures that have been constructed to intentionally create and perpetuate their subordinate status. This knowledge of the origins of oppression helps students go beyond the socially constructed mechanism of self-blame for failure to a conscientious state wherein they realize the potential of their intellectualism. In our students' intellectual pursuits, they discover that their exploitation and subordination serve to perpetuate the interests of the oppressor group. In fact, what comes to light is that maintenance of the racial, social, political, and economic status quo is dependent upon the manufactured failure of our students (Romero 2008). This understanding is what truly helps our students take those first steps toward undoing the chains of intellectual oppression that have historically diminished the capacity for the realization of their truest and deepest potential.

A higher level of thinking provides young people with the analytical and cognitive skills to address problems in their own social context. For example, a young person may be challenged on a personal level at school. He may encounter hostility from an adult that pushes him into resisting education. Critical literacy helps our students understand how the type of resistance they engage in may be self-defeating. An example is a student who skips class because of an abusive or ineffective teacher or irrelevant curriculum. Skipping this class may be a form of resistance, but who benefits from this action? Has the student transformed the system by this action, or has this action created a benefit for the student, his or her family, or the community? In fact, if skipping class leads to failure, the student has simply perpetuated the status quo wherein children of color and poor children are supposed to fall to the wayside, in their appropriate places in our manufactured social order. We hope that our students achieve a higher form of learning, in which they understand that excelling at learning is one of the highest forms of resistance in which they can engage. Given this understanding, students can gauge their resistive actions. It is our hope that they choose actions that are transformative not only for themselves, but for their families and our communities. Students who carry out this understanding often not only realize and embrace their potential but use their talents to serve those around them.

The ability to assist others with their problems emerges only when one changes one's perspective to see the potential in oneself. In other words, after they understand how to improve conditions for themselves, students can improve life conditions for others. This two-step approach of transforming the self and then society is the ultimate goal of critical literacy. A revolution cannot happen without revolutionaries, and we cannot have revolutionaries without the liberation of the mind from the ideologies that suppress creativity and the potential for transformation.

Raza studies is this kind of intellectual revolution that focuses directly on liberating young minds from all the doubts and concerns about their capacity to make the world a more just, equitable, and hope-filled place for their families, their communities, and themselves. By introducing Paulo Freire's work within a raza studies context, we teach students that the struggle for improved educational, social, economic, and political conditions is not only for themselves, but for all. Raza studies breaks down the individualistic paradigm to show young people that important matters should not be limited to the individual. Rather, critical life concerns should extend beyond the individual to include families, communities, and societies. This broadening focus emerges from students' enhanced capacity to liberate themselves from the ideologies that ensconce them in their own immediate minutiae, while simultaneously unlocking their ability to see how life is not a singular or lone experience but a continuous and changing relationship to other people. The real revolution of raza studies is to nurture those epistemological and ontological shifts that teach or help young people to open their minds to the understanding that they can move past narrow individualistic concerns to broader humanistic ones that engender new possibilities and opportunities for those most marginalized.

This revolution of the mind is what Jesus, Freire, Marx, Guevara, or any other humanist would hope to manifest throughout all of human existence. A more just and peaceful world would emerge from people who thought less about themselves and more about others. In the end, we would hope that education would take up this important humanistic goal of altruism. Rather, individualism is the primary ideological paradigm shaping most goals and objectives in traditional education. Our schools teach young people to think only about how they can achieve personal gain. Raza studies operates under a humanistic paradigm in which students comprehend how to connect their personal interests with those of others in need. Therefore, their success is tied to the success of others in ways that help all to experience progress. Raza studies is the revolution we need to overcome the greed that makes us vulnerable, and places our accomplishments in harm's way. Education should follow the lead of raza studies by showing students how they can liberate themselves from the oppression in their lives, because it is in this liberated state that students can participate in the liberation of those around them.

Chapter Outline

Chapter 1, "Critically Compassionate Intellectualism," presents the theoretical convergence that brings humanistic practices to the classroom. Critically compassionate intellectualism (CCI), which combines critical race theory, critical pedagogy, and authentic caring, offers students a comprehensive educational approach that promotes their liberation from oppression while developing their intellectual capacities. Furthermore, chapter 1 highlights the voices of students as a method of conveying the impact of CCI in educational practices. Chapter 2, "Lies, Damn Lies, and Statistics," reveals how the implementation of CCI improves the academic performance of students who take MAS classes in comparison to those who do not. The political context of implementing CCI in the conservative and racist state of Arizona is delineated in chapter 3, "The Battle for Educational Sovereignty and the Right to Save the Lives of Our Children." In this chapter, community members, parents, and students struggle against state officials who feel threatened by the counterhegemonic narrative of raza studies and who implemented a ban on MAS. Chapter 4, "Self-Inflicted Reductio ad Absurdum," reveals how the ban on MAS is par for the course when considering the state's history of anti-Latino legislation and reactionary language policies. Chapter 5, "'When You Know Yourself You're More Confident,'" examines how legislative bills that propose banning MAS have negative psychological effects on college students. In chapter 6, "The Social Justice Education Project," students in raza studies engage in youth participatory action research to put into practice the Freirean approach of critical literacy and praxis. Raza students create and participate in their own original research projects to reflect critically on their schools and determine the best strategies for garnering equity in educational outcomes. Chapter 7, "Encuentros with Families and Students," examines how the Freirean revolutionary principle of dialogue leads to transformation when students and their families collaboratively discuss the historical circumstances that have marginalized their communities. Chapter 8, "Researching the Institute for Transformative Education," discusses the yearly professional development institute held to promote CCI among multicultural educators. Chapter 9, "Deconstructing the Doublethink," is an analysis of the state's discourse against ethnic studies and how certain statements are classic examples of doublespeak in the Orwellian sense. That is, the state of Arizona is trying to tell us that what we thought might be good for students is now bad, such as learning about oppression, closing the achievement gap, and implementing local control over schools. We conclude with chapter 10, "Expanding on Freire," which examines the intersection of Freirean critical pedagogy and indigenous theory and how intersectionality was brought to life in a social justice education project classroom. The chapters present a course offering various ruminations, criticisms, and practices that lead to an understanding of how to educate children who have experienced failure in the traditional education system.

Critical Pedagogy in the Classroom

The use of *Pedagogy of the Oppressed* in raza studies courses is simply about critical pedagogy. We hope to implement a method for learning in which students feel empowered to meet the expectations of becoming true humanitarians. Critical pedagogy lends itself to producing agents who feel capable of transforming circumstances to expand and promote justice and equity. Freire (1998, 492) asserts that a pedagogy based in a critical approach to reality "formulates a scientific humanist conception that finds its expression in a dialogic praxis in which the teachers and learners together, in the act of analyzing a dehumanizing reality, denounce it while announcing its transformation in the name of liberation."

At the core of critical pedagogy is the notion that we become better students or, more importantly, better people by participating in democratic structures for learning. These structures prepare students to treat others with kindness, fairness, and respect. In addition, people learn to contribute, share, and collaborate in ways that render knowledge something they generously and authentically offer as well as something generously and authentically offered to them.

The multilane street in which knowledge moves freely in various directions makes for an elevated intellectual environment that supports the development of everyone participating in raza studies and/or critical pedagogy. People develop their voices, ideas, and modes of perceiving their surroundings that encourage transformative actions for challenging injustices. They begin to see how failure is not the fault of the individual but is manufactured by social structures, political conditions, and economic systems. Individuals become aware that capacities are cultivated and not bequeathed at birth. Everyone has the potential to develop his or her capacities through education and over time.

Through a critical pedagogy that requires learners to become integral to classroom epistemology, students shift from perceiving themselves as unknowledgeable to knowledgeable. In other words, the students' knowledge and experiences represent the measure by which both educators and students understand what they know to be true and valid. When students are at the center of the epistemology, they begin to see themselves as the source and assessor of knowledge. These pivotal roles in the production of knowledge position students as emergent intellectuals who see their agency connected to the process of positive creation. Knowledge becomes a vehicle not only for the students' own personal intellectual development but also to facilitate their ability to be contributors who assist in the evolution of society. The student-derived epistemology changes the purpose of knowledge to humanitarianism in which the goal for learning is to improve the quality of life for all.

The goals for a critical pedagogy and raza studies seem like noble aspirations. But again, Freire saw himself as following in the footsteps of Jesus Christ. This righteous path guides people to perceive and understand that we are all equal in the eyes of our maker, and thus everyone should be treated equally. None should have more wealth and power than others. More importantly, none should have more knowledge than others. We should all share in the production and distribution of knowledge so that intellectualism is a matter of social justice. In other words, denying people their right to know is a grave form of oppression. By democratically sharing the responsibility of producing knowledge, we will make great strides in bringing justice to our world.

References

Duncan-Andrade, J. 2007. "Gangstas, Wankstas, and Ridas: Defining, Developing, and Supporting Effective Teachers in Urban Schools." *International Journal of Qualitative Studies in Education* 20(6): 617–638.
———. 2009. "Note to Educators: Hope Required When Growing Roses in Concrete." *Harvard Educational Review* 79(2): 1–13.
Freire, P. 1993. *Pedagogy of the Oppressed*. New York: Continuum.
———. 1994. *Education for Critical Consciousness*. New York: Continuum.
———. 1998a. *The Paulo Freire Reader*, ed. M. A. Freire and D. Macedo. New York: Continuum.
———. 1998b. "Cultural Action for Freedom." *Harvard Educational Review* 68(4): 476–522.
Romero, A. 2008. "Towards a Critically Compassionate Intellectualism Model of Transformative Education: Love, Hope, Identity, and Organic Intellectualism through the Convergence of Critical Race Theory, Critical Pedagogy, and Authentic Caring." Unpublished PhD diss., University of Arizona.

CHAPTER ONE

Critically Compassionate Intellectualism

The Pedagogy of Barriorganic Intellectualism

Augustine Romero

The following is a dialogue that took place with one of our Chicana students. I believe that it establishes the context in which our educational *lucha* (struggle) is occurring. In this dialogue, a student, Tina, is responding to a question about her educational experiences. Her forthright response portrays the racially hostile environment that she experienced in school and the deep and painful impact it had upon her:

> TINA: You don't feel good about what is happening to you . . . kinda like something bad happened to you, and then they blame you and say it's our fault. Then you feel, ah . . . you feel really bad, and you start feeling like you shouldn't go back, like you need to stay away. Even though it's not good to not be in school, at least when you are not there you don't have that feeling, but then you start feeling guilty because you know you need education for a better life.
>
> ROMERO: Is there one word that you think defines this feeling?
>
> TINA: Damn, that's hard. . . . [silence] The only word I guess is "violated." I guess it could be like when women are raped, something is taken from them.

"In school they take our minds and our souls; they violate us with the way they try to give us school" (Romero 2008, 163).

It is horrifying to think that a young woman would refer to rape to articulate her educational experiences. This is even more egregious when one considers that this young woman in the past had been physically raped, and now she unveiled the intersectionality of physical violence and rape to psychological violence that she faced on a daily basis in our schools at the hands of the administrators, teachers, and staff members.

In this chapter, I describe the experiences and understanding of how we have used critically compassionate intellectualism (CCI), a convergence of critical race theory (CRT), critical pedagogy, and authentic caring, in the Social Justice Education Project (SJEP) and the raza studies classrooms. More importantly, I bring forth the voices of students as a method of conveying the impact of CCI in classroom practices. These practices are parts of three program structures that I created to counter the reality of racism and subordination within the American education system: the SJEP (in partnership with Julio Cammarota; Romero 2008; Romero et al. 2008; Cammarota and Romero 2006a, 2006b); the CCI model of transformative education (Romero 2008; Cammarota and Romero 2006a, 2006b); and CCI's Third Dimension (Romero 2008). An explanation and description of the SJEP and CCI are forthcoming in the next section, and in the last section I examine the tridimensionalization of CCI.

The Social Justice Education Project and the Critically Compassionate Intellectualism Model of Transformative Education

Note: In this section I use "we" instead of "I" in recognition of the collaboration between Lorenzo Lopez Jr., Julio Cammarota, our students, and myself. Tina was a member of the SJEP's first student cohort. The SJEP, which completed its eighth cohort of students in 2011, provides students with all the social science requirements for their junior and senior years of high school. The SJEP enhances and enriches the state-mandated standards with advanced-level readings from critical theory, Chicana/o studies, and CRT. The intent is to help students develop a more sophisticated critical lens through which their level of racial, cultural, historical, and social consciousness is elevated through a curriculum that meets state standards but yet is authentically relevant to their lived conditions and realities. Moreover, when we created this opportunity, we unapologetically did so with the intent to foster a greater sense of educational sovereignty (Moll and Ruiz 2002) for the students, parents, and the community we serve.

The notion of educational sovereignty was paramount within our intellectualization and construction of the SJEP. I believe that if we are going to carry the sword of critical educators, we must engender and embody the essence of liberation, empowerment, and humanization. We must do all we can to center within our own praxis the words, thoughts, hopes, dreams, fears, and needs of the students (as well as the parents and community) we serve. In our praxis, we also recognize the essence of educational sovereignty, which at its core is the need and the empowered state to define the nature and scope of one's own educational experiences. We, like Moll and Ruiz (2002), believe that educational sovereignty is a tool of greater inclusiveness, rather than a tool of exclusion. We recognize that in many cases oppressors do not recognize the evil of their ways. Therefore, in an effort to gain full inclusivity, we must struggle and fight for our opportunity to dictate our own educational as well as social, economic, and political experiences. Educating those who unconsciously or dysconsciously oppress on how educational sovereignty perpetuates greater equity in and of itself becomes an antiracist project.

One of the methods we use in our classrooms, and that I use in this chapter, is counternarratives (Delgado and Stefancic 1993) or counterstories (Delgado 1989). Counternarrative or counterstory is a CRT methodology used to recount and redocument the realities and understandings of the people that have been racially and/or socially excluded from the traditional narrative.

The personal statements in this chapter were gathered through informal interviews, open-ended focus group interviews, open-ended interviews, and informal talking circles as part of my dissertation research. These multilayered methods have helped me develop a richer and deeper understanding of the common ground within the experiences of the SJEP students. The voices that I focus upon represent this common ground. In addition, these voices are the foundation of the epistemological, ontological, and intellectual agenda of the SJEP, the Mexican American/Raza Studies Department, and the CCI model of transformative education (Cammarota and Romero 2006a, 2006b, 2008; Romero 2008).

The SJEP students presented in this chapter were enrolled in Tucson Unified School District (TUSD), a district that is 61 percent Latino and 25 percent Anglo, with an enrollment of nearly 53,000. In the eleven years between 2000 and 2011 in TUSD, the Latino graduating cohort declined between 31 and 49 percent. This means that from the time Latinos enter TUSD as freshmen to their walk across the graduation stage as seniors Latino enrollment fell precipitously.

Before moving forward, it is important to mention that as this book attempts to illuminate the realities of our students, there is the likelihood that others within our system may be facing the same oppressive experiences. Given the dismantling of our program, the intentional exclusion of books and materials, the systemic double standards, and its failure to fully protect the program, the actions and the discourse of our district are firmly entrenched within the realm of oppression, exclusion, irresponsibility, and blatant racism. The actions of our district (with emphasis placed on those of two white males on the governing board and our superintendent) are a result of their lack of critical consciousness, their lack of critical praxis, and their unidimensional reality. This reality hinders their ability to develop an understanding of what our children need and deserve, to develop a deep sense of empathy, and to overcome and remove the racist lenses that inform their understandings and actions.

Through the tridimensionalization of reality, our students are encouraged to critically reflect upon themselves, their families, their community, and their overall lived conditions in order to begin the praxis-based process of constructing a counterstory that can be used as a tool of emancipation. These counterstories help us understand that the experiences of Tina and our students are reality, a reality that is perpetuated by a state of racialized hegemony that becomes one of the primary variables within the ontological and epistemological understanding of not only our students, but all students. This racialized understanding allows people to believe that the experiences of our students are an isolated abnormality. It allows people to excuse themselves from the dialogue because they are uncomfortable or because these realities counter their hegemonic rhetoric and their castle-in-the-sky visions of our society. It allows for the rearticulation of racism that gives racists the opportunity to use the words of Dr. Martin Luther King Jr. as tools of their oppressive projects (Romero 2010).

The SJEP, Mexican American/raza studies, and our CCI model of transformative education were created to counter the racist injustices within our educational system. The CCI model was coconstructed and defined by the students from the SJEP's first cohort. The model is established upon three areas: curriculum, pedagogy, and student-teacher-parent interactions. According to our students, this foundation has helped them develop a strong social, cultural, and historical identity that has allowed many of them to develop for the first time an academic identity, which has also helped them develop a strong sense of academic proficiency (Romero 2008). For many of our students, their experiences with the SJEP and CCI helped to develop the belief that education was something that could be theirs. Additionally, I discovered that the students in the SJEP who experience the CCI pass our state's high-stakes exit exam at a higher rate than all other similarly situated non-SJEP/CCI students at our sites of SJEP and CCI implementation (Romero 2008; also see chapter 2 of this volume).

In addition, I have used the understanding gained from CRT as a foundation for our educational praxis (Freire 1994). CRT has helped us and our students construct an educational experience that deliberately centers the issues of race and racism that resonate in American schools, in American society, and moreover within the lived conditions of our students. Our

Table 1.1. Critically Compassionate Intellectualism Model of Transformative Education

Increased Academic Achievement for Students

=

A Stronger Sense of Academic Proficiency for Students + An Enhanced Academic Identity for Students

=

CURRICULUM	PEDAGOGY	STUDENT-TEACHER-PARENT INTERACTION
• Culturally and Historically Relevant • Social Justice Centered • State Aligned (honors alignment in most cases) Academically Rigorous (+) = CCI Curriculum	• Critical Thinkers • Community Service • Critical Consciousness • Social Transformation (+) = CCI Pedagogy	• Respect • Understanding • Appreciation • Centered in the Creation of an Academic Identity (+) = CCI Student-Teacher-Parent Relations

Source: J. Cammarota and A. Romero. 2006. "A Critically Compassionate Intellectualism for Latina/o Students: Raising Voices above the Silencing in Our Schools," *Multicultural Education* 14(2): 16. Copyright 2006 by *Multicultural Education*. Adapted with permission of the author.

focus has included historically underserved students of color (Latinos, African Americans, and Native Americans) in Advanced Placement courses (Solórzano and Ornelas 2002, 2004), gifted and talented education, and other advanced educational opportunities. Also, our students have focused on the overrepresentation of students of color in shop courses, exceptional education, suspensions, referrals, and so on. In addition, our students have focused on the disparity of programming and the privileges perpetuated and extended to students in those advanced educational programs.

Last, one of our major accomplishments is that through our understanding of CRT we have constructed the ability to foster within our students the understanding that they, their parents, and their communities possess and construct a wealth of knowledge and capital (Delgado Bernal 2002; Yosso 2005, 2006) and they are the fundamental facilitators of their own and their communities' critical transformation (Romero 2008). This understanding as much as any other thing is what I believe has scared the hell of out of the racists within our district and the racist oppressors in our state government. This is the understanding that I unapologetically asked our teachers to nurture in our classrooms. This understanding is critical because it is the force that can and will dismantle the status quo within the US racial and social order. In essence, it is the stepping-stone toward a shift in power, and it sets the path toward greater inclusion of all groups.

The Tridimensionalization of Critically Compassionate Intellectualism

The following six sections are my understanding and explanation of how I have tridimensionalized the CCI model. The six elements of this model were first examined in my unpublished dissertation (Romero 2008). This is an articulation of my understanding of the evolution of the CCI model and, most importantly, it will illuminate the voices of students as they interpret their CCI experiences. In addition, I must thank Jeff Duncan-Andrade for pushing my thinking in this area. The six elements of the tridimensionalized CCI model are the nurturing of blossoming intellectualism (*xinachtli*) through authentic caring; pedagogy de los barrios; students as creators of knowledge; focus on collective and individual agency; organic intellectualism; and academic and personal transformation.

The Nurturing of Blossoming Intellectualism (Xinachtli) through Authentic Caring

Blanca (a member of the SJEP's first cohort) believed that the convergence of CRT, critical pedagogy, and authentic caring (the CCI model) led to a greater sense of relevance, a stronger critically racial consciousness, and a deeper understanding of an educational experience built upon *esperanza, familia,* and *cariño*.[1] This experience is different from the text-driven, silent, lifeless, and artificial classroom experiences that had filled her educational reality prior to the SJEP and the CCI model: "That stays with me. Like I said, it wasn't just like another class where we just sit in class and there's a teacher in front and the whole banking education. . . . It was more interaction and more like student and teacher. We got to know the teacher more, you got to know their life, and we got the chance to fight for a better life; that usually doesn't happen" (Romero 2008, 171).

Through an organically transformative epistemology and a sense of cultural intuition (Delgado Bernal 1998), the CCI teacher, along with students and parents, has a greater capacity to create an authentic caring educational environment that is constructed upon appreciation and respect for the Chicana/o community, its culture, its historic struggle for educational equality, and its social condition (Cammarota and Romero 2006a, 2006b; Duncan-Andrade 2005; Gonzalez 1997; Sanchez 1997; Spring 1997; Valencia, 2002, 2005; Yosso 2006). This appreciation and validation of our students and the knowledge that they hold and create is known as xinachtli (chee-nach-tlee). Xinachtli is an indigenous epistemology, concept, or principle meaning a process of nurturing the *semillas* (seeds) of knowledge. In this sense, the implementation of CCI is a process wherein students and their knowledge are recognized and acknowledged as being precious semillas. Within these semillas are the critical praxis-driven actions, understandings of hope and positive critical transformation. Moreover, CCI reaches deeper into the students' being by using xinachtli as a platform upon which students are critical of their own epistemology and ontology.

A few of the primary critical consciousness-building exercises used in CCI classrooms are: My History, Four Tables, and I Am poems. My History is usually offered during the second or third week of school, after some CCI context has been built and student-teacher relationships have had time to form. This exercise consists of five sections: the History of My Life, My Family's History, My History at High School, My Views of My Community and the World, and My Future. Each section includes a series of questions from which students choose what to address. These questions are simply starting points or thought provokers. For many of our students, the questions are the first engagements of the critiques of their epistemology and ontology. I strongly encourage teachers to invest in some one-on-one time with students as they explore their responses, and, in some cases, as they reinvent the questions they are answering. I believe that dialogue in this space is critical. Through dialogue students become familiar with the questioning process, as questions about their questions enter into the dialogue.

My History is not overly complex; however, the ontological and epistemological depth required is often deeper than students are accustomed to. Nevertheless, students should be encouraged to ask questions regarding their questions, and to ask questions about their answers, and as they dialogue with parents and other family members, students should be encouraged to ask questions about the thoughts and perspectives held by their family. A few simple but provocative questions are: Why do you believe this? Where did that belief come from? Who does that belief benefit? Who are we? Why do we do these things? What is our identity? How was our identity constructed? In my experience, "Why?" has been an extremely powerful tool in the quest to push the intellectual capacity of our students. I have watched students search deeply for the answer to that question and the question that follows their immediate response, and so on.

As students start to construct their histories or counterhistories, it is important that teachers build in both group dialogue time and one-on-one time with students. The group dialogue will cover many questions and concerns, and will help students move toward a greater social, cultural, and historical reality because these are their counterhistories. However, the one-on-one offers a more intimate dialogue, which is often needed when covering authentic hard-core social realities. Moreover, these processes give students the opportunities they need to construct their counterhistories. This is often the introduction to the notion of counternarratives or counter-storytelling (Delgado 1989).

For teachers, this exercise presents the opportunity to see into the lives and the thoughts of our students. This is paramount to our development of truly authentic relationships and essential to the ongoing enhancement of our critical consciousness and our epistemological and ontological understandings of who we are as teachers.

Given the recent developments of racist movements of the right, such as the tea party movement, counterstories are even more critical in opposing the story and the racist political discourse that legitimizes the Anglo story as the only American story. It is important that our students understand that their stories and those of their families and communities are legitimate American stories and that they are significant, vital, and enriching components of the fabric that makes America and Americans.

In the creation and telling of our counterstories, I am not saying that our story is more important than the current narrow narrative; however, I am saying that it is equally important. I am also saying that the inclusion of our counternarratives creates an American narrative that is more inclusive, enriched, and honest. Unfortunately, my experiences with race and racist politics is that the truth is irrelevant and lying is typical and is without accountability. Nevertheless, as a method of strengthening our war of position (Gramsci 1999), our students must continue to create and articulate their counterstories.

This ability to remake or re-create their schooling experiences offers Chicanas/os the opportunity to realize and strengthen their humanity. It is for this reason that engaging students in the Chicano epistemological practice of Tezcatlipoca is vital. In this liberatory moment students are moved toward realizing their humanity through self, familial, and community critical reflections. Without their humanity, Chicanas/os struggle to gain a critical consciousness. Without humanity and a critical consciousness, these students become the premier prey for cultural and capitalist predators (McLaren and Gutierrez 1995).

> TINA: You guys were like our *tíos* . . . like my dad even. There was that love, there was that *cariño*, there was that touch; you guys could relate to us. It was a relief. Finally, somebody that understood where we were coming from; we didn't have to make this big ol' explanation to try to make you understand us. . . . There was still that type of security and it was there and a lot of love, a lot of love for all of us to you guys and from you guys to us because you guys show it to us how much you guys went through for us. You guys did . . . *hicieron lo imposible* [did the impossible] . . . to make us get back on our feet and to make us want something out of life. (Romero 2008, 206)

In this exercise our students analyze and interpret a list of concepts, theories, and key words that become the theoretical foundation of our courses, which include, but are not limited to, the following: hegemony, social reproduction theory, theory of surplus equality, schooled by social class, cultural capital, subordinate group, dominant group, colonization, theory of inequality of language, racial justice theory, resistance theory, race, racism, class, strategic conjuncture, oppression, fatalism, privilege, subtractive schooling, agency, transformation, resistance, dystopian parody, habitus, scapegoat, and power-knowledge. As a race-conscious Freirean educator, I have studied and directly experienced the same conditions as many of our students. These words help construct the themes of our lived struggles and the context and content through which we define ourselves and our lived conditions (Freire 1994). Moreover, these are the very words and themes that help us (student, teacher, and, in many cases, parents and community) construct our transformative critical praxis.

Our praxis helps us to understand that the opportunity to create a picture that represents the students' interpretation of the concept, theory, or key word is the opportunity to construct new understandings and added meanings. The most critical part of the Four Tables exercise is the four-table dialogue between student and teacher. In most cases, the definition and word associations are self-explanatory, but the most meaningful is the students' articulation of their picture that represents the word, theory, or concept.

A few years back, a student that I will call AC was discussing his artistic expression of the concept of a subordinate group. Drawing from his experiences as a disc jockey, AC's picture had a turntable with some small speakers, a control for the volume, and one other knob. I said, "AC, how is this subordinate group?" He said, "Romero, that is all about subordinate group. Can't you see?" I said, "*Mijo*, I can't see it." AC said, "Romero, it is all right there." I said, "I'm trying, but how do you get subordinate group from this turntable with a few controls?" He responded, "Okay, look at my dominant group picture. Maybe you will get it." I turned to the dominant group picture. He had drawn a box with three turntables, lots of controls, and two huge speakers. I said, "Mijo, I still don't see it." AC said, "Come on, Romero. Look, subordinate group, less power and control: small speakers, one turntable, and only a few controls. Dominant group, more power and control: lots of turntables, big powerful speakers, and lots of controls. Now do you see it?" Yes, I did see it, and I did see how AC and other students were reinventing the ways in which each of these concepts, words, or theories could be explained in more meaningful and authentic ways.

I Am poems present another opportunity to nurture greater critical consciousness and to engage in critical praxis. You need a statement about the purpose of the poems, such as, "Students express where they are situated in the world and what their deepest hopes and concerns are." These poems offer teachers and students the opportunity for self-reflection and self-discovery. I Am poems also provide another opportunity for teachers and students to utilize the tridimensionalization process by asking them to explore and analyze the past and present conditions that have helped construct who they are at that moment, as well as what they presently see in their futures. After all I Am poems have been completed, each one is presented and read in class. Equally important, CCI teachers share their poems with students, which is another opportunity for teachers to reveal their hearts and souls. The reciprocation of thoughts, concerns, fears, desires, and so on presents an opportunity for both teachers and students to establish greater connections, and it provides teachers with the opportunity to gain interpersonal capital with the students.

The expansion of humanistic, social, and cultural capital (Bourdieu 1986) is experienced during I Am poems. Humanistic capital is the greater realization of one's humanity and the sociohuman investment and reinvestment that students make in those around them including their teachers, peers, and family. As students grow in their critical consciousness and their humanity, the capacity of these sociohuman investments expands and intensifies. In addition, we use a Bourdieuan lens to define social and cultural capital, which we define as assets that are developed and enhanced by alliances, group membership or relationship, and education, knowledge, or skills that are considered valuable by the dominant group. Moreover, both social and cultural capital are used by most as tools of upward mobility. However, in our classrooms social and cultural capital are used between teachers and students as a means of developing a stronger familial-like bond.

If students see their teachers as human beings, they are more likely to invest their humanistic capital in that teacher. Once the teacher has gained this humanistic capital, the relationship between teacher and student can become reciprocating and authentic (Valenzuela 1999). Social capital and cultural capital are gained from the teacher's understanding and appreciation of the social and cultural assets students bring with them from their homes, barrios, and communities (Gonzales et al. 1995; Yosso 2005; Romero 2008). The incorporation of these assets into the daily functions of the classroom helps create a scenario in which students can invest greater humanistic capital into their teacher. As a result, the authentic relationship between teacher and student is intensified. The following is an excerpt from our talking circle in which the topic was I Am poems:

OLIVIA: Do you remember when you did those I Am poems in class last year?

ROMERO: Yes, I do them every year.

OLIVIA: Do you know how much the other students really like doing those? Some would complain because, even though they seem simple, they are real hard.

ROMERO: I think that most students have difficulty with the idea that they have to read them in class.

LOZANO: Yeah, students do not like that.

OLIVIA: But it was a lot different in our class because you [AR] read your poem in front of everybody. The part when you were talking about your dad and you got tears in your eyes really changed everything. You were not this perfect, fake teacher—you were real, you were human. After that day me and a lot of students took our poems home and really thought about what we were going to say. In other classes your students were talking about their poems; I know people were working on their poems in other classes.

CAMMAROTA: So Olivia, what are you saying?

OLIVIA: We need to do I Am poems, but you guys need to do them too, and you need to read them in class in front of all the students. Like with Mr. Romero, after you show your human side, the students will have an easier time opening their human side to you and the whole class. For me and other students, that was when we knew that you were different than other teachers. . . . Basically, we knew that you guys really cared about us as people; you guys wanted what was best for us without judging us, and that helped me and other students to open our eyes and minds to what you were saying and how you were trying to guide us to have more consciousness. (Romero 2008, 237)

The I Am poems gave us (students and teachers) the opportunity to reveal ourselves to the students. It gave us an opportunity to show them our souls, to show them that we cry, that we have fears, that we have desires, that we have dreams, and that we can and do love. This is an example of an I Am template:

FIRST STANZA

I am (two special characteristics about person)
I wonder
I hear

I see
I want
I am (first line of the poem repeated)

SECOND STANZA

I pretend
I feel
I touch
I worry
I cry
I am (first line of poem repeated)

THIRD STANZA

I understand
I say
I dream
I try
I am (first line of poem repeated)

Moreover, the second and third submissions of I Am poems often transcended the template as students felt more and more willing to express the depths of their critical consciousness.

Sonia Zumosa transformed her I Am poem into the following poem about her perception of oppression and critical praxis:

BIG COLORFUL PLACE

I and the big colorful place,
I see beautiful bright colors, bright flowers blooming with pride, I see nature as green as can be, then I see people.

The people that I see are tall and small, thin and thick. The looks are different and unique in every individual.

I can't help but watch all these people interacting with each other. Some just talk, other people fight with an anger so deep that it fills their head with a rage.

They seem unhappy. The people living unhappy lives know what's going on, they know how it is to live in an unjustice [sic] place. Can you really blame them?

But I also notice one thing. I notice how some human beings seem to think their *pinche cabezas* that they are higher than another human being, that they are of big value, and I notice how they spit in the face of these people whose skin is red and burnt from the flames of the sun and step on the hands that don't stop working, the ones that have blisters and their skin so rough and peely.

I hear the yells; I hear the altercations and the sayings.

They talk about society and illegal aliens coming in left and right to a Whites only place.

We all know who they call illegal aliens, but would they call a person from Europe an alien?

I listen to all this bullshit and I just think to myself.

They express it in the way of whoever doesn't have their color, falls beneath their shoe.

I think of just knocking the s*** out of them with the power that has been building up more and more and asking how does it feel to be down there.

They imagine that people like me are trouble and we evolved just to serve them.

But I try to believe and think positive.

We know their [sic] a lot of people out their [sic], with this attitude, so what do I do? Theirs [sic] only the way to think outside the premises and say something!

Santos Ricardo's I Am poem advocates that conscious rap be used as a tool to elevate the consciousness of the oppressed, as a lever to help the oppressed rise to the quest for humanization:

LETHAL INJECTION

we call it the land of the free
or is this hell, every breath that we breathe
land of pain, suffering, greed and mysery [sic]

they haven't gave [sic] nothing to us
so we have to fight and take it
everytime [sic], we step, they just hate it

but everytime you hold us down
will come up twice as strong
so you better hate it

were [sic] here to stay
here to play
here to do those games
will leave you confused and traped [sic] in a maze

we can't be color on color
and be self-destructive
we got to see each other as
friends and be self-productive

but who will come up . . .
luther king and X plus pac
all steped [sic] up, got lit up and rid of

and with the microphone piece, all those rappers
only want to rap about hoes, money and now
he or she killed that ese or nigga in the streets

I know there will never be peace
but at least, rap about something positive
so your fans can here [sic] on your beat

they take whatever they want
cops, governments, the whole system
so they are comitting [sic] a theft
we will rise out of depth, fight till there's no one left

my words are weapons
deadly as venomous
porject [sic] my voice into your mind
with a lethel [sic] injection

Pedagogy de los Barrios

The approach of authentic caring of blossoming intellectuals is nurtured through our barrio pedagogy (Duncan-Andrade and Morrell 2008). *Camarada* Jeff Duncan-Andrade, through his work with our department, has helped us define and name this barrio pedagogy. Within this pedagogy are the Freirean elements of problematization, true words, and tridimensionalization (Freire 1994). It is also crucial that I define these critical intellectual engagements taking place both in the barrio/ghetto/reservation and in the school. Moreover, the third space (Bhabha 1994; Moje et al. 2004) that is created in our classrooms is a convergence of the barrio/ghetto/reservation and the institution. This third space challenges the status quo and the stereotypes that exist within our educational institutions and within our society in general. This newly created pedagogical and intellectual space is driven by the need to challenge the epistemological and ontological understandings of our students and in some cases their parents. Furthermore, CCI is grounded in the understanding that race and racism are dominant variables within the tridimensionalized reality of our students, their parents, our communities, and us as emancipatory educators (Romero 2008).

As I reflected upon the voices of the students, it was clear that our true words influenced their ability to find their true words, and through their true words they try to tridimensionalize their realities. I have interpreted true words to mean the actions that are informed by a high level of reflection that takes place through a lens of respect and love (Romero 2008). Moreover, in a number of cases the students created true words through conflict or through an evolution of understanding that opened the door for the creation and re-creation of true words that established for them a transformed reality:

> Ansenia Valenz: I liked the class 'cuz they helped a lot because like they made me realize that I really need . . . I need to go to college and if I really want to change and help people, . . . but what can they do? The media, the, what's that word? I can't say it.
>
> Cami Nieto: Hegemony?
>
> Ansenia Valenz: Yeah, that word. It prevents people from believing that things can change. People are scared to speak because they think if they make noise or shine the light someone will get them. But after awhile my family, even my mom started to be different. Anyways, my family and me now [we] see things different; and yeah I'm going to be somebody, but somebody who helps. (Romero 2008, 246)

As I reflect upon this process, I understand that students and teacher created and re-created new spaces as we demonstrated an appreciation for each student's reflections and perceptions, and we offered guidance on actions taken by students that was transformative rather than self-defeating.

Solórzano and Delgado Bernal (2001) have helped me conceptualize and operationalize transformative actions as those that directly name, assess, and engage oppression in a manner that perpetuates social justice.

In this pursuit of social justice, both the students and I constantly engage in the exercises of problematization and tridimensionalization of reality. I borrow both exercises from Freire (1994), and I have modified them to meet the needs and context of our students. The problematization process is broken into four phases: (1) naming or identifying the problem; (2) analyzing causes of the problem; (3) finding solutions to the problem; and (4) reflecting on the process (Freire 1994). I have modified this process in a deliberate attempt to "racially problematize" it by asking our students to insert the race and racism variables.

It is my belief that in the historical and social reality of the United States the exclusion of the racial problematization process is a huge mistake that historically and presently places teachers of social justice in the role of agents of injustice. Moreover, teachers add deeper contextualization to the racial problematization process by helping students through the tridimensionalization of their realities. I describe tridimensionalization as an active intellectual endeavor that helps our students create the nexuses between the past, present, and future, and especially what meaning these nexuses have within antiracist and antioppression projects. Blanca clearly articulates this tridimensionalization as she explains her nurturing of an academic identity: "Yeah, the project helped me develop it [an academic identity] more because I didn't have my *tía* saying 'did you do your homework?' I was on my own. It helped me say 'you're doing this for yourself, for your dad, and your grandmother, and everyone else who struggled with you, and now it's your turn and you have to carry on'" (Romero 2008, 187).

I see tridimensionalization in Tina's explanation of how she developed a deeper understanding of how she could engage and transform her epistemology and ontology, while simultaneously developing her academic identity:

> We were being taught way advanced curriculum that you guys would teach at a university, and we were juniors and seniors in high school and reading out of critical race theory books, Paulo Freire. Looking at our own history and culture was really important, it gives you pride and makes you feel like you belong. It also helped us become Chicanas or Chicanos, the way we see [understand] things was really important. I really liked that stuff, but the critical [pedagogy] stuff was the stuff that

really opened my eyes. It helps you to have a deeper understanding, and makes you see through the surface. It helps you ask questions, and helps connect this stuff to right now, our history, and like it helped us connect those things to the future. That is what made it real, like nothing ever before. This made more sense. It helped us understand the fucked up shit we did, *pero* it helped us understand that we could fuck them up if we studied our shit.

If our shit [critical socially and culturally relevant course work and research] was tight, they could not stop us. Yeah, we had to play some of their game, but like you said, nothing is better than beating them at their own game. Look at us now, we won. Look at where we started, and look at me, us, now. Shit, so many of my teachers told me to just drop out. You know they actually told me to drop out, and they told it to Rolando, Ramiro, Ansenia—I mean all of us they told to drop out. The class helped us understand that we could fight them, and it taught us that doing good in school and graduating was the way we could win. But, Romero, it taught us that the way to really win is when we make changes in our community or in our school. (Romero 2008, 204)

Students as Creators of Knowledge

Dolores Delgado Bernal (2002) has helped me understand that our students are constructors of knowledge versus simply receivers of the trivial information that the state recommends with the intent of domesticating and quashing their consciousness. It is through this process that the state becomes an agent of the social and racial status quo. The antithesis is a state of authentic caring, wherein my colleagues and I have developed and employed what Delgado Bernal (1998) refers to as a Chicana/o epistemology. This epistemology reflects the unique experience that arises from historic and current social, political, and cultural conditions that are encountered by Chicanas/os. The intersectionality of these two spaces has helped me recognize and operationalize the epistemology, ontology, and consciousness that help us help our students recontextualize their educational and social reality. In many cases our students have defined this epistemology and consciousness as being built upon a sense of inferiority, fear, and hopelessness (Romero 2008). Most often, all that is created from the oppressor group's epistemology and consciousness is the perpetuation and rearticulation of itself. However, our students have articulated that in their recontextualized ontology, a different reality has been created, and what is possible within their world has been positively and more hopefully redefined (Romero 2008).

Our students have articulated their belief that the development of a recontextualized way of knowing and thinking helped them to engage their world and their social condition more effectively. Our students believe that in their newly recontextualized epistemological or ontological understandings, they can and do contribute positively to society; and each believes that he or she has the capacity to change his or her present and future reality (Romero 2008). For the unconscious or dysconscious, these recontextualizations may seem insignificant, but for students who are caught in the state of hopelessness and despair, these transformations have led to a new state of hope and critical consciousness. The beauty of this state is the students' understanding that it is from these conditions that they can truly create new realities for themselves (Romero 2008). In this regard, Rolando stated, "At the time we couldn't understand the things they were saying, but now I know. The class, the project, I mean you guys showed the students that we could say something; we didn't have to be scared. We know that we need to stand up. We are conscious, and we need to use our conscience for justice, and to fight racism. Damn Mister, this was the best part, one of the best parts" (Romero 2008, 121).

Focus on Collective and Individual Agency

Another area of significant impact for our students is the understanding of the agency they possess and can create in their engagements in antiracist projects. Blanca explained that with the impact and understanding gained from the CCI model, she now knows that she can help "provide a change . . . to help kids, to help other students see that there are options out there and that we could better our community, to better ourselves" (Romero 2008, 194). This acting upon and countering of injustice to create change and to rehumanize the students and those around them is also framed within an indigenous framework of Huitzilopochtli (weet-zee-lo-poch-tlee). In the classes where CCI is implemented, the students' culture is continuously validated through identification and engagement in this process. It is through the epistemological process of Huitzilopochtli that students act upon *la voluntad* (the will) to be positive, progressive, and creative to bring about justice and rehumanization for themselves as well as for those who have the power and position to dehumanize. Critical consciousness and organic intellectualism are the two Freirean pedagogical strands within Blanca's expression, and reveal the impact that the CCI model had upon her.

Blanca also focused upon the idea of engagement created by the social relevance of the SJEP and the CCI model. She stated that this relevance created a stronger sense of connectedness to the overall experience of the class: "It was very interesting. I just enjoyed going to your class and seeing what experience they [would] have to say about their life. It was an eye opener. . . . It was so relevant to our thinking and our lives" (Romero 2008, 186).

Organic Intellectualism

I have defined transformative actions as the type of interactions that nurture and foster within students, parents, and teachers the courage and understanding needed to change the racial and social order inherent within the US educational system and society. Through the use of true words these transformative interactions were used as mechanisms to create a war of position and to inspire a strong sense of organic intellectualism within the students, the parents, and the teachers.

The pursuit of organic intellectualism is the means by which CCI students and teachers transcend the liberal notion of good and just. The organic intellectual defines justice, goodness, and even godliness by the essence of his or her lived reality in the context of creating something that many may consider utopian but which he or she understands as the essence that brings all of us closer to our true humanity. This understanding of organic intellectualism may transcend that established by Gramsci (1999); however, both at their core are driven by the need to use their entire intellectual and humanistic capacity to transform the social condition of their community and their people. Through CCI, intellectuals from the barrios, the ghettos, the reservations, and places in between are nurtured by critical praxis and true words. Through these intellectual and humanistic exercises, social and political reality is problematized and racismized through the exercise of praxis, and with the intent of fostering self, social, and structural transformation (Solórzano and Delgado Bernal 2001).

In her explanation of the impact CCI had upon her, it is obvious that the academic identity and proficiency that were nurtured within Blanca helped her develop her critical consciousness and her sense of organic intellectualism, which are evident through her desire to learn more and more as a means of advancing her community: "Yeah, it [CCI] helped me relate to education more. It helped [me] grow stronger in my other classes because I wanted to do something that would help. I felt like doing the work in the other classes would give me a chance to do more for the people; it gave [me] a chance to do more, to help more. I mean, the more I knew, the more I could help. Like you said, the things we learned would become our weapons because our mind and our words would be stronger" (Romero 2008, 198).

Tina's final statement during her interview centered on the principles within organic intellectualism in that she connected the development of her intellectualism to the development of community and responding to those who are in need: "You guys made us learn to live and love life. You guys taught us that and from now on I'm going to carry those intellectual weapons, like you say, and all the things that I learned from the project to help me succeed in life and to help others" (Romero 2008, 198).

Academic and Personal Transformation

In explaining the impact and understanding she gained from our project, Blanca explained that she now understands that she has the power to create change, and she has embraced her role as an organic intellectual:

> The Project [CCI] helps us because we learned a new way of thinking. We took the pill [laughing]. Now we can't go back, but this is better because now we see the matrix. They can't fool us. Sometimes it hurts more because we can see everything, well now we can fight it too. Before, we were fighting the wrong way. I love the project, it was great, and it helped me feel smarter and know that I could challenge the teachers, and the project gave the idea that I could help my community, and that is what I am going to do with my life. (Romero 2008, 208)[2]

When the SJEP was created the primary intent was to help students develop an identity, an understanding of their purpose in this world, and a strong sense of hope. Through these fundamental characteristics, I believed that our students could develop a critical consciousness and a strong sense of organic intellectualism. Through this process students develop an academic identity, and through an evolution of consciousness and identity formation our students become more academically proficient (Romero 2008).

In our conversations with our students, very seldom, if ever, did we talk about doing better in this class, much less other classes. The same is true about the notion of academic identity; the dialogue regarding identity is that of the social, cultural, and historic self. In essence we discussed who the students are, where they come from, and what this means in the present-day context, as well as how this understanding could transform their lives and help them engage their epistemology today and transform the ontology they will carry into tomorrow.

As we engaged in these conversations, it is important to note that we, along with our students, evolved in our epistemological and ontological understandings. This transformation of student and teacher galvanized the intellectual nature of CCI. One of CCI's most critical projects is its intent to nurture intellectuals, which Said articulates as constituting "a clerisy . . . since what they uphold are eternal standards of truth and justice that are precisely not of this world" (1994, 5). CCI in its praxis seeks to nurture intellectuals that are products of the oppressed groups, and who use, for these oppressed groups, all of their skills and power to engage and transform the oppressor group's hegemony. In this engagement is the potential of untested feasibility, or the truth or justice that may exist just beyond the walls of our consciousness.

In this transformation the vast majority of our students grasp the necessity to commit themselves to a transformational resistance orientation (Solórzano and Delgado Bernal 2001). The nature and scope of their research and the way they have led their lives are articulations of their commitment to social justice and the dismantling of society's structures of inequality.

It is in this tridimensionalized state that our SJEP students started to experience greater academic success, and it is therein that our students developed their academic identities. It is in this space that Olivia began to think about education in a different manner:

> Your class got me really interested in learning and like education because, like before, I probably wouldn't have graduated on time because I was already really behind. . . . I had a lot of family problems and I ended up not going to school for a whole year. After I became involved with the project, I had a lot of motivation to get finished, and like the class really made an impression on me that without education, without a high school diploma and going on to college, you really wouldn't be successful in life. I did better in all my classes; I think I knew that if I could do all the college assignments in our class, I could do the other BS stuff in my other class. I realized that I wanted an education. (Romero 2008, 186)

Conclusion

The tridimensionalized version of our CCI model, like the original version of CCI, is a creation that has evolved from the voices of our students. Our students have been critical in our education and our transformation and evolution toward becoming liberatory educators and organic intellectuals. In fact, it is my belief that if it were not for our students, our practical and real-world knowledge would be significantly diminished, and therefore our evolution would not be possible.

As we evolve in our teaching and as our students better educate us, we look forward to the transformations and evolutions that await our students and us. Moreover, we look forward to experiencing the social and educational transformations that will be made by our students, and other students and teachers who are engaged in the pursuit of racial and social justice in the United States and all over the world.

This dimension or relationship between students, teachers, and the social condition is one of the key variables almost always excluded from the discourse of school reform. As a result, this discourse is often contaminated by failed paradigms of the past that are often reconstituted with different names or in polished and shiny new versions even though they failed those who needed the greatest amount of help.

Educators must understand that the traditional methods of schooling for children of color have been nothing more than false generosity at best, and in many cases have been a sophisticated version of the smallpox-infested blankets that were offered to Native Americans as gifts. If those in educational leadership and most colleges of education were truly concerned with the life trajectory of those students in the ghettos, in the barrios, and on the reservations they would throw all those old and ghastly ideas back in their tyrannical box and once and for all burn that box.

Many transformational answers can be found in our tridimensionalized version of the CCI model. Unfortunately, within the field of educational leadership and teacher preparation programs, paradigms such as social justice, cultural and social responsiveness, authentic caring, and critical consciousness are absent from the discourse and dialogue. This is regrettable, because very little if anything within the development of teachers and educational leaders prepares them to authentically and equitably meet the needs of students like ours, the ones who have often been lost on the margins, forgotten in the numbers, left behind, and simply neglected.

CCI and its tridimensionalization have many answers. If you are truly concerned, take them off these pages and implement them in our classes, in our schools, but before you do that, place them in your heart and soul and let them transform and redefine whom you are. Otherwise please get out of our way!

Notes

1. The English translation is hope, family, and love.
2. The "pill" is a reference to the film *The Matrix*, in which the character Neo is asked to take a red or blue pill. If he takes the red pill, he will be able to see the world in its truest form; however, if he takes the blue one he will continue to see the world only as it has been constructed for him. I found that this scene helped our students better understand the notion of a critical consciousness. Our students came to understand that if they took the pill of critical consciousness they, like Neo, who took the red pill, would be able to see the world in the most critical or truest form. However, if they did not take the pill, they would remain in their naive or magical realities.

References

Bhabha, H. 1994. *The Location of Culture*. London: Routledge.
Bourdieu, P. 1986. "The Forms of Capital, trans. R. Nice. In *Handbook for Theory and Research for the Sociology of Education*, ed. J. G. Richardson, 241–58. New York: Greenwood.
Cammarota, J. 2006. "Disappearing in the Houdini Education: The Experience of Race and Invisibility among Latina/o Students." *Multicultural Education* 14(1): 2–109.
Cammarota, J., and A. Romero. 2006a. "A Critically Compassionate Pedagogy for Latino Youth." *Latino Studies* 4(3): 305–12.
———. 2006b. "A Critically Compassionate Intellectualism for Latina/o Students: Raising Voices above the Silencing in Our Schools." *Multicultural Education* 14(2): 16–23.
———. 2008. "The Social Justice Education Project: A Critically Compassionate Intellectualism for Chicana/o Students." In *Handbook for Social Justice in Education*, ed. W. Ayers, T. Quinn, and D. Stovall, 465–76. New York: Routledge.
Darder, Antonia, Rodolfo Torres, and Henry Gutierrez, eds. 1997. *Latinos and Education: A Critical Reader*, 158–72. New York: Routledge.
Delgado, R. 1989. "Storytelling for Oppositionists and Others: A Plea for Narrative." *Michigan Law Review* 87: 2411–41.
Delgado, R., and J. Stefancic. 1993. "Critical Race Theory: An Annotated Bibliography." *Virginia Law Review* 79: 461–516.
Delgado Bernal, D. 1998. "Using a Feminist Latina Epistemology in Education Research." *Harvard Education Review* 68: 555–82.
———. 2002. "Critical Race Theory, Latino Critical Theory, and Critical Raced-Gendered Epistemologies: Recognizing Students of Color as Holders and Creators of Knowledge." *Qualitative Inquiry* 8(1): 105–26.
Duncan-Andrade, J. 2005. "An Examination of the Sociopolitical History of Chicanos and Its Relationship to School Performance." *Urban Education* 40(6): 576–605.
Duncan Andrade, J., and E. Morrell. 2008. *The Art of Critical Pedagogy: Possibilities for Moving from Theory to Practice in Urban Schools*. New York: Peter Lang Publishing.

Freire, P. 1994. *Pedagogy of the Oppressed*. New York: Continuum.
Gonzalez, G. 1997. "Culture, Language, and the Americanization of Mexican Children." In *Latinos and Education: A Critical Reader*, ed. A. Darder, R. Torres, and H. Gutierrez, 158–72. New York: Routledge.
Gonzalez, N., L. Moll, F. Tenery, A. Rivera, P. Rendon, R. Gonzales, and C. Amanti. 1995. "Funds of Knowledge for Teaching in Latino Households." *Urban Education* 29: 443–70.
Gramsci, A. 1999. *Selections from the Prison Notebooks*. New York: International.
McLaren, P., and K. Gutierrez. 1995. "Pedagogies of Dissent and Transformation: A Dialogue with Kris Gutierrez." In *Critical Pedaogy and Predatory Culture: Oppositional Politics in a Postmodern Era*, ed. P. McLaren, 145–76. New York: Routledge.
Moje, E. B., K. McIntosh Ciechanowski, K. Kramer, L. Ellis, R. Carrillo, and T. Collazo. 2004. "Working toward Third Space in Content Area Literacy: An Examination of Everyday Funds of Knowledge and Discourse." *Reading Research Quarterly* 39(1): 38–70.
Moll, L., and R. Ruiz. 2002. "The Schooling of Latino Students." In *Latinos: Remaking America*, ed. M. Suarez-Orozco and M. Paez, 362–74. Berkeley: University of California Press.
Romero, A. 2008. "Towards a Critically Compassionate Intellectualism Model of Transformative Education: Love, Hope, Identity, and Organic Intellectualism through the Convergence of Critical Race Theory, Critical Pedagy, and Authentic Caring." Unpublished PhD diss., University of Arizona.
———. 2010. "At War with the State in Order to Save the Lives of Our Children: The Battle to Save Ethnic Studies in Arizona." *Black Scholars* 40(4): 7–15.
Romero, Augustine, Julio Cammarota, Kim Dominguez, Luis Valdez, Grecia Ramirez, and Liz Hernandez. 2008. "'The Opportunity if Not the Right to See': The Social Justice Education Project." In *Revolutionizing Education: Youth Participatory Action Research in Motion*, ed. J. Cammarota and M. Fine, 131–51. New York: Routledge.
Said, E. 1994. *Representations of the Intellectual*. New York: Pantheon.
Sanchez, G. 1997. "History, Culture, and Education." In *Latinos and Education: A Critical Reader*, ed. A. Darder, R. Torres, and H. Gutíerrez, 158–72. New York: Routledge.
Solórzano, D., and A. Ornelas. 2002. "A Critical Race Analysis of Advanced Placement Classes: A Case of Educational Inequality." *Journal of Latinos and Education* 1(4): 215–29.
———. 2004. "A Critical Race Analysis of Latina/o and African American Advanced Placement Enrollment in Public High Schools." *High School Journal* 87(3): 15–26.
Solórzano, D., and D. Delgado Bernal. 2001. "Examining Transformational Resistance through a Critical Race Theory and LatCrit Theory Framework: Chicana and Chicano Students in an Urban Context." *Urban Education* 36(3): 308–42.
Spring, J. 1997. *Deculturalization and the Struggle for Equality: Brief History of the Education of Dominated Cultures in the United States*. New York: McGraw-Hill.
Valencia, R. 2002. *Chicano School Failure and Success: Past, Present, and Future*. New York: Routledge/Falmer.

——. 2005. "The Mexican American Struggle for Equal Educational Opportunity in Mendez v. Westminster: Helping to Pave the Way for Brown v. Board of Education." *Teachers College Record* 107(3): 389–423.

Valenzuela, A. 1999. *Subtractive Schooling: U.S.-Mexican Youth and the Politics of Caring*. Albany: State University of New York Press.

Yosso, T. 2005. "Whose Culture Has Capital? A Critical Race Theory Discussion of Community Cultural Wealth." *Race, Ethnicity and Education* 8(1): 69–91.

——. 2006. *Critical Race Counterstories along the Chicana/Chicano Educational Pipeline*. New York: Routledge.

CHAPTER TWO

Lies, Damn Lies, and Statistics

The Impact of Mexican American Studies Classes

Nolan L. Cabrera

Mark Twain famously wrote, "There are lies, damn lies, and statistics." While Twain's pithy comment contains a great deal of truth, it should not be construed to mean all statistical analyses are created equal or are equally valid. An example of this involves the heated debates over Mexican American studies (MAS) in the Tucson Unified School District (TUSD). One of the primary arguments in favor of this program is that the lowest-performing students in the district (low-income, first-generation Latina/os) who take these classes outperform those who do not.[1] This is all the more important given the national context where "almost half of Latinos do not receive a diploma four years after entering high school" (Gándara and Contreras 2009, 23).

This argument took center stage February 23, 2011, when TUSD statistician David Scott released a report detailing the 2010 graduating cohort and their matriculation rates. Finding that all students in TUSD (those who take an MAS course and those who do not) graduate at approximately an 83 percent rate, Doug MacEachern (2011) of the *Arizona Republic* wrote, "now, the district's own statisticians have—finally—examined the claims [of improved academic performance] and found them lacking." MacEachern was not alone in his criticism as commentators throughout Arizona routinely used equivalent graduation rates as evidence that the MAS program was educationally ineffective (or "only" as effective as non-MAS courses in TUSD). These pronouncements stemmed more from ideology than empirical analysis, but they do warrant a more nuanced explanation than a ten-second sound bite affords. Therefore, in this chapter

I outline conceptually how to assess programmatic impact. I then detail the available data and offer a descriptive, empirical analysis of MAS participation for the 2010 graduating cohort.

Conducting an Impact Analysis

Impact and effect are two very tricky words when dealing with statistics because they require the analyst to have some pretreatment measures (Astin 1993). This rarely occurs when the term "impact" enters public discourse. For example, Princeton University frequently touts its four-year graduation rate of 87 percent as evidence of excellence in teaching and student learning.[2] Upon closer examination, Princeton traditionally recruits the most academically prepared applicants from across the country (sometimes the world); students with GPAs above 4.0 and perfect SAT scores, who are school leaders, accomplished athletes, and renowned musicians. From this applicant pool, the admissions office then admits approximately 10 percent. With these characteristics of entering students, one would expect astronomically high graduation rates. In fact, it would be surprising if these students did not graduate at such high levels.

Without making a statement about the quality of education at Princeton University, the discourse surrounding quality of education tends to focus on outcomes without taking account of inputs. This occurs frequently when largely white, affluent parents assess the quality of education their children will receive by examining the standardized test scores produced by individual schools (Apple 2001; Kozol 2005). This common practice misunderstands high test scores as an indication of higher-quality teachers. What these parents tend to overlook is that high test scores, graduation rates, and college attendance rates are highly correlated with the concentration of affluent and white students who have college-educated parents (Apple 2001; Lewis 2004; Kozol 2005). Therefore, these shotgun analyses surrounding test scores are primarily measures of race and class instead of educational quality because they do not account for incoming student characteristics.

Comparing Apples to Apples

The other issue in MacEachern's analysis, one that has not yet been addressed in analyses conducted by the district, is the issue of making appropriate comparisons between students who take MAS classes and those who do not. Returning to the issue of matriculation, the 2010 graduating cohort for all TUSD high schools had a graduation rate of 82.5 percent according to publicly available data provided by the district ("Graduation Rate" 2010). Disaggregating these data, white students graduated at a rate of 87.1 percent while Latina/o students graduated at a rate of 79.5 percent. Similar gaps exist across Socioeconomic Status (SES) lines. TUSD students who received free or reduced-price lunch in the 2010 cohort graduated at a rate of 77.8 percent, compared to a rate of 85.7 percent for those who were not on free or reduced-price lunch.[3] Therefore, dramatic differences exist in the academic performance of TUSD students along racial and SES lines.

According to district-provided data (Department of Accountability and Research 2011b), the students in the 2010 MAS graduating cohort tended to be both Latina/o and low income. Specifically, 83.6 percent of students who took an MAS course in this cohort were Latina/o and 55.5 percent came from families that were district defined as low or very low income. In contrast, only 43.8 percent of TUSD students not taking an MAS course were Latina/o in this cohort, and 66.5 percent came from families that were district defined as medium, high, or very high income. Therefore, the most appropriate comparison when assessing programmatic impact would use a random sample of students from the district who matched the demographic profile of the students who took MAS courses. Instead, the district compared MAS students with the rest of the district, which meant these comparisons were confounded by issues of race and class that are not easily disentangled from MAS class impact. While the district could provide a better comparison group, they would not voluntarily release these data under the guise that it would be "too political." In addition, the data released offer a conservative definition of completion of an MAS course. The district-provided data count anyone who took one semester of an MAS course in the MAS cohort, but these courses were designed to be year-long. To determine the program's true impact, it would be necessary to include only those students who completed a full year of MAS study. Despite the sampling limitations, which likely produce conservative estimates of the true impact of MAS courses, some very compelling results emerged.

Examining MAS Course Impact

To begin the assessment process, I had to determine if there were measures of student performance before students took an MAS course. The state's standardized test, Arizona's Instrument to Measure Standards (AIMS), provided this opportunity as students take it for the first time during the second semester of their sophomore year in high school.[4] In TUSD, students do not take MAS courses until their junior year. Therefore, I was able to determine whether an achievement gap between MAS and non-MAS students existed before students were able to take these courses (see table 2.1). Within the 2010 graduating cohort, students who eventually took an MAS course passed the AIMS test at substantially lower rates than those who never took these courses.

The achievement gap ranged from 10 percentage points (writing) to 16 percentage points (math). Students who did not pass the AIMS test on their first attempt had multiple other chances to pass these tests, and this created the opportunity to begin assessing the impact of MAS courses.

If MAS courses were less effective or just as effective as non-MAS courses, I would expect these gaps to persist because all students would be developing at approximately similar rates. For students who never took an MAS course, these trends hold along the lines of race/ethnicity and SES (see table 2.2). There were persistent gaps, such as a 16-percentage-point difference between the final passing rates of white students and their Latina/o peers. In addition, there was a full 28-point gap between the final AIMS passing rates of non-MAS low-income and high-income students.

The differences become even more stark when including very low-income (63 percent AIMS passing rate) and very high-income (96 percent AIMS passing rate) students in the analysis. The gap persists also for medium-income students—they have a final AIMS passing rate of 78 percent; a full 16 percentage points higher than their low-income peers. Thus, the initial gaps in student performance persist and sometimes widen for those students who never took a MAS course.

Returning to the analysis of MAS students, instead of a gap, I found relative parity in terms of final AIMS passing rates (see table 2.3). The achievement gaps in initial AIMS passing rates were in double digits for all

Table 2.1. Initial AIMS Passing Rates, 2010 Graduating Cohort (%)

	MAS Students	Non-MAS Students	Difference (Non-MAS vs. MAS)
Math	61	77	16
Reading	66	80	14
Writing	65	75	10

Note: Data for this table derived from TUSD Department of Accountability and Research (2011a).

Table 2.2. Non-MAS AIMS Final Passing Rates, 2010 Graduating Cohort (%)

	Final AIMS Passing Rate	Difference
White	87	16
Latina/o	71	
High income	90	28
Low income	62	

Note: The data for this table are derived from data requested of TUSD on September 14, 2011.

Table 2.3. Final AIMS Passing Rates, 2010 Graduating Cohort (%)

	MAS Students	Non-MAS Students	Difference (Non-MAS vs. MAS)
Math	86	90	4
Reading	92	94	2
Writing	93	95	2

Note: Data for this table derived from TUSD Department of Accountability and Research (2011a).

subject areas (see table 2.1). These shrank to a maximum gap of four percentage points in math and a minimum of two percentage points in reading and writing.

To put this in perspective, if only six more MAS students passed the reading section of the AIMS test, there would be no gap at all. The most surprising result of this analysis is the closing of the achievement gap in AIMS math, because a class such as "Chicano algebra" does not exist. This might indicate that MAS courses not only improve skills such as reading ability, but also might impact student orientation toward learning regardless of subject matter.

On the specific tests, MAS students demonstrated substantially greater gains in AIMS passing rates than their non-MAS peers (see figure 2.1). On all three tests, their improvement far surpassed that of their non-MAS peers.

However, these numbers likely overestimate the impact of MAS classes because MAS students had substantially more room for improvement than their non-MAS peers. With greater room for improvement, I would expect the absolute gains of MAS students' AIMS passing rates to exceed those of their non-MAS peers. Therefore, I wanted to determine if the rate of improvement differed between these two groups.

I operationalized the AIMS passing rate of improvement as follows. I calculated the possible improvement score by subtracting the initial AIMS passing rate from 100 percent (the maximum passing rate). I then calcu-

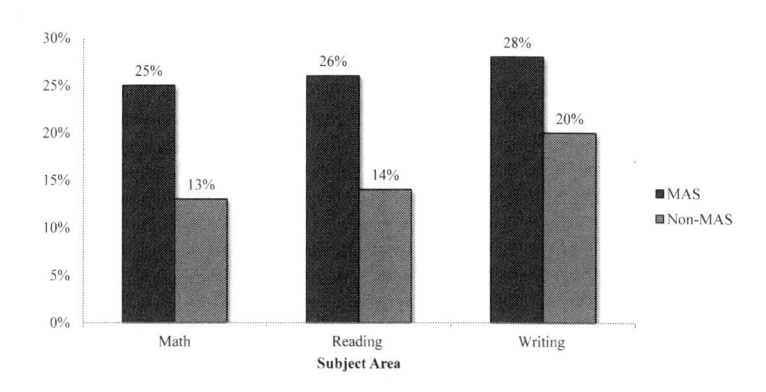

Figure 2.1. Improvement in AIMS passing rate, 2010 graduating cohort.

lated the actual improvement score by subtracting the initial AIMS passing rate from the final AIMS passing rate. Finally, I calculated a ratio of the actual improvement to the possible improvement. I wanted to do this to take a more conservative estimate that primarily examined rates instead of absolute improvement. Finally, I subtracted the non-MAS rates of improvement from the MAS rates of improvement to see if, when controlling for the amount of improvement possible, MAS students outperformed their non-MAS peers (see table 2.4). The short answer is yes.

In both AIMS reading and math, MAS students passed AIMS at substantially higher rates than their non-MAS peers, although writing showed no difference. Even though MAS students improved their writing passing rate by 28 percentage points compared to 20 percentage points for non-MAS students, their relative rates of improvement were comparable (80 percent). Regardless, in both absolute (figure 2.1) and relative (table 2.4) terms, MAS classes appear to substantially, positively affect student achievement. To further explore this issue, I also critically examined graduation rates.

Passing the AIMS tests is important, but the primary measure of success is whether or not the students graduate from high school. As previously discussed, the 2010 MAS graduating cohort had graduation rates virtually identical to those of their non-MAS peers (82.6 percent for the former and 82.5 percent for the latter). However, this was only one part of the story because the MAS cohort has a high concentration of low-income

Table 2.4. Rates of AIMS Passing Improvement, 2010 Graduating Cohort (%)

		Initial Passing Rate	Possible Improvement in Passing Rate	Actual Improvement in Passing Rate	Rate of Improvement	Difference (MAS vs. Non-MAS)
MAS	Math	61	39	25	64	8
	Reading	66	34	26	76	6
	Writing	65	35	28	80	0
Non-MAS	Math	77	23	13	57	—
	Reading	80	20	14	70	—
	Writing	75	25	20	80	—

Note: Data for this table derived from TUSD Department of Accountability and Research (2011a).

Table 2.5. Graduation Rate Differences, TUSD 2010 Graduating Cohort (%)

	Graduation Rate	Difference
White	87.1	7.6
Latina/o	79.5	
No free or reduced-price lunch	85.7	7.9
Free or reduced-price lunch	77.8	
MAS	82.6	0.1
Non-MAS	82.5	

Note: Data derived from "Graduation Rate" (2010) and TUSD Department of Accountability and Research (2011b).

and Latina/o students, two groups who have persistently lower TUSD graduation rates than their affluent and white peers (see table 2.5). The gap in graduation rates between white and Latina/o students within TUSD was almost eight percentage points, and a similar gap exists between those who receive free or reduced-price lunch and those who do not.

If the MAS courses had no discernible impact, one would expect a similar gap between the largely low-income and Latina/o MAS students in relation to their non-MAS peers. Similar to the AIMS analysis, instead of a gap I found relative parity.

Further disaggregating these data by SES highlighted an emerging achievement gap that actually favored students who took MAS classes. District-defined low- and very low-income students who took MAS classes graduated at substantially higher rates than their non-MAS peers (see table 2.6). For the 2010 graduating cohort, low-income MAS students

Table 2.6. Graduation Rate Differences, TUSD 2010 Graduating Cohort by SES (%)

		Graduation Rate	Difference (MAS vs. Non-MAS)
Low income	MAS	82.7	7.8
	Non-MAS	74.9	
Very low income	MAS	78.9	14.6
	Non-MAS	64.3	

Note: Data derived from TUSD Department of Accountability and Research (2011b).

graduated at a rate 7.8 percentage points higher than their non-MAS peers while very low-income MAS students graduated at a rate 14.6 percentage points higher.

To put this in context, there were 3,338 TUSD students in the 2010 graduating cohort who did not take an MAS course during their high school careers. If the low- and very low-income students in this population graduated at the same rate as their MAS peers, 103 more students would have graduated from TUSD in 2010.[5]

Further Exploring Graduation Rates

If low-income MAS students graduate at substantially higher rates than their non-MAS peers, and if the graduation rates for all students are relatively similar, then it would follow that TUSD upper-income students outperform MAS upper-income students. This is true, but it is also an issue that requires deeper examination. For example, there is a dramatic difference between upper-income MAS and non-MAS students in terms of taking Advanced Placement (AP) courses. For the 2010 graduating cohort, only 1 percent of MAS students earned any AP credit regardless of income level, compared to 20 percent of high-income, non-MAS students and 25 percent of very high-income non-MAS students. These statistics are important for a number of reasons.

First, many AP courses were not available to students who eventually took an MAS course because of their early high school academic performance. Therefore, a huge selection bias favors those already on a college track in terms of opportunities to take AP courses. Second, there are a number of structural reasons one would expect very high educational outcomes for those able to take AP courses above and beyond the academic prowess of the students.

The schools that offered MAS courses had dramatic differences in class size between AP and non-AP course offerings. For example, there were dramatically different class enrollments in Tucson Magnet High School. Sometimes the differences were relatively small, such as the four-student difference in history offerings (see table 2.7). Sometimes they were large, as in the eight-student difference between Latino literature and AP English language (see table 2.7).

Even in the case of small differences in enrollment, this still means educating 14 percent fewer students per class. This trend is relatively consistent throughout TUSD: the AP courses tend to have lower enrollments relative to general education and MAS courses. In addition, there tends to be a significant, inverse relationship between class size and educational outcomes. In slight simplification of existent literature, the fewer students in a class, the better the students perform (Ehrenberg et al. 2001; Pritchard 1999).

In addition, AP courses occupy a unique place within public high schools. They tend to be offered by teachers with the highest levels of professional training (Milewski and Gillie 2002, 1). Additionally, there

Table 2.7. Tucson Magnet High School, MAS and AP Class Size

Subject Area	Class	Sections	Average Class Size
Government	American government/ Social Justice Education Project 1,2 (MAS)	2	32.3
	AP US government and politics 1,2	2	25.7
History	American history/ Mexican American perspectives 1,2 (MAS)	5	27.3
	AP US history 1,2	2	23.5
English	Latino literature 7,8 (MAS)	3	32.3
	Latino literature 6,7 (MAS)	5	26.2
	AP English literature 1,2	3	25.2
	AP English language 1,2	2	18.7

Note: Data derived from TUSD Department of Accountability and Research (2011c). "Sections" refers to two class semesters of the specific offering.

are frequently entrance requirements for students such as high standardized test scores, faculty recommendations, or taking a prerequisite course—an honors course, for example (Milewski and Gillie 2002, 5). Returning to TUSD, this means that the upper-income students in the district (who are largely white with college-educated parents) have unparalleled access to the most academically rigorous courses, with the smallest size, among peers who are ostensibly college bound, and taught by the best-trained instructors. With these structural inequalities, I would be surprised if I did not find achievement gaps at the upper end of the income spectrum.

Conclusion

Students taking MAS courses begin their academic endeavors far behind their peers who never take an MAS course as evidenced by achievement gaps between the two groups in terms of initial AIMS passing rates. If MAS courses were as effective at teaching students as non-MAS courses, I would expect these achievement gaps to persist. Instead, the end result is educational parity in terms of AIMS passing and graduation rates. When students begin their careers in TUSD, affluent and white students overwhelmingly graduate and go to college. For low-income and Latina/o students, just graduating high school is in question. These differences are highlighted by the persistent achievement gaps along the lines of race and class (see table 2.2) that have been at the center of discussion in TUSD for decades. As previously outlined, the data available are conservative in nature because the available statistics compare MAS students to all other students in the district without taking account of race, SES, and differing levels of incoming student academic preparation. However, a word of caution is warranted. These statistics are descriptive in nature, not inferential, so they only highlight the possibility of an impact as opposed to definitively identifying one. Future studies should employ multivariate analyses to more clearly isolate the impacts of MAS classes when controlling for potential confounding hypotheses. Even with these obstacles and limitations, one key conclusion became clear: the achievement gap is, for all intents and purposes, closed for MAS students. The underlying question therefore becomes: what is causing this gap to close?

Notes

1. A number of terms are used to describe people of Latin American descent in Arizona (e.g., Hispanic, Mexican American, Chicano, or Latino). For consistency, I use the term Latina/o throughout this chapter to refer to one pan-ethnic identity while avoiding the sexism embedded within the term "Latino."
2. "Princeton University," *U.S. News and World Report,* http://colleges.usnews.rankingsandreviews.com/best-colleges/princeton-university-2627.
3. The graduation rate for those on free or reduced-price lunch was provided, but it was not for those not on free or reduced-price lunch. So I calculated it using the following formula: $[(N_{FullCohort})(Graduation\ Rate_{FullCohort}) - (N_{FreeorReducedLunch})(Graduation\ Rate_{FreeorReducedLunch})]/(N_{FullCohort} - N_{FreeorReducedLunch}) = (Graduation\ Rate_{StudentsNotOnFreeorReducedLunch})$. While it is an estimate, a more precise figure would not eliminate an 8 percentage point gap.
4. http://www.azed.gov/standards-development-assessment/.
5. This calculation was made using the following formula: take the number of students in the low- and very low-income quintiles who did not take an MAS course, multiply it by the MAS graduation rate for the specific income quintile, and subtract the actual number of non-MAS graduates in the specific quintile.

References

Apple, M. W. 2001. *Educating the "Right" Way: Markets, Standards, God, and Inequality.* New York: RoutledgeFalmer.

Astin, A. W. 1993. *Assessment for Excellence: The Philosophy and Practice of Assessment and Evaluation in Higher Education.* Westport, CT: Oryx.

Department of Accountability and Research. 2011a. "AIMS Achievement Comparison for Students Taking One or More Ethnic Studies Classes: Initial Passing Rate versus Cumulative Passing Rate by AIMS Subject and Cohort Year." Tucson, AZ: Tucson Unified School District, January 6.

———. 2011b. "Selected Statistics—2010 (Four Year) Graduation Cohort." Tucson, AZ: Tucson Unified School District, January 6.

———. 2011c. "2010–2011 School Year MASD Average CORE Class Size Compared to Non-MASD Average CORE Class Size." Tucson, AZ: Tucson Unified School District, April 22.

Ehrenberg, R. G., D. J. Brewer, A. Gamoran, and J. D. Willms. 2001. "Class Size and Student Achievement." *Psychological Science in the Public Interest* 2(1): 1–30.

Gándara, P., and F. Contreras. 2009. *The Latino Educational Crisis: The Consequences of Failed Social Policy.* Cambridge, MA: Harvard University Press.

"Graduation Rate." 2010. TUSDStats, http://tusdstats.tusd.k12.az.us/paweb/aggD/graduation/gradrate.aspx.

Kozol, J. 2005. *Shame of the Nation: The Restoration of Apartheid Schooling in America.* New York: Crown.

Lewis, A. E. 2004. *Race in the Schoolyard: Negotiating the Color Line in Classrooms and Communities*. New Brunswick, NJ: Rutgers University Press.

MacEachern, D. 2011. "Bogus Arguments for Tucson Ethnic Studies Finally Debunked." *Arizona Republic*, March 6, http://www.azcentral.com/arizonarepublic/opinions/articles/20110305maceachern-ethnic-studies-0306.html.

Milewski, G. B., and J. M. Gillie. 2002. *What Are the Characteristics of AP® Teachers? An Examination of Survey Research*. Princeton, NJ: College Board.

Pritchard, I. 1999. "Reducing Class Size: What Do We Know?" Washington, DC: National Institute on Student Achievement, Curriculum and Assessment, Office of Educational Research and Improvement, US Department of Education.

CHAPTER THREE

The Battle for Educational Sovereignty and the Right to Save the Lives of Our Children

Augustine Romero

Question: what would you expect a state to do with a successful academic program that has (a) inverted the achievement gap between Mexican American students and their peers (regardless of ethnicity); (b) inverted the graduation rate between Mexican American students and their Anglo peers; (c) raised the college matriculation rates for Mexican American students to a level significantly higher than the national average; and (d) virtually eliminated suspensions and expulsions of Mexican American students?

Over the last eight academic years (2003–2011) the Tucson Unified School District's (TUSD's) Mexican American/raza studies program (MAS), the Social Justice Education Project (SJEP), and the critically compassionate intellectualism (CCI) model have created and nurtured the academic environment described above. Yet before I go into detail about the program, I return to my opening question. I believe that most rational and soundminded people would say, "Replicate that program." However, remember I live in Arizona.

Let me tell you what the state of Arizona did. On April 29, 2010, the Arizona state legislature gave House Bill 2281 final approval status, thus sending it to the governor for her signature. On May 11, 2010, Jan Brewer signed HB 2281 into law as Arizona Revised Statute (ARS) 15-112. I believe the sole intent of HB 2281 was to abolish the liberatory, counterhegemonic, and transformative structures within CCI, SJEP, and MAS. This was an attack on equity in education, and this was an attack on a model that has many of the answers needed to truly counter and remedy the historically unjust, unequal, and in many cases, the racist American educational system.

Although the media and even some in the legislature have deemed ARS 15-112 to be anti–ethnic studies legislation, the attacks from the racist Right and in some cases the dysconsciously racist (King 1997) Left have been waged solely on MAS, SJEP, and CCI. From its inception, MAS has been different than its three ethnic studies siblings. These departments, Native American studies, African American studies, and pan-Asian studies, have what I refer to as an "associated academic services" orientation, which involves mostly tutoring, mentoring, and student advocacy. Mexican American studies has a "direct academic service" orientation that focuses primarily on direct classroom instruction, with some attention given to teacher mentoring and continuing education. It is my belief that MAS has also been singled out for its transformative, holistic, and consciousness-raising nature. Quite truthfully, many nonprogressives have a negative view of the fact that CCI, SJEP, and MAS enrich and enlighten the American historical narrative, because this disrupts and erodes the fabric of their fictitious and self-serving narrative. For these people the truth is irrelevant; for these people the level of academic success is irrelevant; and for these people the fact that CCI, SJEP, and MAS have saved, do save, and will save the lives of many children is irrelevant. These critical factors are irrelevant because they all have the potential of disrupting the status quo within America's historical racial and social order (Romero 2008).

This chapter highlights the context in which this unethical, immoral, dishonest, and antihumanistic political battle is being waged against us in the name of patriotism, morality, and "American" values. Moreover, this chapter constitutes a counternarrative (Delgado 1989; Yosso 2006) that highlights the academic, social, and cultural transformations taking place within our students and in our communities.

Overview

I begin with a brief narrative of the creation of MAS and its roots within Tucson's Mexican American community. I also discuss the numerous legislative attempts to abolish the MAS program during 2008, 2009, and 2010. The next section discusses some of the counterstrategies I have used to preserve MAS. The last section interrogates HB 2281's implications and discusses our national outreach campaign.

Tucson Unified School District is 61.6 percent Latino and 26 percent Anglo, with an enrollment of nearly 58,000. For the last eleven graduating classes within TUSD, over the four years of high school Latino enrollment has declined by anywhere from 32 percent to 49 percent. This means that from the time Latinos enter TUSD as freshmen to their walk across the graduation stage as seniors, Latino enrollment has fallen by as much as 49 percent (class of 2000) to as little as 32 percent (class of 2007) (TUSD Department of Accountability and Research 2010).

Creation

TUSD's Mexican American Studies Department was created in July 1998 as a result of a grassroots movement for greater academic achievement for the Chicana/o children in the district. For many Chicanas/os in Tucson the establishment of the MAS Department was a victory in battles fought nearly thirty years earlier when community organizers such as Raúl Grijalva, Guadalupe Castillo, Salomón Baldenegro, and Eduardo Olivas led a series of school walkouts in 1969.[1] The creation of Chicano studies was one of the primary demands of community and student activists. Beyond the Chicano studies issue, the student organizers were distressed by a school system that was truly separate and unequal. The majority of the district's resources flowed to the predominantly white east-side schools, with very few resources going to the immensely African American and Chicano westside schools.

Despite the issuance of a federal desegregation order in 1978, the social and educational conditions for Chicanos in TUSD would change very little. As a result, in 1996, community groups, community members, educators, and academics began to organize in support of the creation of a Mexican American studies program. The unification of these groups of community members, educators, and educational advocates and their relentless efforts were hugely instrumental in the realization of a community dream, the creation of MAS.

The creation of MAS and the Chicana/o educational struggle in Tucson is part of a larger legacy. The Mexican American/Chicana/o quest for educational justice, sovereignty, equal opportunity, and freedom can be traced back seventy years to legal cases such as *Romo v. Laird* (1925), *Independent School District v. Salvatierra* (1931), *Alvarez v. Lemon Grove* (1931), *Mendez v. Westminster* (1947), and *Delgado et al. v. Bastrop Independent School District et al.* (1948). In fact, the Mendez case demonstrates the strong relationship between the Mexican American and African American liberation struggles, as it was one of the precedents used by future Supreme Court Justice Thurgood Marshall in the landmark *Brown v. Board of Education* case, which he successfully argued before that court in 1954 (Romero and Arce 2010).

In 2003, in the effort to honor the voices of those who struggled for its existence, and in concert with the No Child Left Behind Act, as director of MAS, I implemented CCI as a means of ensuring an equitable educational experience for Mexican American/Chicana/o students. This model was created from student voices and established on the basis of educational equity, educational sovereignty, and student empowerment. The model expresses what our students said they and others like them needed to obtain educational equity and a method through which they and others could achieve greater academic success. Equally important, this model gave our students the opportunity to realize their potential as organic/barrio intellectuals (Romero, Arce, and Cammarota 2009). This opportunity to realize their potential as intellectuals is a manifestation of their educational sovereignty.

The Actions of the Hegemonic Group

In 2008, 2009, and 2010 bills were introduced into the Arizona legislature to abolish the MAS and all ethnic studies programs from the state's secondary schools. I must make it clear that TUSD is the only district in the state that has an ethnic studies program. Moreover, during his testimony to the Arizona Senate's Education Committee on April 7, 2010, State Superintendent of Public Instruction Tom Horne stated that his only concern was the "Raza Studies Department in TUSD" (Arizona State Legislature 2010).

The first bill made clear the true intent of our attackers. In the spring of 2008, Senate Bill 1108 (SB 1108) was introduced in the Arizona state legislature. In essence, SB 1108 would prohibit the use of any curriculum centered in the voices and experiences of people of color. The authors of SB 1108 argued that these voices "denigrate American values" and "overtly encourage dissent" against American values. Moreover, the underlying rationale within this bill becomes crystal clear with the knowledge that SB 1108 was a Homeland Security bill. The understanding that the abolishment of our program was being promoted as a matter of national or state security fully exposes the level of hate, paranoia, and fear revealed in the actions of our attackers. We were fortunate that this bill was the most egregious, hateful, and the broadest of the three bills, including not only K–12 education but also all of the community college and university ethnic studies programs. It also included any and all K–12, community college, and university clubs and organizations that had any kind of ethnic orientation. Therefore, clubs such as the Association of Black Engineers or Latino/a sororities or fraternities would have been abolished by this piece of legislation. We were able to recruit the support of the three major Arizona universities, and many of their ethnically rooted clubs and organizations.

The vast, broad-based opposition to SB 1108 led to its death on the Senate floor. However, we knew that this was just the beginning. We knew that in the future the political will would be greater, and we knew that when the time was right there would be conservatives that would use the devastation of our program, our communities, and our children for political gain.

In 2009, Senate Bill 1069 was introduced in the Arizona State Senate. Although SB 1069 was less egregious than SB 1108, it still forwarded a discourse of dishonesty and fearmongering. This bill established some of the language that would appear in 2010's Senate Bill 2281—"A school district or charter school in this state shall not include in the program of instruction any courses or classes that either: 1. Are designed primarily for pupils of a particular ethnic group. 2. Advocate ethnic solidarity instead of the treatment of pupils as individuals" (Arizona State Legislature 2010).

In 2010, House Bill 2281 (HB 2281) was introduced in the Arizona House of Representatives. Once this bill passed in the House, it was heard in the Senate Education Committee on April 7, 2010. At this hearing Arizona's superintendent of public instruction, Tom Horne, stated in his testimony that he sponsored this bill because he believed that Mexican American studies promoted anti-American sentiment and resentment toward white people. In a 4–3 vote that went right down party lines (Republicans yes and Democrats no), SB 2281 moved out of the committee. However, the most repulsive part of the hearing was that despite the presence of numerous groups and individuals supporting the MAS program, the chairman of the Education Committee, Republican John Huppenthal, denied them the opportunity to testify, despite having given our adversaries all the time they needed to fully articulate their lies. In fact, he did so despite the fervent protest of the committee's three Democratic members. Huppenthal arrogantly ignored the protest and called for the vote. Adding to the level of arrogance and ignorance, the Republicans cast their votes without hearing the testimony of the numerous pro-MAS individuals and organizations that had officially stated their desire to testify. None of them had any real understanding of our program other than what they had most likely read in Phoenix newspapers and the lies they heard during the testimony of our adversaries. As stated above, HB 2281 was signed into law by Governor Jan Brewer, who herself does not have any firsthand knowledge of our program; moreover, she was not willing to meet with us to gain an honest understanding of the nature and scope of our program or its educational and social merits.

HB 2281 states that classes in Arizona public schools cannot (1) promote the overthrow of the US government; (2) promote resentment toward a race or class of people; (3) be designed primarily for pupils of a particular ethnic group; or (4) advocate ethnic solidarity instead of the treatment of pupils as individuals. The fact of the matter is that CCI, SJEP, or MAS do not do any of the things prohibited by HB 2281. However, in this case, CCI, SJEP, and MAS have been declared guilty until proven innocent, contrary to the core American legal principle that one is innocent until proven guilty.

On December 31, 2010, HB 2281 became ARS 15-112, making it law in Arizona. On December 30, 2010, the TUSD governing board issued a resolution stating that its ethnic studies program was in compliance with ARS 15-112. On January 3, 2011, in his final moments as Arizona's superintendent of public instruction, Tom Horne declared that TUSD's Mexican American Studies Department was in violation of ARS 15-112. Horne's action was not a surprise, nor was the January 4, 2011, action of the newly seated superintendent of public instruction, John Huppenthal. On that day he announced that TUSD's MAS Department was in violation of ARS 15-112. The purging of MAS was a primary element of both Horne's and Huppenthal's political platforms. Both used and fed into the anti-Latino sentiments that mirror the racist climate of the post–civil rights era.

In early March 2011, Huppenthal announced that he would sanction an audit of TUSD's MAS Department by Cambium Learning Incorporated. On March 17, 2011, news broke that the person Huppenthal hired to conduct the audit had recently pleaded out of eleven criminal charges. This person's plea agreement included a lifetime ban on working in the state of New Jersey. This was yet another example of the lack of integrity and diligence at the core of Huppenthal's and Horne's actions and motives. It is my belief that at some point the majority of Arizonans and Americans will rise above the racist rhetoric and recognize the truth that I and my colleagues have been telling for years.

An editorial on March 21, 2011, by governing board member Mark Stegeman in the *Arizona Daily Star* announcing his belief that MAS courses should be elective rather than maintaining their elevated status as core classes is a great example of dysconscious racism and naïveté. In essence, this recommendation would relegate our courses to second-class status. It would be okay to offer European history for Advanced Placement credit, but our students would be forced to take Mexican American history, social justice government, or Latino literature for elective credit.

What is most incredible is how most people fail to recognize the dysconscious racism of this opinion. In addition, most of the same people naively believe that if the status of these courses were changed, the state would thereafter leave us alone. These people have failed and continue to fail to accurately assess the level of racist politics in play, which will maintain itself at least for the foreseeable future. It is this naïveté that has caused the greatest divisions between TUSD leadership and MAS leadership and its community advocates.

Above all, and with all due respect, none of the people operating from this state of naïveté understands what needs to be delivered to our historically underserved students in order to ensure they receive an equitable and excellent education. In most professions these people would not have had the option, much less the power, to make such decisions. In most professions such actions would be considered malpractice and blatant acts of professional and ethical negligence.

In this section, I discuss the actions of May 3, 2011. The events of April 26, 2011, are covered later. On May 3, 2011, a special board meeting was held with a limited thirty minute "call to the audience." During the call to the audience speakers are given no more than three minutes to offer their message. This protocol limited the community voice to only ten speakers. This was highly problematic given that there was an enormous amount of people who were denied the opportunity to speak by the District. What is glaringly obvious to me is the fact that District consciously diminished the voice and perspective of the pro-MAS community. To escalate the level of tension, TUSD leadership ordered the presence of well over one hundred Tucson Police Department officers, many of whom were dressed in full riot gear, outside the boardroom. At the same time, the police department's helicopter flew overhead for hours, while, for the first time ever, people had to pass through metal detectors before they could enter the building. At the request of TUSD Superintendent John Pedicone, seven community members who only wanted to have their voices heard by the TUSD governing board were arrested. Among those arrested were three community elders and civil rights champions: Raquel Rubio-Goldsmith, Lupe Castillo, and Salomón Baldenegro Sr.

Toward the end of the evening, protesters were trying to block the transport of some of the community members who had been arrested. These protesters decided to form a human chain through which the transport needed to pass. Over time, Tucson police became frustrated and decided to physically move the protesters from the street. This led to some people being punched, kicked, and thrown to the ground.

This was an attack on our community; more specifically, this was an attack on TUSD's Latino community. The TUSD leadership decided that it could silence the voice of our community members and criminalize our entire community, and then at the end of meeting they gave license to the police to beat down our community members. For those who share the historical and ideological lenses of community members such as myself, this day will forever live in infamy, and we will never forget or forgive those who sanctioned and imposed these acts of violence upon our community.

The hypocrisy and immorality of the state continued. On June 16, 2011, after holding the Cambium audit for forty-five days, in a press conference at the state capitol, Huppenthal issued his findings, stating that TUSD's Mexican American studies was in violation of ARS 15-112. On June 17, different media sources, including the *Huffington Post*, reported that despite Huppenthal's statement, the audit found that MAS was in total compliance with the statute. Huppenthal made claims of noncompliance despite the lucid, cogent, and unambiguous results of the $175,000 audit that he commissioned. In fact, Cambium clearly articulated that MAS was in full compliance with ARS 15-112. Moreover, the Cambium report lauded MAS for its impact on achievement, and for the humanity-based element of its pedagogy.

Counters

Over the course of this racist cultural war, CCI, SJEP, and MAS supporters used a variety of tactics to counter the proposed anti–ethnic studies legislation. In 2008, I was a member of Governor Janet Napolitano's Latino Advisory Board. In April 2008, I made a presentation on MAS at the governor's monthly meeting. After the presentation, Governor Napolitano guaranteed the entire Latino Advisory Board that if the bill made it to her desk she would veto it without hesitation. Fortunately, the bill died on the House side of the legislature, and the supporters of CCI, SJEP, and MAS did not have to rely on the governor's veto.

In 2009, SB 1108 passed out of the Judicial Committee in the Senate and went to the third of its required three readings, which made SB 1108 eligible for a vote on the Senate floor. Fortunately, with the help of TUSD's lobbyist, Sam Polito, we were able to negotiate our way out of this bill. On Father's Day 2009, two of my colleagues, two of our students, a good friend of the teachers' union, and I met with the primary Republican player, and in this meeting it was agreed that the bill would be killed (details of this meeting are confidential). Despite this agreement, a coalition of community groups wanted to demonstrate their support for MAS. This coalition decided that it would sponsor a run from Tucson to Phoenix in the middle of summer. On June 27, 28, and 29, 2009, over fifty Tucsonans (youth, students, parents, community members, educators, and district administrators) ran over 130 miles in the Equality and Justice Run, in heat of up to 117 degrees, across the desert from Tucson to Phoenix. Over the course of the event, hundreds of supporters from the barrios and communities of Tucson, Eloy, Casa Grande, Guadalupe, and Phoenix joined our runners. The run culminated on June 29 with a 300-person march to the State Capitol Building.

It must be noted that one of the most critical aspects of the Equality and Justice Run was the spiritual support given by the Yoeme and Akimel O'odham nations as the students, teachers, and CCI, SJEP, and MAS supporters ran through their lands. In addition, it must be understood that this run was about healing and it was linked to sacred traditional indigenous practices. The run was used as a channel for positive change in our communities and in our state. It was not a march, a rally, or a race, but rather an opportunity for our supporters, teachers, and students to unite for the purpose of healing, and to do so through an indigenous tradition that generates change through prayer. The Yoeme and Akimel O'odham nations believe the energy that is projected from the momentum of the run, its runners, their intentions, and their constant connection to the earth will be reciprocated in the form of a healing and ultimately a blessing.

It is important to recognize the spiritual support given for many years by Jesus "Chucho" Ruiz and the Calpulli Teoxicalli, which has been paramount to our spiritual well-being and to our ability to ground ourselves and to maintain our focus on students, parents, and community.

In 2010, we did not have a friendly governor. The tea party movement heightened and further normalized racist politics and it totally purged the political will and sensibility of moderate Republicans. Therefore, we had absolutely no leverage to negotiate HB 2281's withdrawal or defeat. As a result, we were left to the mercy of demagogues that planned to use our program to advance their political platforms and careers. After the bill passed out of committee on April 7, we knew the end result was a foregone conclusion. On May 11, 2010, Governor Jan Brewer signed HB 2281, making it Arizona law effective December 31, 2010.

On October 18, 2010, Save Ethnic Studies, a group of former MAS teachers, filed a lawsuit challenging the constitutionality of HB 2281. The most effective district-level counter to HB 2281 to date took place on April 26, 2011. On that Tuesday, the TUSD governing board was holding a special meeting wherein they were to discuss and devalue the MAS courses by officially making them elective. However, in a heroic act of social justice and righteousness, the student group UNIDOS took over the TUSD governing board meeting room by chaining and locking themselves to chairs on the dais. This act of true justice led to the cancellation of the entire meeting, which caused the vote to be postponed. Hundreds of students and community members cheered the UNIDOS students and sang songs of unity, love, and hope.

With regard to the legal battle, on October 18, 2011, Save Ethnic Studies submitted a motion for summary judgment, in essence requesting that Judge A. Wallace Tashima find ARS 15-112 unconstitutional based upon provisions established in the First and Fourteenth Amendments of the US Constitution.

Implications

The most troublesome reality is that due to ideological conflicts, not only has our program been dismantled, but the ideological and theoretical foundation on which it was created has been deemed illegal in the state of Arizona. Our enemies are right when they say this war has nothing to do with education. They are right because this war is yet another manifestation and rearticulation of the racist projects that perpetuate the racial, social, and political order that is rooted in white privilege and white oppression. Some may not like, understand, or even believe the statements in this chapter, but as God is my witness, they are the truth.

Viva justicia, amor, y esperanza.

Notes

1. The 1969 TUSD walkouts were products of the Chicano movement. Among the primary requests of the 1969 protesters, the most relevant was their demand for Chicano studies. It is my belief that the seeds of the MAS Department were sowed during the 1969 walkouts.

References

Arizona State Legislature. 2010. Arizona State Legislator Bills. http://www.azleg.gov/.
Delgado, R. 1989. "Storytelling for Oppositionists and Others: A Plea for Narrative." *Michigan Law Review* 87: 2411–41.
King, J. 1997. "Dysconscious Racism: The Cultural Politics of Critiquing Ideology and Identity." In *Critical White Studies: Looking behind the Mirror*, ed. R. Delgado and J. Stefancic, 640–641. Philadelphia: Temple University Press.
Romero, A. 2008. "Towards a Critically Compassionate Intellectualism Model of Transformative Education: Love, Hope, Identity, and Organic Intellectualism through the Convergence of Critical Race Theory, Critical Pedagogy, and Authentic Caring." Unpublished PhD diss., University of Arizona.
Romero, A., and M. S. Arce. 2009. "Culture as a Resource: Critically Compassionate Intellectualism and its Struggle Against Racism, Fascism, and Intellectual Apartheid in Arizona." *Hamline University School of Law Journal of Public Law and Policy*, 31: 179.
Romero, A., S. Arce, and J. Cammarota. 2009. "A Barrio Pedagogy: Identity, Intellectualism, Activism, and Academic Achievement through the Evolution of Critically Compassionate Intellectualism." *Race, Ethnicity, and Education* 12(2): 217–33.
Tucson Unified School District. 2010. AIMS Data [Data file]. Retrieved from http://tusdstats.tusd.k12.az.us/planning/profiles/aims/multyeareth_front.asp.
Yosso, T. 2006. *Critical Race Counterstories along the Chicana/Chicano Educational Pipeline*. New York: Routledge.

CHAPTER FOUR

Self-Inflicted Reductio ad Absurdum

Pedagogies and Policies of the Absurd in the State of Arizona

Mary Carol Combs

In recent years the state of Arizona has provided the rest of the country with considerable levity. It is, after all, the state whose governor claimed that severed heads routinely turn up in the desert ("Brewer Shows She Has the Chops" 2010), whose publicity-loving sheriff of Maricopa Country dresses immigrant inmates in pink underwear and striped pajamas (Boehnke 2008; Wagner 2007), and whose state education officials believe that ethnic studies courses promote the overthrow of the US government (Reinhart 2011). These are the same officials who would also like to prohibit teachers with heavy accents from instructing English-language learners, even though these teachers may share similar cultural and linguistic backgrounds with their students, and thus may be able to connect on a deeper level with students' language learning experiences (Jordan 2010; Strauss 2010).

Levity aside, the policies described above are outlandish, even bizarrely humorous, but they also are symptomatic of a darker, more troubling side to politics in the state. While other chapters in this book illuminate the multiple assaults against the Mexican American studies classes in the Tucson Unified School District—and by extension against the Latino students enrolled in them—this chapter discusses the effect of state policies on another vulnerable and marginalized group in state schools—English language learners (ELLs). In Arizona, the public discourse surrounding the education of ELLs is inextricably bound to larger political concerns about immigration, border crime, the environment, and international law. To wit, one cannot address issues of pedagogy or curriculum for students acquiring English as a second language without also considering the fact that many people in Arizona, including elected officials, believe the vast majority of ELLs are undocumented, and thus undeserving of state-funded services.

The immigration-education interface provides a context for a more focused examination of one of the most backward and egregious of the state's education policies, an ethnically and linguistically segregated four-hour grammar and reading program for students developing proficiency in English. I describe the segregated program and explain why it exists, although there is no research basis for it and school districts, teachers, and students strongly oppose the program. There is credible evidence that these policies specifically target Latinos, particularly immigration, education, and language policies. Considered as a whole, these polices represent a reactionary political response of state government to two major shifts in population demographics: (1) the increasing numbers of Latinos in the state, especially young Latinos, and (2) a growing, predominantly Anglo, elderly population.

Arizona's Legislative Theater of the Absurd

Passage of bizarre laws in Arizona has become almost routine. In early 2011, for instance, the State Senate voted to declare an official state gun—the Colt single-action army revolver. University faculty and students can now feel safe since another law would allow us to carry concealed weapons on campus (and in bars as well). Both gun laws were introduced after the horrific January 8, 2011, shootings in Tucson that killed Judge John Roll, severely wounded Congresswoman Gabrielle Giffords, and killed and wounded many others. They certainly advance the Wild West image our legislators in Phoenix aspire to, as evidenced in such other proposals as these:

The Freedom to Breathe Act, which protects Arizona residents from the Clean Air Act.[1]

The Nullification of Federal Laws Act, which frees Arizonans from living under any federal legislation that a simple majority of the legislature deems unconstitutional.[2]

The Nullification of International Law, exempting Arizona from having to abide by international law.[3]

The Federal Registration Act, requiring all federal agencies to register their presence in any Arizona county with that county's sheriff.[4]

The Arizona Citizenship bill, which recognizes a child's US citizenship status only if the child has at least one parent who is already a US citizen.[5]

The "Birther" bill that would have required President Obama to produce his birth certificate in order to get on the state's ballot in 2012.[6]

The Border Crime Funding bill, which defines a county eligible for state funds as one that has a population of more than 3 million (only Maricopa County) or between 300,000 and 500,000 people (only Pinal County). The funding law explicitly prohibits funding to a county with more than 500,000 but fewer than 2,000,000 residents (only Pima County).[7]

The Susan B. Anthony and Frederick Douglass Prenatal Nondiscrimination Act of 2011, requiring physicians to swear in an affidavit that they are not performing an abortion for the purpose of sex or race selection (even though there's not a shred of evidence that anyone in Arizona has elected the procedure for these reasons).[8]

Requirements for School Science Instruction, a bill encouraging science teachers to provide alternative perspectives about global climate change.[9]

The retaliatory nature of some of these proposals is clear. The most obvious example is the Border Crime Funding bill, which explicitly punishes Pima County because of comments its sheriff made after passage of SB 1070, the anti-immigration/racial profiling law passed by the state legislature in March 2010. Sheriff Clarence Dupnik declared he would not enforce parts of the law because of the potential for inconsistent or idiosyncratic enforcement from county to county, particularly the racial profiling aspect of SB 1070, which allows the apprehension of an individual on the basis of the arresting officer's "reasonable suspicion" that the individual was undocumented (McCombs 2010). Dupnik, a Democrat, also antagonized Republican legislators after the January 8, 2011, assassination attempt on Congresswoman Gabrielle Giffords by stating that Arizona had become a "mecca of prejudice and bigotry" (Fischer 2011a, 2011b). Excluding Pima County was "by design," explained Senate president and cosponsor Russell Pearce (R-Mesa): "The sheriff says he's not going to enforce the law. Why would I fund him?" (quoted in Fischer 2011b, A2).

Another example of retaliatory legislation is the Arizona Citizenship bill, or the sardonically named "Anchor Babies" law, which challenges the Fourteenth Amendment's guarantee of citizenship by birth in the United States. Sponsors of anti-immigrant proposals sometimes refer to the US-born children of undocumented immigrants as "anchor babies" because when they turn twenty-one, they may sponsor their parents for legal permanent residency (Gonzalez 2005). The Arizona Citizenship bill bestows Arizona and US citizenship upon a child born in the United States only if one or both parents are US citizens. In an interview with the *Arizona Republic*, one of the bill's principal sponsors argued that court attention to this issue was necessary "so we can figure out how to treat these kids" (Rau 2011c, A1).[10]

Other proposals are downright silly. The Freedom to Breathe Act and the "Birther" bill are examples, the former challenging the existence of global climate change and the latter requiring all presidential candidates to produce certified birth documents in order for their names to appear on the state ballot. State senator Sylvia Allen (R-Snowflake) introduced the Freedom to Breathe Act to forestall regulation of greenhouse gases by the Environmental Protection Agency. Allen declared there was no evidence that carbon dioxide from power plants or vehicle emissions harmed anyone (Fischer 2011c). The "Birther" bill mirrored the obsession of national tea party members with the belief that President Barack Obama was not a US citizen. HB 2177 required all presidential candidates on the state ballot to produce a certified copy of their long-form birth certificate, signatures of witnesses in attendance, baptismal or circumcision certificates, hospital birth records, or their mothers' postpartum medical records signed by the individual who delivered them at birth. If they refused to supply the documentation, their names would not appear on the state ballot (Rau 2011a).

Federalism or Sedition?

Three proposals introduced in early 2011 reflect a strong states' rights perspective. SB 1433 creates a twelve-member Joint Legislative Committee on Nullification of Federal Law empowered to "vote by simple majority to nullify in its entirety a specific federal law or regulation that is outside the scope of the powers delegated by the people to the federal government." According to the Senate Research Office, this means that Arizona citizens are not required to recognize or live under any federal legislation nullified by the committee. SB 1433 also empowers the nullification committee to ensure that the state legislature adopts and enacts "all measures necessary to prevent the enforcement of any nullified federal legislation" (Arizona State Senate 2011).

Related legislation (HB 2077) would require all federal regulatory agencies conducting business in any of Arizona's fifteen counties to register with the sheriffs of those counties. Such agencies must also pay a registration fee and turn over any fines, fees, or penalties they impose on individuals, businesses, or industries (for deposit into the state's general fund). Sylvia Allen, sponsor of the Freedom to Breathe Act, also supported the nullification laws: "We are trying everything legally given to us . . . to start back on the path to restore our country," she said. "The states don't even have rights anymore. Private people don't have rights" (quoted in Rough 2011, A1).

Finally, Senate Concurrent Resolution 1010, introduced by twenty-one Republican legislators, would prohibit Arizona courts from considering international law or legal precepts of other nations or cultures when making judicial decisions. Though subject to voter approval, this particular law reveals the obstreperous character of the state legislature and current governor Jan Brewer, who likened nullification proposals to her own efforts to limit federal authority on health care and environmental regulation: "We need to be able to make the decisions that control the destiny of our populations. And if the government would step back and give us the opportunity, we would do a great job" (quoted in Rough 2011, A1).

Adherence to federalist principles commonly reflects the belief that the federal government should be smaller, that its legislative and judicial influence should be limited, and that power and governance should be greater at the state level. Arizona's support for states' rights is not especially surprising given the spate of bills in 2011 that assert its sovereignty. Still, the nullification bills hint at more than mere state chauvinism. A legislative declaration of independence from federal law, which SB 1433 essentially made, can be viewed as windmill chasing (the US Constitution trumps state law), as treasonous (no state can refuse to abide by the US Constitution or federal law), or simply laughable (introduced by a fringe element in the legislature), though as *Arizona Republic* columnist E. J. Montini has ruefully noted, "Those of us who have lived in Arizona for a long time know that the fringe element represents a very small percentage of the overall population. That's the good news. The bad news? Just about all of them are in the Legislature" (2011, B1).

Fortuitously, the governor vetoed the guns-on-campus and "Birther" bills, and the Arizona Senate rejected five restrictive immigration bills (including the "Anchor Babies" bill) because they jeopardized the state's economic interests (Rau 2011b), and a committee of lawyers and politicians in Pima County, where I reside, countering absurdity with absurdity, has launched a move to secede from the rest of Arizona in order to become the fifty-first state (Bodfield and Kelly 2011). A new name has not yet been selected, but the front runner is Baja Arizona. Other suggestions coming from *Arizona Daily Star* cartoonist David Fitzsimmons include Arizonistan, the Kingdom of Pima, the People's Republic of Screw Phoenix, and Mexifornia. He also suggests naming everything north of the Gila River as Southern Utah (Fitzsimmons 2011, A15).

Arizona's Procrustean Bed: The English Language Development Block

Let me begin this section with a parable. In ancient Greek mythology, Procrustes was a cruel and lawless blacksmith and bandit who tormented travelers along a ten-mile stretch of road between Athens and Eleusis. Procrustes, whose name means "the Stretcher," lured unsuspecting travelers to his house by offering them a good meal and a night's rest in a very special bed that would magically resize itself to the exact length of all guests who lay down upon it. Procrustes withheld a dreadful truth, however: it was not the bed that would change shape, but the guests. If the guests were too long for the bed, Procrustes would chop off their legs and feet. If they were too short, he would stretch them until they fit. Procrustes's reign of terror ended when Theseus captured and punished the bandit by fitting him to his own bed The moral of this parable, of course, is that one size does not fit all, and, in fact, attempts to fit all to one size may have fatal consequences (*Encyclopedia of Greek Mythology* 2001).

The Procrustean bed is an appropriate metaphor for the way in which ELLs are currently educated in the state of Arizona. The bed in this case is the state's mandatory language program for all English learners, which since 2009 has forced students into Structured English Immersion (SEI) programs, which the Arizona Department of Education (ADE) has idiosyncratically designed as a segregated four-hour daily grammar and reading block. Students remain in the block for an entire year or more, until they are able to pass the AZELLA (Arizona English Language Learner

Self-Inflicted Reductio ad Absurdum · 69

Assessment)—the state's English proficiency test. With the typical school day comprising six to six and a half hours, four hours of English grammar instruction is a huge portion. While students do not literally lose their limbs along the way, they risk losing other intimate parts of their developing identities—their languages, cultures, confidence, and a healthy sense of place in the world.

Arizona's English Language Development (ELD) program focuses on an idiosyncratic curriculum model that ADE calls the "Language Star" (see figure 4.1). Each of the five points represents a domain of language that students must learn before anything else: phonology, morphology, syntax, lexicon (vocabulary), and semantics. ADE officials reason that if students acquire the linguistic skills associated with each point, they will become proficient enough in English to learn content subjects like science, social studies, language arts, and math.

ADE officials argue that ELLs have to learn about English before they can effectively learn content in English. The PowerPoint slides in figures 4.2 and 4.3, from an ADE professional development presentation to administrators in 2009, indicate the department's conceptualization of the

ELD Components

Phonology: Speech, sounds

Semantics: Meaning of words or sentences

Morphology: Parts of words, prefixes, suffixes and roots (base), verb tenses

Vocabulary

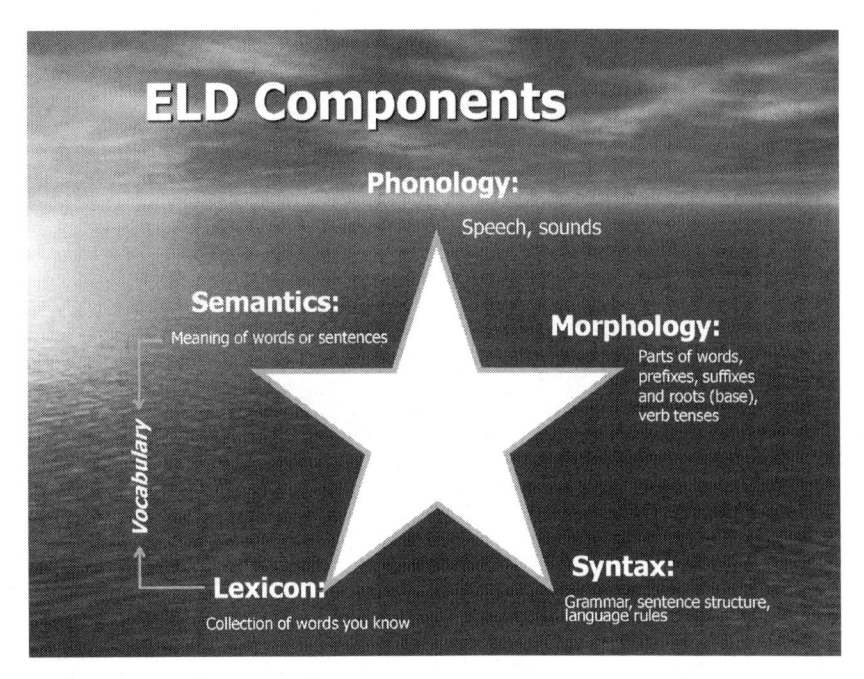

Lexicon: Collection of words you know

Syntax: Grammar, sentence structure, language rules

Figure 4.1. The Language Star: The Five Components of Arizona's English Language Development Program

ELD is ....

- NOT a math lesson
- NOT a science lesson
- NOT a social studies lesson
- NOT optional in an SEI classroom

Figure 4.2. What English Language Development is NOT According to the Arizona Department of Education

Principles for Accelerating English Language Learning

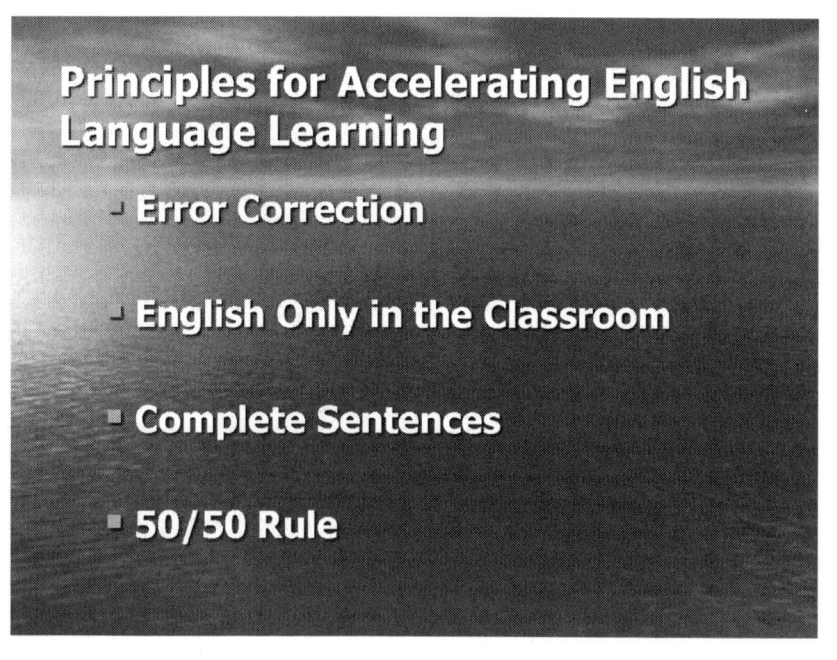

- Error Correction
- English Only in the Classroom
- Complete Sentences
- 50/50 Rule

Figure 4.3. How to Accelerate English Language Learning

ELD block as a program that features only the linguistic aspects of English (Arizona Department of Education 2009). The slides emphatically discourage instruction in content areas and require teachers to overtly correct errors that students make. Students must answer and speak in complete sentences at least 50 percent of the time.

State education department officials claimed the new program would meet the mandates of House Bill 2064, a law that required students to learn English in one year.[11] They reiterated that a prescriptive program would enable the state to accomplish this ambitious goal. Included in the new model were a prescriptive curriculum and methodology (the Discrete Skills Inventory, discussed later), rigid allocations of time for grammar, vocabulary, reading and writing instruction, a prohibition against content

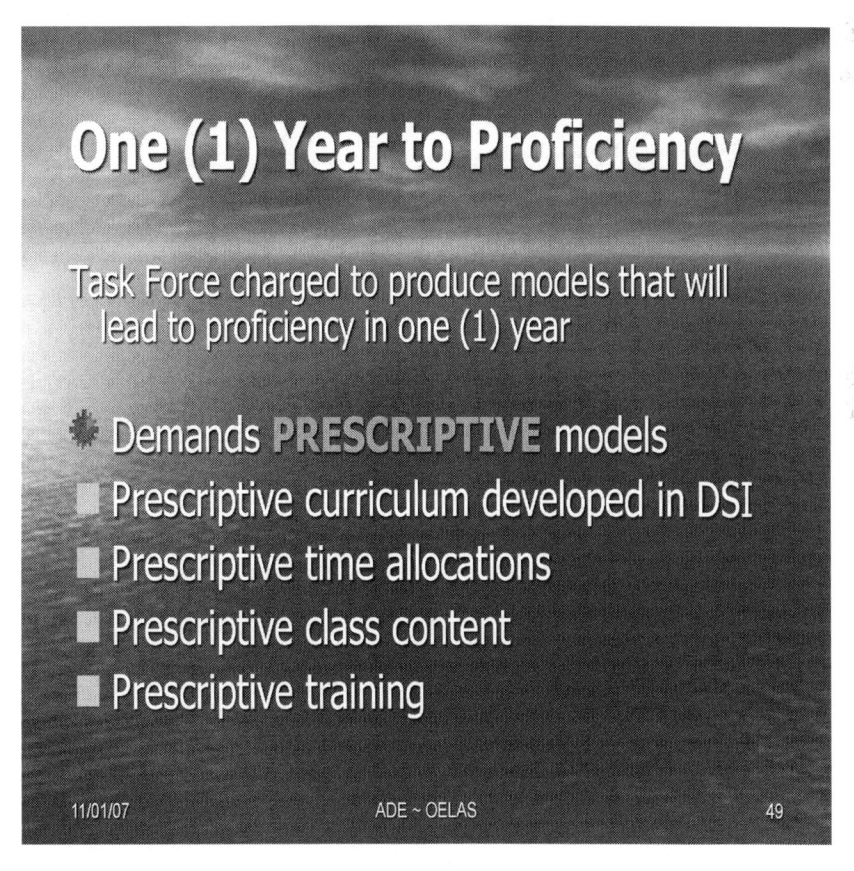

Figure 4.4. How to Learn English in One Year

(no subjects other than language development), and, finally, prescriptive training for ELD teachers.

The Four-Hour ELD Block in a Typical School Day

As noted earlier, the ELD program must be implemented for four hours per day. At the elementary level, these hours can be sequential or scheduled after or before other daily routines (lunch, recess, etc.), math instruction, or, if a school offers them, "specials" (art, physical education, music, etc.). Generally, students must be grouped by proficiency level (rather than by age or grade level, for example). If a school enrolls smaller numbers of English learners, it may combine them in one multigrade classroom (Arizona Department of Education 2008). Alternatively, the school can develop an Individual Language Learner Plan (ILLP) for the few English learners present. The ILLP permits the placement of ELLs in mainstream classrooms, but students should still receive four hours of English language development as required by ADE policy:[12]

> The ILLP language was included in the SEI Models to address the special circumstance created at schools with low numbers of ELL students where it is not possible to provide Highly Qualified teachers assigned to provide the required four hours of English Language Development. It is important to note that the use of the ILLP is permitted, not required. The preferred method for the delivery of ELD is for all four hours to be provided in an SEI classroom by a Highly Qualified teacher in Elementary content at the Elementary level, Language Arts or English at the Middle School level and English at the High School level, and who is trained in the use of the ELP Standards and Discrete Skills Inventory (DSI). (Arizona Department of Education 2008, 2)

In the secondary grades, English learners are grouped by proficiency levels if there are enough students to compose an ELD classroom. Schools with fewer ELLs may convene an ELD classroom of multiple grades or proficiency levels. ADE secondary ELL policy, however, awards a single academic English credit for all four hours (students need four credits to graduate). Consequently, there is a real possibility that ELLs will lag behind their peers for a couple of years, at best, assuming they attend summer school every year from at least the tenth through the twelfth grade; at worst, English learners may become so frustrated about their lack of progress that they drop out of school.

Explicit Time Allocations

Within the ELD program, teachers are required to devote explicit allocations of time to oral English, grammar, vocabulary development, and reading and writing. The amount of time students receive for each area depends upon their proficiency in English (see tables 4.1 and 4.2). For example, elementary English learners at the preemergent and emergent levels must receive sixty minutes each of grammar, reading, and vocabulary, but only forty-five minutes of oral English development and fifteen minutes of prewriting. Why ADE officials would prioritize grammar instruction over oral language development for students at these proficiency levels is unclear. ADE ELD policy also permits a 10 percent flexibility in the time allocations for each area, though this hardly seems flexible: if students can only engage in prewriting activities for fifteen minutes, a 10 percent increase is a mere minute and a half.

Table 4.1. Time Allocations for Elementary School Levels (10% Flexibility)

Students Testing at AZELLA Preemergent and Emergent

Conversation	Grammar	Reading	Vocabulary	Prewriting
45 min.	60 min.	60 min.	60 min.	15 min.

Students Testing at AZELLA Basic

Conversation	Grammar	Reading	Vocabulary	Writing
30 min.	60 min.	60 min.	60 min.	30 min.

Students Testing at AZELLA Intermediate

Conversation	Grammar	Reading	Vocabulary	Writing
15 min.	60 min.	60 min.	60 min.	45 min.

Source: Structured English Immersion Models of the Arizona English Language Learners Task Force (May 14, 2008), p. 5. Arizona Department of Education, Office of English Language Acquisition Services. http://www.azed.gov/wp-content/uploads/PDF/SEIModels05-14-08.pdf

Table 4.2. Time Allocations for Middle School and High School (20 Hours per Week/10% Flexibility)

Students Testing at AZELLA Preemergent and Emergent Levels

Conversational English and Academic Vocabulary 60 min.	English Reading 60 min.	English Writing 60 min.	English Grammar 60 min.

Students Testing at AZELLA Basic

Academic Oral English and Vocabulary 60 min.	English Reading 60 min.	English Writing 60 min.	English Grammar 60 min.

Students Testing at AZELLA Intermediate

English Language Arts (SEI) 60 min.	English Language Arts 60 min.	Academic English Reading 60 min.	Academic English Writing and Grammar 60 min.

Source: Structured English Immersion Models of the Arizona English Language Learners Task Force (May 14, 2008), p. 6. Arizona Department of Education, Office of English Language Acquisition Services. http://www.azed.gov/wp-content/uploads/PDF/SEIModels05-14-08.pdf

The Discrete Skills Inventory

Arizona state education officials have argued repeatedly that the four-hour block would facilitate the acquisition of English within the one-year time frame required by the state legislature. Because the need to accelerate English learning was so critical, they also prescribed a methodology that ostensibly would accomplish this: the Discrete Skills Inventory (DSI; Arizona Department of Education n.d.). Designed as "a sequential series of English language skills," the DSI represented a framework that teachers could use in conjunction with the state English Language Proficiency Standards and the state proficiency test (AZELLA).

The DSI is described as "a guide to teaching the grammatical foundations necessary" for students to acquire English and meet academic standards in language arts. As such, it focuses explicitly on parts of speech and

Table 4.3. How English Is Taught through the Discrete Skills Inventory (An Example)

Parts of Speech	Review		ELL II Skill Progression	
Nouns	Singular common nouns Plural common nouns Proper nouns Plural proper nouns Articles	Common nouns with determiners (a bird, an animal, the zoo) Plural nouns (friends, teachers)	Proper nouns of locations and objects (Flagstaff, Arizona) Irregular plural nouns (see level-appropriate list)	Singular possessive nouns (friend's, teacher's) Plural possessive nouns (friends', teachers')
Verbs	Simple present tense Simple past tense Simple future tense Present tense of "to be" Present progressive tense Imperatives	Present tense of "to have" (have, has) Present participle (walk-walking, run-running) Past tense of "to be" (was, were) Irregular past tense (see attached chart for level-appropriate list Infinitives ("to" plus simple present: "to buy") Linking verbs of sensation (smell, sound, taste, feel: "soup tastes good")	Present tense of "to do" (does, do) and "to go" (goes, go) Present progressive tense ("to be" plus present participle: "is swimming") Past negative of "to be" ("I was not") Past progressive tense (past tense of "to be" plus present participle: "was running") Future tense "am going to" ("am going to play") Linking verbs of being (act, seem, appear, become: "boy seems tall")	Present simple negative ("do not run") Present progressive negative ("am not talking") Past simple negative ("did not walk") Past progressive negative ("was not running") Future negative ("will not play"/"am not going to play") Modal auxiliaries (may, might, must, can, could, shall, should, will, would, ought to) Demonstrative (this, that, these, those) Interrogative (who, what, where, when, why, how)
Pronouns	Personal subjective pronouns	Personal possessive singular (my-mine, your-yours, his, her-hers, its) Personal objective singular (me, you, him, her, it)	Personal possessive plural (our-ours, your-yours, their, theirs) Personal objective plural (us, you, them)	

Source: Arizona Department of Education (n.d.), Discrete Skills Inventory.

other grammatical aspects of English. Although teachers may incorporate reading and writing activities into the ELD blocks, their academic emphasis must be the structure and use of English.

The DSI provides a logical and linear ordering of English language concepts and skills to assist teachers in the design, development, and implementation of ELD instruction for English learners who have been placed in SEI classrooms. The concepts and skills identified in the DSI are the building blocks for English learners in their journey toward English mastery. They provide a comprehensive grammatical foundation necessary for meeting the ELP standards at each stage of a student's development.

The skills presented in the DSI make lesson planning easier for teachers. Using the DSI, teachers can fashion lesson plans and implement classroom activities that provide their students with an understanding of the parts of speech, how they combine to form phrases and sentences, and the overarching structure of the English language. For example, if students are expected to describe items in the classroom, they need first to be taught certain parts of speech such as nouns, adjectives, and verbs, as well as how to conjugate verbs, and then learn how to assemble different types of words in proper grammatical order (table 4.3; Arizona Department of Education n.d.).

The ADE has organized DSI training sessions for teachers and administrators in which trainers emphasize the prescriptive nature of the methodology. First, language itself is narrowly defined as comprising five discrete, interdependent elements that must be taught overtly (phonology, morphology, syntax, lexicon, and semantics). Accordingly, a basic skills approach would provide the foundation for proficiency in reading, writing, listening, and speaking. Second, the four-hour ELD blocks and the segregation of ELLs from non-ELLs within them are nonnegotiable. Third, grouping students by proficiency levels (rather than by age or grade levels) is mandatory.

Why Is This Happening in Arizona?

In spite of criticism of the four-hour block from researchers, administrators, and teachers alike, as well as a legal challenge in federal court, why do state officials persist in forcing this Procrustean bed on ELLs and the schools that serve them?[13] One obvious answer to this question is the clear disconnect between research in second language acquisition and the ways in which state policymakers have constructed language and education policies toward English learners. For example, there appears to be little interest from state policymakers in learning what the research literature actually says about how children acquire a second language, or how long it may take them to learn it in informal or formal settings. Similarly ignored are robust discussions about the role of first language literacy in second language acquisition, how parental economic status and education determine their children's access to privileged instructional discourse, or the linguistic and cultural resources ELLs bring to classrooms. Former Arizona Superintendent of Public Instruction Tom Horne, a staunch supporter of English-only education in the state, was asked about his views on bilingual education research by the *Advocate*, a publication of the Arizona Education Association: "Where I'm a strong opponent of bilingual education is where they have students who don't speak English at school or at home and as a result it takes forever to learn English. I sat on a committee where a bilingual education expert said it takes seven years to learn English. That makes me boil. It doesn't take seven years to learn a language. You should be able to do it in a year if you focus on it. [These experts] are sacrificing their kids for their theory" (Arizona Education Association 2003, 11).

Horne did not provide any evidence for his statement that anyone should be able to learn English in one year, probably because there is none. On the contrary, an extensive body of research indicates that the acquisition of English as a second language is a complex process. How quickly and how well English learners acquire fluency in English depends on many factors, including how one actually defines proficiency. Applied linguists and second language acquisition researchers generally agree that English proficiency has different dimensions and that children acquire these dimensions at different speeds. For example, children tend to acquire social or conversational language more rapidly than academic language. The former is aided by numerous contextual clues, like nonverbal communication in face-to-face interactions and visual or graphic support in a classroom, and is generally thought to be less cognitively demanding (Combs 2012). Academic language, on the other hand, is characterized by fewer contextual clues and relies on more advanced knowledge of English vocabulary, word order, grammar, and pragmatics, or knowing how to act and interact in the second language in different environments (Kasper and Roever 2005; Wong Fillmore and Snow 2000). On average, ELLs tend to acquire social language in one to three years and academic language in four to seven years (Combs 2012). The former superintendent's insistence that students should learn English in one year is based on an abstraction contrary to reasoned theory and experience.

Besides the disregard of second language acquisition and applied linguistic research, there are other reasons why state policymakers have taken such a narrow view of the education of English learners. Let me propose at least five:

1. A fierce anti-immigrant discourse in the state
2. A widening "gray versus brown" demographic divide
3. A unique, contradictory, and evolving nexus between state education policies and federal case law
4. Uninformed and ideologically motivated state officials (swayed by popular folk theories of language acquisition)
5. Time-on-task notions of curriculum and instruction

Anti-immigrant Discourse in Arizona

It is not a coincidence that Arizona's language policies are occurring at a time of great hostility toward immigrants in general and undocumented immigrants in particular. Animus toward Spanish speakers is ubiquitous on talk radio, in the print and broadcast media, and in public discourse. The verbal hostility has resulted in harsh anti-immigrant legislation, such as SB 1070, the racial profiling law that passed through the legislature in April 2010 (and whose most controversial parts were declared unconstitutional by a federal court). Although the numbers are hard to pin down, the percentage of US-born English learners has been estimated at approximately 80 percent (Gándara and Hopkins 2010). This makes them citizens of the United States. Nonetheless, as noted earlier, there is a widespread belief among members of the state legislature that Arizona's ELLs are undocumented, and as such deserve no support. During the debates around HB 2064, in fact, the speaker of the Arizona House of Representatives declared that additional school funding for English learners would turn Arizona into "Mexico's best school district north of the border" (Hogan 2006).

Other legislators reject any state responsibility for educating noncitizens and insist that children born in the United States to undocumented parents are not citizens despite the US Constitution's explicit language to the contrary and the Supreme Court's decision in *Plyler v. Doe* (providing a free, public education to the children of undocumented immigrants).[14] One legislator suggested that the children "should be deported, along with their parents" (Hogan 2006, 16).

Gray and Republican: The Gray versus Brown Divide

Arizona, like other Western states, is experiencing what William Frey of the Brookings Institute calls the "gray versus brown cultural generation gap." Put simply, white residents in the state are aging while the numbers of young Latinos are increasing. In fact, over the past two decades Arizona's Latino population has grown by 180 percent, shifting the state's racial composition from 72 to 58 percent white (Frey 2010). The demographic changes in Arizona provide a context for the white backlash there, as well as evidence for the widening cultural generation gap between Latino young adult and child populations and the largely white baby boomers and older populations (Frey 2010). Nationally, the average for this group is 25 percent; in Arizona, however, the gap is 40 percentage points. In other words, 43 percent of the state's youth population is white compared to 83 percent of its senior citizens. Older Arizonans tend to conform to a certain demographic—retired, aging, white, and Republican—the same demographic, Frey suggests, that "predominates in the recent Tea Party protests." Table 4.4 shows the six states with the greatest gaps between white youth and aging white populations. These states also happen to have the highest numbers of Latino residents in the United States. Of the six, Arizona leads the nation with the largest gap (Frey 2010).

Table 4.4. Gray versus Brown Cultural Generation Gap

| | | Percent White | | |
Rank	State	Under Age 18	Age 65+	Gap
1	Arizona	43	83	40
2	Nevada	43	77	34
3	California	30	63	33
4	Texas	37	68	32
5	New Mexico	29	60	31
6	Florida	49	78	29

Source: Frey. 2010. "Will Arizona Be America's Future?" Brookings Institution, http://www.brookings.edu/opinions/2010/0428_arizona_frey.aspx#.

The cultural generation gap is increasing in large urban areas, where racial demographics have also shifted. Frey reports that of the 100 largest metropolitan areas in the United States, twenty have cultural generation gaps of over 30 percent. Phoenix, Arizona, is at the top of the list, and Tucson is third (table 4.5).

The overwhelming majority of Arizona's residents reside in Maricopa County (where Phoenix is located), and its population numbers dwarf those of all other counties in the state, including Pima (where Tucson is located). According to the 2010 Census, there were 6,392,017 people in the state; 3,817,117 resided in Maricopa County, a population total nearly four times higher than in Pima County, the second most populous county with 980,263 (US Census 2010). The cultural generation gap in Arizona suggests a parallel ideological divide. The Arizona state legislature consists of 90 elected members: 21 Republicans and 9 Democrats in the Senate; 40 Republicans and 20 Democrats in the House. Of these legislators, 83 percent are white, 14 percent are Latino, 3 percent are Native American,

Table 4.5. Metropolitan Areas with the Largest Cultural Generation Gaps

Rank	Metro Area	Percent White Under Age 18	Age 65+	Gap
1	Phoenix-Mesa-Scottsdale, AZ	44	85	41
2	Riverside, San Bernadino–Ontario	27	67	40
3	Tucson, AZ	39	79	40
4	Fresno, CA	23	61	38
5	Bakersfield, CA	30	68	38
6	Modesto, CA	37	74	37
7	Cape Coral–Ft. Myers, FL	56	92	36
8	Stockton, CA	27	62	34
9	Dallas–Ft. Worth–Arlington, TX	42	76	34
10	San Diego–Carlsbad–San Marcos, CA	37	71	34
11	Las Vegas–Paradise, NV	38	72	34
12	Albuquerque, NM	30	62	32
13	Lakeland–Winter Haven, FL	55	87	32
14	Los Angeles, Long Beach, Santa Ana, CA	22	53	32
15	Oxnard, Thousand Oaks, Ventura, CA	39	71	31
16	Houston, Sugar Land, Baytown, TX	33	64	31
17	Orlando-Kissimmee, FL	45	76	31
18	Bradenton-Sarasota-Venice, FL	65	95	30
19	San Jose, Sunnyvale, Santa Clara, CA	28	58	30
20	Austin–Round Rock, TX	46	75	30

Source: Frey. 2010. Will Arizona Be America's Future?" Brookings Institution, http://www.brookings.edu/opinions/2010/0428_arizona_frey.aspx#.

and 2 percent are African American. Sixty-four percent of the Arizona legislature is male, while 35.6 percent is female. The legislature is also aging, with 67 percent over the age of 50 (48 percent are 50–64, and 19 percent 65 years or older; National Conference of State Legislatures, http://www.ncsl.org/legislatures-elections/legisdata/legislator-demographic-map.aspx). As of June 2011, the Maricopa County Recorder listed 713,599 registered Republican voters and 538,549 registered Democrats in twenty legislative districts (Maricopa County Recorder's Office 2011).[15] In Pima County's six legislative districts, registered Democrats dominate in four.

Just before SB 1070 was scheduled to take effect, an *Arizona Republic* poll of registered voters indicated that support for the anti-immigration law was heavily dependent upon political affiliation, age, income, gender, and ethnicity. For example, individuals with household incomes greater than $50,000 supported the law by a 2:1 ratio, while those earning less were divided 45 to 44 percent in favor of SB 1070. Additionally, 66 percent of men favored the law, while 28 percent of men did not. Women were evenly divided at 44 percent each. Finally, Latinos overwhelmingly opposed the law, 76 to 16 percent (Hansen 2010). Nearly 90 percent of Republicans supported the law, compared with 30 percent of Democrats. Of voters age 55 years or older, 63 percent favored SB 1070; 64 percent of voters between 35 and 54 favored the law. In contrast, 52 percent of voters between 18 and 34 years old opposed the law (table 4.6).

Table 4.6. *Arizona Republic* Poll of Voter Support and Opposition to SB 2010 (%)

[In response to the question] Do you support or oppose Senate Bill 1070?			
	Support	*Oppose*	*Neutral/Don't Know*
Overall	55	36	9
Registered voters	61	31	10
Republicans	88	10	3
Democrats	30	58	12
Independents	60	31	10
18–34	36	52	12
35–54	64	26	11
55+	63	31	6

Source: Hansen, R. 2010. "Poll: Politics, Age Sway Opinions on Immigration Law." *Arizona Republic*, July 25, 2010.

Note: Margin of error: 3.89 percentage points. Numbers may not add to 100 percent because of rounding.

A Unique and Contradictory Policy Nexus

Arizona's education policies regarding English learners have evolved from a complicated confluence of state and federal legislation, case law, and policies that both determine and confound educational choices for English learners. This confluence represents a legal and policy conundrum for schools and school districts. It is one that continues to confuse, challenge, or justify the educational decisions districts make for their ELL students (Combs 2012).

In January 2000, a federal court judge ruled in a class action lawsuit (*Flores v. Arizona*) that the state of Arizona had violated the Equal Educational Opportunity Act by underfunding school districts serving large numbers of ELLs.[16] In the subsequent consent decree between the plaintiffs and the state of Arizona, state officials agreed to provide ELLs with access to the core curriculum as well as English language development. The decree outlawed the widespread practice of "pullout" programs in which ELLs were pulled out of content classes for a variable period of time in order to receive English as a second language (ESL) instruction. Because the pullout approach was eliminated, school districts interpreted the new policy to mean that ELLs must receive content instruction and language development at the same time, in the same classroom.

In November 2000, Arizona voters approved Proposition 203, a ballot initiative that replaced bilingual education and ESL with a predominantly English-only program called Structured English Immersion. Teachers in SEI classrooms had to be trained in sheltered instruction and other strategies designed to make their content area teaching more comprehensible to English learners (Combs et al. 2005).

After resisting the court's school funding order for five years, the state legislature passed HB 2064, which minimally increased the funding for English learners. The new law also reconceptualized SEI as a four-hour intensive English grammar block, and authorized an English Language Learners Task Force, which among other duties was charged with "developing and adopting research-based models of structured English immersion." The English Language Learner Task Force was composed of nine members, seven of whom were appointed by Republican elected officials, and two by the Democratic governor. Of the nine individuals, only two consistently questioned the wisdom of a segregated program, and only one had extensive research expertise in the education of ELLs: both were appointed by the governor.[17] The seven other members differed only in the degree of their opposition to bilingual education (from somewhat opposed to emphatically opposed): one of them had been cochair of English for the Children, the organization that sponsored Proposition 203. The rest included a school vice principal, a high school ESL coordinator, a retired Latin and ESL teacher, an investment banker, a public accountant, and a health care administrator.[18]

Uninformed and Ideologically Motivated State Officials

For the most part, elected officials in Arizona are uninformed about the way children acquire a second language and about the most effective means of teaching English. During the rancorous debates about Proposition 203, some were vocally opposed to effective second language teaching approaches like bilingual education (see, for example, "Arguments for Proposition 203" in Arizona Secretary of State 2000; Wright 2005). For instance, the notion of using students' first language to teach a second appears counterintuitive to some, ill-advised and unpatriotic to others. Elected officials also tended to take literally the following declarations in Proposition 203:

> Young immigrant children can easily acquire full fluency in a new language, such as English, if they are heavily exposed to that language in the classroom at an early age.
>
> [These children] can be educated through Sheltered English Immersion during a temporary transition period not normally intended to exceed one year.[19]

These declarations are not supported by research in applied linguistics and second language acquisition theory. In addition to the officials' faith in these particular folk theories of language acquisition, the process for determining ELL policy in the state is highly political (see, for example, Florez 2012; and Goldenberg and Rutherford-Quach 2012, for exposés of the manipulation of cut scores for the AZELLA, the state's proficiency test for ELLs, and the serious underidentification of ELLs due to state-imposed changes to the Home Language Survey).

It is perhaps not surprising that the elected officials who approved HB 2064 (imposing the ELD block on English language learners) are the same individuals who voted to "il-legalize" Mexican American studies classes in the Tucson Unified School District, in spite of compelling evidence that the program was inspiring students to stay in school, work hard on class projects, graduate from high school, and attend college (see chapter 2 of this volume). An unscientific analysis of the voting records of the elected officials who introduced and supported the bills described earlier indicate that they opposed Mexican American studies as well. These officials represent conservative constituencies that tend to vote Republican, including those in rural towns in the state, affluent districts in Maricopa and Pima counties, and large incorporated retirement communities (Sun City West, for example).

The "Time-on-Task" Principle

Members of the English Language Learner Task Force defended an obligatory enforcement of the four-hour ELD block because districts were implementing too many different programs, and teachers were not providing enough direct instruction in ESL. A single model of ELL education was necessary to ensure that ELLs acquired enough English in one year to master other subjects (Kossan 2007). Another explanation for the new approach was based on the "time-on-task" or "maximum exposure" principle, that is, the belief that the more time students spend learning something, the better they will learn it. Applying the adage to second language acquisition sounds something like this: the more time students spend learning in English, the more (and better) they will learn English.

The conviction that more exposure to English equals more acquisition of English underlies much of the historical opposition to bilingual education (Baker 1998; Chavez 1991; Clark 2000; Epstein 1977; Imhoff 1990; Porter 1990, 2000, 2001; Rossell 1990; Siano 2000; Walberg 1986). With regard to the acquisition of English, time-on-task principles advance three general assumptions, at least in Arizona:

1. SEI in English is more effective than other alternatives.
2. SEI settings will enable ELLs to acquire the language in one year.
3. Young children are ideally suited for immersion because they are better at learning languages than older children or adults.

These assumptions reflected the attitudes of the majority of task force members, including its head, an economist and investment banker who justified the state's approach this way: "More time on task. That's a tried-and-true educational standard. If you want to learn how to play the piano, what do they tell you to do? They tell you to practice" (Alan Maguire, quoted in Kossan 2007, A1).

Arizona's Procrustean Bed

Let us return to the metaphor of the Procrustean bed. There is undeniably a mythological feel to the discourse of Proposition 203 and the policy documents arising from the Flores case and HB 2064. In the monumental—and impossible—effort to reclassify all of Arizona's English language learners in one year, the state has crafted a Procrustean policy mandating a one-size-fits all program. The metaphor also serves as an example of one of the multiple policies of the absurd in the state of Arizona.

The paradox is that the text of Arizona's education and language laws, originating in vaguely worded ballot initiatives and uninformed legislation, is now codified in the Arizona Revised Statutes as law. And as law, the text—misleading and false though it may be—has become part of the official state discourse about the education of ELLs. And as official discourse, cum law, it has become fact. Reductio ad absurdum.

Notes

I am indebted to William Combs and Salvador Gabaldón for their suggestions on earlier versions of this chapter.

1. The "Freedom to Breathe Act," or Senate Concurrent Resolution 1050, asserts state sovereignty over federal regulation of greenhouse gases. SB 1050, 41-1294, §4 (Declaration of exclusive sovereign authority and sanction), 4C: "Any effort by any governmental official to enforce within the borders of the state of Arizona federal laws or federal regulations purporting to restrict intrastate emissions of anthropogenic carbon dioxide or other greenhouse substances is herewith declared a violation of civil rights and unlawful under Arizona state law." Second Regular Legislative Session, 2010: Passed in the Senate, held in the House of Representatives.

2. SB 1433 asserts, among other declarations: "This act serves as a notice and demand to the Congress and the federal government to cease and desist all activities outside the scope of their constitutionally designated powers." First Regular Legislative Session, 2011: Failed in the Senate.

3. SCR 1010, subject to voter approval, constitutionally prohibits courts from considering international law. Declares: "The courts shall not look to the legal precepts of other nations or cultures. The courts shall not consider international law." First Regular Legislative Session, 2011: Held in the Senate Judiciary and Rules Committees.

4. HB 2077 states that any federal agency "that comes into a county to conduct authorized business shall register its presence with the county sheriff." First Regular Legislative Session, 2011: Held in the House Rules Committee.

5. HB 2561 and SB 1309 challenged the Fourteenth Amendment's declaration of citizenship: "all persons born or naturalized in the United States, and subject to the jurisdiction thereof, are citizens of the United States and of the State wherein they reside." These bills redefine citizenship status by bestowing it only upon children with "at least one parent who owes no allegiance to any foreign sovereignty, or a child

without citizenship or nationality in any foreign country." First Regular Legislative Session, 2011: HB 2561 was held in the House awaiting a first reading. SB 1309 failed in the Senate.

6. SB 1526 specifies "citizenship qualification requirements for a presidential candidate's name to be placed on a ballot in Arizona." First Regular Legislative Session, 2011: Held in the Senate Judiciary and Rules Committees. The title is my own characterization.

7. SB 1621 requires "various statutory and session law changes to enact the fiscal year (FY) 2011–2012 budget as it relates to criminal justice." The sheriffs of Maricopa and Pinal Counties have been outspoken supporters of the state's anti-immigration laws. Pima County Sheriff Clarence Dupnik has criticized the laws and announced he would not enforce some of their provisions. Section 9 22-117 amended the definition of counties eligible for crime-costs compensation. First Regular Legislative Session, 2011: Passed in both the House and Senate. Signed by the governor on April 5, 2011.

8. HB 2443 provides "that a person who knowingly performs an abortion, with the knowledge that the abortion is sought based on the sex or race of the child or the race of the parent of the child, is guilty of a Class 3 felony." First Regular Legislative Session, 2011: Passed in both the House and Senate. Signed by the government on March 29, 2011.

9. SB 1213 stated that "the teaching of some scientific subjects, including biological evolution, the chemical origins of life, global warming and human cloning, can cause controversy" and therefore, teachers should "review in an objective manner the scientific strengths and scientific weaknesses of existing scientific theories covered in the course being taught." Explained principal sponsor Senator Judy Burgos, "Students should be given all sides of the story . . . [and] there should be an opportunity for teachers to step up to the plate and give their opinion if they have scientific proof that [climate change] isn't happening, that it's a natural phenomena [sic], without retribution" (Fischer 2013; Roberts 2013). First Regular Legislative Session, 2013: Held in the Senate Education and Rules Committees.

10. Senator Ron Gould (R-Lake Havasu City) and John Kavanagh (R-Fountain Hills) were the principal sponsors of SB 1309 and HB 2561, the Arizona Citizenship bill.

11. HB 2064, Section 15-756.01C, passed by the state legislature in 2006, specifies that SEI models "shall be limited to programs for English language learners . . . not normally intended to exceed one year." Second Regular Legislative Session, 2006.

12. ADE's ILLP policy applies to "schools with 20 or fewer ELLs within a three grade span, including Kindergarten." (Nonetheless, each ILLP must adhere to the time allocations specified for all other ELLs.) See *Individual Language Learner Plan* at the Arizona Department of Education website: http://www.azed.gov/english-language-learners/files/2012/10/illp-guidance-document-complete-revised.pdf.

13. See for example the nine reports published in July 2010 by the Civil Rights Project of the University of California, Los Angeles. They are available at http://civilrightsproject.ucla.edu/research/k-12-education/language-minority-students. These reports represent a collaborative critique of Arizona's program by teachers, researchers, and graduate students. In March 2011, Arizona ELL teachers voiced their concern about the ELD block at the National Conversation on English Learner Education, sponsored by the US Department of Education and held in Los Angeles.

The "SOS" (Arizona Is Sinking) document they presented stated, among other things: "the educational program currently in place for English Learners does not meet their needs and prevents them from gaining access to core content while also segregating them from the school population. Despite positive press about the SEI program, there is much doubt as to its actual success." "What Makes for Quality Education for English Learners in the 21st Century?" http://www.ncela.gwu.edu/files/uploads/24/SOS _Arizona.pdf.

14. *Plyler v. Doe*, 457 US 202 (1982).

15. Other political parties in Arizona include the Green, Libertarian, Independent, Reform, and Socialist parties.

16. *Flores v. Arizona*, 48 F. Supp. 2d. 937, US District Court, District of Arizona, 1999.

17. John Baracy, former superintendent of Scottsdale Unified School District, and Dr. Eugene Garcia, dean of the Arizona State University College of Education.

18. The Task Force chair is Alan Maguire, an economist and investment banker. Other members appointed by Republican elected officials were Jim DiCello, a public accountant; Eileen Klein, chief operations officer at United Health Group; Margaret Garcia Dugan, former cochair of English for the Children; Karen Merritt, Glendale Union High School district ELL coordinator; Anna Rosas, vice principal of A.J. Mitchell School (Nogales Unified School District); and Johanna Haver, retired ESL and Latin teacher.

19. Arizona Revised Statutes, Title 15 (Education), § 3.1 (English Language Education for Children in Public Schools), 751-756.01.

References

Arizona Department of Education. 2008. "Structured English Immersion Models of the Arizona English Language Learners Task Force." http://www.azed.gov/wp-content/uploads/PDF/SEIModels05-14-08.pdf.

———. 2009. "Administrator's Model Implementation Training." PowerPoint presentation, http://www.azed.gov/english-language-learners/files/2013/02/administrators modelimplementationtraining.pdf .

———. n.d. "Discrete Skills Inventory." http://www.azed.gov/wp-content/uploads/PDF/DSIAllLevels.pdf.

Arizona Education Association. 2003. "New Superintendent Sees Job as Helping the Classroom." *AEA Advocate* (February/March): 10–11.

Arizona Secretary of State. 2000. "Voter Education Pamphlet: 2000 Ballot Propositions." http://www.azsos.gov/election/2000/Info/pubpamphlet/english/contents .htm.

Arizona State Senate. 2011. *Fact Sheet for S.B. 1433.* www.azleg.gov. See under First Regular Session, 2011, Senate Bills.

Baker, K. 1998. "Structured English Immersion: Breakthrough in Teaching Limited-English-Proficient Students." *Phi Delta Kappan* 80(3): 199–204.

Bodfield, R., and A. Kelly. 2011. "Could Baja Arizona Be 51st State in US?" *Arizona Daily Star*, February 24, A1.

Boehnke, M. 2008. "Sheriff's Popularity Safely in the Pink." *Arizona Republic*, February 15, 2.

"Brewer Shows She Has the Chops to Run Our State." 2010. *Arizona Republic*, July 21, B4.

Chavez, L. 1991. *Out of the Barrio: Toward a New Politics of Hispanic Assimilation*. New York: Basic Books.

Clark, K. 2000. "The Design and Implementation of an English Immersion Program. In *The ABC's of English Immersion: A Teacher's Guide*, 24–30. Washington, DC: Center for Equal Opportunity.

Combs, M. C. 2012. "Everything on Its Head: Re-inventing Theory and Practice in a Structured Immersion Classroom." In *Implementing Educational Language Policy in Arizona: Legal, Historical and Current Practices in Structured English Immersion*, ed. B. Arias and C. Faltis. Clevedon, U.K.: Multilingual Matters.

Combs, M. C., C. Evans, T. Fletcher, E. Parra, and A. Jiménez. 2005. "Bilingualism for the Children: Implementing a Dual Language Program in an English Only State." *Educational Policy* 19(5): 701–28.

Encyclopedia of Greek Mythology. 2001. "Procrustes." Retrieved August 1. http://www.mythweb.com/encyc/entries/procrustes.html.

Epstein, N. 1977. *Language, Ethnicity, and the Schools: Policy Alternatives for Bilingual-Bicultural Education*. Washington, DC: Institute for Educational Leadership.

Fischer, Howard. 2011a. "Brewer Vetoes Gun, Birther Bills." *Arizona Daily Star*, April 19, A1.

———. 2011b. "Pima Excluded from Border-Crime Funding." *Arizona Daily Star*, March 18, A2.

———. 2011c. "Legislator to Feds: Hands Off of Our Air." *Arizona Daily Star*, February 2, A1.

———. 2013. "AZ Bill Would Let Teachers Dismiss Global Warming." *Arizona Daily Star*, February 5, A1. http://azstarnet.com/news/science/environment/az-bill-would-let-teachers-dismiss-global-warming/article_4bec9422-44b6-5b49-b0da-78513c959433.html.

Fitzsimmons, D. 2011. "If We Secede, Should We Be 'Arizonistan' or 'Mexifornia'?" *Arizona Daily Star*, March 5, A15.

Florez, I. R. 2012. "Examining the Validity of the Arizona English Language Learners Assessment Cut Scores." *Language Policy* 11: 33–45.

Frey, W. H. 2010. "Will Arizona Be America's Future?" Brookings Institution, http://www.brookings.edu/opinions/2010/0428_arizona_frey.aspx#.

Gándara, P., and M. Hopkins. 2010. *Forbidden Language: English Learners and Restrictive Language Policies*. New York: Teachers College Press.

Goldenberg, C., and S. Rutherford-Quach. 2012. "The Arizona Home Language Survey: The Under-identification of Students for English Language Services." *Language Policy* 11, 21–30.

Gonzalez, D. 2005. "Citizens by Birth? Perhaps Not; GOP Out to Alter Law on Migrants' Babies." *Arizona Republic*, November 25, A1.

Hansen, R. 2010. "Poll: Politics, Age Sway Opinions on Immigration Law." *Arizona Republic*, July 25, http://www.azcentral.com/news/articles/2010/07/25/20100725immigration-poll-demographic.html#ixzz1HS2sfkNl.

Hogan, Tim. 2006. *Flores v. State of Arizona: History, Status, and Implications*. Phoenix: Arizona Center for Law in the Public Interest.
Imhoff, G. 1990. "The Position of U.S. English on Bilingual Education." In *English Plus: Issues in Bilingual Education*, ed. C. B. Cazden and C. E. Snow, 48–61. Annals of the American Academy of Political and Social Science. Newbury Park, CA: Sage.
Jordan, M. 2010. "Arizona Grades Teachers on Fluency." *Wall Street Journal Eastern Edition*, April 30, A3.
Kasper, G. and C. Roever. 2005. "Pragmatics in Second Language Learning." In *Handbook of Research in Second Language Teaching and Learning*, ed. E. Hinkel, 317–34. Mahwah, NJ: Lawrence Erlbaum, Inc.
Kossan, P. 2007. "New Learners Must Spend 4 Hours a Day on English." *Arizona Republic*, July 15, A1.
Maricopa County Recorder's Office. 2011. "Maricopa County Voter Registration Totals." http://recorder.maricopa.gov/voterregnet/redirect.aspx?view=congressional.
McCombs, B. 2010. "200+ Gather to Push for Immigration Bill's Veto." *Arizona Daily Star*, April 21, A4.
Montini, E. J. 2011. "Arizona to Secede (Unofficially) from Union?" *Arizona Republic*, February 3, B1.
Porter, R. 1990. *Forked Tongue: The Politics of Bilingual Education*. New York: Basic Books.
———. 2001. "Introduction. The Cost of English Acquisition Programs: The Arizona Department of Education English Acquisition Cost Study." *READ Perspectives* 8: 5–10.
Porter, R. P. 2000. "The Benefits of English Immersion." *Educational Leadership*, 57(4): 52–56.
Rau, A. B. 2011a. "House Passes 'Birther' Measure." *Arizona Republic*, April 15, B1.
———. 2011b. "5 Migrant Bills Rejected." *Arizona Republic*, March 18, A1.
———. 2011c. "Birthright Citizenship Fight Begins in Arizona." *Arizona Republic*, January 28, A1.
Reinhart, M. K. 2011. "Horne: TUSD Runs Afoul of State Ethnic Studies Law." *Arizona Republic*, January 3, A1.
Roberts, L. 2013. "Senator Helps Us Zap Real Science." *Arizona Republic*, February 11, B1.
Rossell, C. 1990. "The Effectiveness of Educational Alternatives for Limited English Proficient Children." In *Learning in Two Languages: From Conflict to Consensus in the Reorganization of Schools*, ed. G. Imhoff, 71–122. New Brunswick, NJ: Transaction.
Rough, G. 2011. "Arizona Taking Up Fight to Limit Feds' Authority." *Arizona Republic*, February 4, A1.
Siano, J. 2000. "Teaching Juan and Maria to Read." In *The ABC's of English Immersion: A Teacher's Guide*, 16–19. Washington, DC: Center for Equal Opportunity.
Strauss, V. 2010. "Heavily Accented Teachers Removed from Arizona Classrooms." *Washington Post*, May 2. http://voices.washingtonpost.com/answer-sheet/teachers/heavily-accented-teachers-remo.html.
US Census. 2010. State Population Profile Maps/Arizona. http://www.census.gov/2010census/data/.

Wagner, D. 2007. "Triumphs, Troubles in 15 Years as Sheriff; Maricopa County's Joe Arpaio: Admittedly Brash, Always Divisive." *Arizona Republic*, November 3, A1.

Walberg, H. J. 1986. "Letter to Frederick Mulhauser, September 22." In *Bilingual Education: A New Look at the Research Evidence*, 71–72. Washington, DC: US General Accounting Office.

Wong Fillmore, L., and C. E. Snow. 2000. "What Teachers Need to Know about Language." US Department of Education, Office of Educational Research and Improvement, ED-99-CO-0008. http://faculty.tamu-commerce.edu/jthompson/Resources/FillmoreSnow2000.pdf.

Wright, W. E. 2005. "The Political Spectacle of Arizona's Proposition 203." *Educational Policy* 19(5): 662–700.

CHAPTER FIVE

"When You Know Yourself You're More Confident"

Resilience and Stress of Undergraduate Students in the Face of Anti–Ethnic Studies Bills

Andrea J. Romero and Anna Ochoa O'Leary

I woke my five-year-old son up at 5:30 a.m. in the dark; he was already dressed and we ate tortillas in the car. By the time we arrived at the school district building, the sun was starting to come up and the people were gathering—there were children, parents, teenagers, college students I recognized from my classes, and elders. Everyone was moving slowly and many were sitting on the ground waiting. My son and I had done several walks that spring together, including the Susan G. Komen walk for breast cancer awareness, because my mom is a survivor. This crowd did not look that different from the crowds at other walks. There were people of all ages, ethnicities, and backgrounds, but the feeling in the air was as festive as the breast cancer walk, where cheerleaders dressed all in pink. The crowd this morning was gathering to send off a group of runners who would run from Tucson to Phoenix in June, when temperatures regularly reach up to 115 degrees in the desert (Running for Our Lives: In Pursuit of Our Educational Dreams). The gravity of the undertaking of running across Arizona in the summer was clear, and the feeling that morning was one of quiet concentration and preparedness for the runners. Our collective intention was to bring attention to the anti–ethnic studies bill (AZ SB 1069) that was proposed that summer (2009) to end ethnic studies and Movimiento Estudiantil Chicano de Aztlán (Movement of Chicano Students of

Aztlán or MEChA) student organizations in public schools. We walked the first three miles together and then gathered at a local park to send off the runners. People spoke passionately about the intention for the run and shared their reasons for being there; some might assume it was to keep jobs, or it was vengeful in response to the hate rhetoric espoused by opposing groups, but the talk was of respect and was given respectfully. No, the intentions given were personal, heartfelt, and emotional. I was there because Chicano studies helped keep me in graduate school and I wanted my children to have the same opportunity to have Mexican American studies in public school settings. Students spoke of how Mexican American studies changed their lives and helped them believe in themselves and stay in school. The resilience, engagement, and strength of the young people were so powerful at those moments that I felt compelled to look at this in more detail in my research on mental health. So little research has investigated the individual effect of policies on health and well-being, and even less has investigated the resilience of young people within negative political contexts.

Youth Responses to SB 1108

The youth of today, as compared to young people of the 1960s, are often portrayed as less concerned with ethnic-based issues and more apathetic in terms of civic engagement around these topics. Yet there was widespread involvement and organizing of youth in the immigration marches of 2005–2007 (Pallares and Flores-Gonzalez 2010). Thus, perhaps a broader view of civic and political participation is useful for understanding the behaviors of the youth of today, which includes actions that can be taken regardless of citizenship status or voting ability (Marcelo, Lopez, and Kirby 2007; Montoya 2002). Civic activities that may influence political outcomes, include the equity and justice run to mobilize and bring attention, but also may include wearing buttons with political messages, taking part in demonstrations, voicing concerns to or trying to persuade registered voters, and volunteering to help mobilize communities (Marcelo, Lopez, and Kirby 2007; Verba, Schlozman, and Brady 1995). Membership in organizations based on ethnic, racial, or ideological identity (McIlwain 2007), or values such as responsibility or obligation to community can advance the development of civic and political voice through coalition building, collaboration, outreach, and consciousness raising that are fundamental to exercising civic rights (Fox 2005). The current study thus adopted this broader view of political and civic engagement to understand contemporary activities of Latino youth and their response to SB 1108.

In the current study, we were interested in how young adults, Latinos and non-Latino whites, responded to the proposal of SB 1108, a later reincarnation of the SB 1069 bill, known as the "Anti–Ethnic Studies Bill." We took a stress and coping approach to measuring and understanding youth strategies and how responses were associated with self-esteem and depressive symptoms among undergraduate students. Psychological research theory has found that mental well-being is the result of a balance between stress and healthy coping resources (Compas et al. 2001). Studies have found that Mexican-descent youth report stress due to discrimination and intercultural conflict (Romero and Roberts, 2003). We investigated the degree to which students reported feeling stress as a result of the anti–ethnic studies bill and their coping responses to it. Two primary forms of coping strategies are well documented among young people. Engagement coping strategies involve directly coping with the stressor or one's emotions and include problem solving, emotional expression, and emotional modulation (Compas et al. 2001). On the other hand, coping through disengagement distances one's thoughts, emotions, and physical presence from the stressor, such as denial and wishful thinking. Compas and colleagues (2001) have noted that engagement strategies are generally associated with fewer behavioral and emotional problems among youth. Edwards and Romero (2008) found that Latino youth have better mental health when they are directly and actively engaged in coping with discrimination through engagement coping, which we define as talking, praying, learning, and activism. Thus, we anticipated that a stress response to SB 1108 and disengagement coping would be associated with worse mental well-being, and that engagement coping would be associated with better mental health.

Chicana/o studies were truly rooted in the civil rights movement and the Chicana/o movement and the mobilization of student organizations, such as MEChA. MEChA had its beginnings in the period of civil rights struggle (Muñoz 1989) and it was during the historic Denver Conference that discussions planted the seeds for the implementation of Chicano studies programs in higher education. MEChA and allies of diverse ethnic backgrounds would play an important leadership role advocating for meaningful curricula within US colleges and universities by integrating Chicana/o culture, history, and politics (Muñoz 2007). The mobilization of student groups who were able to influence national, state, and local policies to create Chicana/o studies was a major source of empowerment for generations. A knowledge of history and consciousness of culture and social injustice through education was a central element of the Chicana/o movement and the empowerment of youth of all backgrounds. Current ethnic identity development models identify and measure the maturation of identity based on knowledge of history and traditions and acceptance of one's ethnic group membership in a manner that is based on a deeper sense of belonging and a positive view of one's ethnic group overall (Phinney et al. 1990–1991). It is this approach to understanding ethnic identity that we used in this study, which is relevant for all ethnic backgrounds (Roberts et al. 1999).

Ironically, in 2008, the same year that we celebrated the forty-year anniversary of Chicano studies, Arizona Senate Bill 1108 threatened to eliminate race- or ethnic-based groups (such as MEChA) from operating on college, university, and high school campuses. This bill was proposed by Russell Pearce (R-Mesa) as an amendment to a Homeland Security bill that would effectively eliminate ethnic studies and ethnic-related student groups in public schools in Arizona. Pearce, an architect of many anti-immigrant proposals since 2004, was reported as saying that he did not oppose diversity instruction but rather the use of taxpayer dollars to indoctrinate students in what he depicted as anti-American, seditious thinking. As such, the bill sought to undo the civil rights achievements at publicly funded schools by eliminating ethnic studies, based on the perception that these programs espoused "anti-Western values." SB 1108 specifically stated: "A primary purpose of public education is to inculcate values of American citizenship. Public tax dollars used in public schools should not be used to denigrate American values and the teachings of Western civilization."

For institutions found in violation, state funding could be withheld by an authority vested in the state system of public instruction. Although the measure did not pass in 2008, nor when it was introduced a year later (SB 1069), it did pass in 2010 as HB 2281 (O'Leary et al. 2012). What remains in question, however, is the effect of the hostile discourse on the social and political climate surrounding the measure given it that targets specific student groups and classes. Given that Native American groups and courses were excluded from this legislation, and that the largest ethnic minority in Arizona is of Mexican descent (32 percent of the state, and 40 percent of the K–12 population), it appeared that this legislation was primarily targeting Chicana/o studies.

During the 1960s, two major fundamentals of the Chicana/o movement were civic engagement and ethnic identity; thus, we also investigated the relation between these factors and coping strategies among undergraduate students of Latino and non-Latino white backgrounds. We anticipated that a more conscious and positive ethnic identity and more civic engagement would be associated with more engagement coping. A more mature ethnic identity would lead to more civic engagement, which would buffer negative effects of SB 1108. In the current study, undergraduate students at an Arizona university completed online surveys to provide individual-level perceptions of the SB 1108 bill, civic engagement, ethnic identity, discrimination, self-esteem, and depressive symptoms.

Our research questions were:

Do students report stress due to SB 1108?

Is SB 1108 stress associated with engaged coping, disengaged coping, ethnic identity, or civic engagement?

Are self-esteem and depressive symptoms associated with any of the following factors: SB 1108 stress, engaged coping, disengaged coping, ethnic identity, or civic engagement? Does engaged coping buffer the effect of stress on well-being?

Research Design and Participants

Methods

The study, conducted in the fall of 2008, used a cross-sectional self-report design. Undergraduate students completed an online survey at one time point. Students were recruited from undergraduate courses in Mexican American studies, family studies and human development, and psychology at a four-year institution in Arizona. Undergraduate research assistants read a five-minute recruitment script in each of these classes at the beginning of class, and students were asked to write down their e-mail address on a list if they were interested in being contacted for the study. The recruitment script not only contained details about the survey but also let the students know that it was confidential and anonymous, and that they would only be contacted twice via e-mail. As an incentive, students were offered extra credit in most of their courses for participating in the study. Students were also able to enter a raffle for an MP3 player for their participation; one MP3 player was given out. Students who provided e-mail addresses were sent individualized links to the web-based survey; if they did not respond to the first e-mail contact, they also received one follow-up e-mail twenty-four hours before the end of data collection. In total, 513 e-mail addresses were collected, 51 e-mails bounced, and 7 students opted out of the study; 326 completed the survey online, which was 71 percent of the valid e-mail addresses that were sent an invitation.

Procedure

Undergraduate students completed an online survey on a wide range of student issues using the program SurveyMonkey.com. The program is readily available using the Internet. Students were sent individualized e-mail links for the survey to ensure that they completed it at only one time point. Once students completed the survey, they were not able to go back to make changes or to forward the link to other students. The online survey was completed at students' convenience at computers of their choice. Prior to beginning the survey, participants read and agreed to an informed assent. At this point students were also able to opt out of the survey. The survey took approximately forty-five minutes to complete. All surveys were completely in English. After completing the questionnaire, participants were able to print out a confirmation page to give to their professors in order to receive extra credit. Students were entered into a raffle for an MP3 player upon completion of the survey. One MP3 player was given to one student upon the completion of the study. This study was approved by the Human Subjects Committee at the University of Arizona.

Demographics

Participants self-reported their age, gender, and generation level: 154 (61.8 percent) were white (non-Hispanic) and 104 (38.2 percent) were of Mexican descent (OMD = Of Mexican Descent). See table 5.1 for a description of demographics by ethnic group.

Civic Engagement

Civic engagement items were modified from scales by Flanagan and colleagues (2007). A total of nineteen questions were asked, including items such as, "How often have you used the following strategies when you feel there is problem in your community? Write an opinion letter to local newspaper, contact an elected official, get other people to care about the problem, participate in a boycott, vote on a regular basis, or wear a campaign button." A Likert scale ranged from 1 = never, 2 = a few times, 3 = sometimes, 4 = a lot. The alpha for all items for non-Latino whites was $\alpha = .92$, and for individuals of Mexican descent was $\alpha = .93$. All items were combined to create an overall average score of civic engagement, with a higher score indicating more frequent civic engagement behaviors.

Table 5.1. Description of Demographic Sample

	Non-Latino White (n = 154)	Mexican Descent (n = 104)
Gender		
Male	34 (22%)	28 (27%)
Female	119 (78%)	76 (73%)
Age	19.58 (1.67)	20.26 (1.77)*
Generation		
Immigrant	1 (.7%)	10 (10%)
Child of immigrant parents	15 (11%)	44 (42%)
Later generation	126 (89%)	50 (48%)
Language preference		
English mean	3.94 (.21)	3.66 (.49)
Spanish mean	1.37 (.44)	2.39 (.83)
First in family to go to college		
Yes	14 (9.2%)	35 (34%)
No	139 (91%)	67 (66%)

Note: Age means were significantly different based on t-test, $t(256) = -3.14$, $p < .01$. Language preference means were significantly different based on t-test, $t(256) = 6.39$, $p < .001$ for English and $t(256) = -12.67$, $p < .001$ for Spanish. *$p<.05$.

Stress and Coping Strategies for SB 1108 Anti–Ethnic Studies Proposed Legislation

The following vignette explaining SB 1108 was provided for the questionnaire: "In the spring of 2008, some Arizona senators proposed a law (SB 1108) that would ban curricula that conflict with Western values (such as raza studies) and 'race-based' organizations (such as MEChA) from public school campuses, including colleges and universities." Participants read the vignette and were asked, "To what degree do the following describe your response to the proposed law/these events?" A Likert scale ranging from 1 = strongly Disagree to 4 = strongly agree was provided for each of the responses. The responses a, b, and i were grouped to create a "disengage" variable and the responses d, e, f, g, and h were grouped to create an "engage" variable, and variable j was used as an individual item to represent stress (table 5.2).

Ethnic Identity

Ethnic identity was assessed with twelve items of the Multigroup Ethnic Identity Measure (Phinney 1992), which represent the degree to which

Table 5.2. Variables Used to Determine Engaged Coping and Disengagement

Responses Used to Determine Engaged Coping	Responses Used to Determine Disengagement
(d) I talk to friends and family about it	(a) I realize I have to live with how things are
(e) I learn all I can about it	(b) I try not to think about it
(f) I concentrate on positive things	(i) I don't know what I feel
(g) Pray or meditate to calm myself	
(h) Participate in activism (e.g., petitions, marches, rallies, etc.)	

Note: The internal reliability for Engaged Coping was $\alpha = .79$ for non-Latino whites and $\alpha = .71$ for Mexican Americans. The internal reliability for Disengagement was $\alpha = .63$ for non-Latino whites and $\alpha = .66$ for Mexican Americans.

individuals have explored their ethnic history and traditions and have committed and resolved their feelings about their ethnic group, as well as seven affirmation items (Marsiglia et al. 2004) that represent the positive or negative emotional valence of ethnic identity. Response items ranged from 1 = strongly disagree to 4 = strongly agree. The twelve identity items were averaged for a mean score, with a higher score indicating more agreement. A mean value of the affirmation items was taken and standardized from –1 to 1 in order to create a valence for the positive or negative effect of the affirmation of identity. Thus, in order to represent positive ethnic identity development, a variable was created by multiplying the identity mean with the standardized affirmation mean. The internal reliability for non-Latino whites was $\alpha = .89$ and for individuals of Mexican descent it was $\alpha = .90$.

Depressive Symptoms

Depressive symptoms were measured with ten items from the Center for Epidemiologic Studies–Depression Scale (CES-D; Radloff 1977). Participants rated how frequently they experienced each symptom during the past week, on a scale from 1 (rarely) to 4 (most of the time). Items included: "I felt that I could not shake off the blues, even with help from my family or friends; I had trouble keeping my mind on what I was doing; I felt lonely; and I felt hopeful about the future" (reverse scored). Higher mean scores denoted higher depressive symptoms. The scale was reliable ($\alpha = .79$).

Self-Esteem

The Rosenberg Self-Esteem Scale was used to measure self-esteem. The seven-item scale (1 = never through 5 = almost always true) was reliable in previous studies with adolescents (Rosenberg 1965, 1979) and particularly with Mexican Americans. Cronbach's alpha ranged from .73 to .87 (Cervantes et al. 1990, 1991; Joiner and Kashubeck 1996). A sample item is "I feel that I have a number of good qualities." For this sample the internal reliability was .62. An average self-esteem score was computed.

Results

Test Values

Test values for variables of interest by ethnic group are provided in table 5.3 with results from *t*-test analysis for significant differences between ethnic groups. White students were more likely to report disengaged coping and Mexican-descent students were more likely to report engaged coping strategies. Students of Mexican descent were significantly more likely to report more positive ethnic identity development. There were no significant ethnic differences for civic engagement, stress response to SB 1108, self-esteem, or depressive symptoms.

Pearson product moment correlations are provided for both whites and Mexican Americans in table 5.4. Students of Mexican descent had

Table 5.3. *t*-Test Values for Ethnic Group Differences in Variables of Interest

	Non-Latino White M(SD)	Mexican Descent M(SD)	t Value	p Value
Disengaged response to SB 1108	2.31 (.68)	1.94 (.65)	4.17	.001
Engaged response to SB 1108	2.28 (.58)	2.67 (.51)	−5.52	.001
Stress response to SB 1108	2.07 (.85)	2.27 (.94)	−1.75	.082
Positive ethnic identity development	−.22 (2.75)	1.27 (2.68)	−4.31	.001
Civic engagement	1.53 (.55)	1.50 (.50)	.40	.692
Self-esteem	4.13 (.65)	4.22 (.60)	−1.06	.291
Depressive symptoms	1.92 (.52)	1.93 (.51)	−.26	.797

Note: *p* value less than .05 is considered a significant difference between groups. A higher score indicates more agreement.

Table 5.4. Pearson Product Moment Correlations between Variables of Interest by Ethnic Group

	1. Engaged	2. Disengaged	3. Stress	4. Civic Engagement	5. Ethnic Identity	7. Self-esteem	8. Depressive
Engaged	1.00	-.30**	.36***	.27**	.14	.04	.09
Disengaged	.07	1.00	-.11	-.19	-.38***	-.07	-.05
Stress	.42***	.02	1.00	.14	.04	-.25*	.32**
Civic engagement	.29***	-.12	.21*	1.00	.02	.07	.06
Ethnic identity	.00	.05	-.21*	.17*	1.00	.27**	-.24*
Self-esteem	-.05	-.12	-.29**	-.08	.41***	1.00	-.56***
Depressive	.04	-.03	.28**	.02	-.24**	-.62***	1.00

Note: *$p < .05$, **$p < .01$, ***$p < .001$. Correlations above the 1.00 diagonal line indicate correlations are for individuals of Mexican descent and bottom correlations are for non-Latino whites.

significant correlations as follows. An engaged response to SB 1108 was associated with being less disengaged, feeling more stress in response to SB 1108, and more civic engagement. A more disengaged response was associated with a lower ethnic identity. Higher self-esteem and fewer depressive symptoms were associated with lower SB 1108 stress and higher ethnic identity. For white students, a more engaged response to SB 1108 was associated with more SB 1108 stress and more civic engagement. More stress in response to SB 1108 was associated with lower ethnic identity, more civic engagement, lower self-esteem, and more depressive symptoms. More civic engagement, higher self-esteem, and fewer depressive symptoms were associated with higher ethnic identity.

Student Responses to SB 1108

Multiple linear regression analyses were conducted to answer the basic research questions (see table 5.5). The three responses to SB 1108 were disengaged, engaged, and stress. The predictor variables of civic engagement, ethnic identity, and discrimination stress were entered into the models at the same time. Given the number of ethnic differences in previous analyses, it was decided that each model should be run separately for non-Latino whites and Mexican-descent individuals.

Disengaged Coping

The model for the disengaged response was not significant for non-Latino whites. It was significant for Mexican-descent individuals ($p < .001$), with the overall model accounting for 16 percent of the variance. The only significant predictor variable was positive ethnic identity, which was negatively associated with disengagement ($\beta = -.37$, $p < .001$). Thus, more positive ethnic identity development among Mexican-descent individuals was associated with a less disengaged response to SB 1108.

Engaged Coping

The models predicting the engaged response were significant for both ethnic groups, accounting for 8 percent of the variance for non-Latino whites and 7 percent of the variance for Mexican-descent students. More civic engagement significantly predicted more engagement for both non-Latino whites ($\beta = .30$, $p < .001$) and Mexican-descent students ($\beta = .20$, $p < .05$).

Table 5.5. Multiple Linear Regression Analyses for Responses to SB 1108 by Ethnic Group

	Non-Latino White		Mexican Descent	
	Std. β	t	Std. β	t
1. Disengaged	$F(3, 138) = 1.39, p = .250$; $R = .17$, adj. $R^2 = .01$		$F(2, 95) = 10.26$, $p = .001, R = .42$, adj. $R^2 = .16$	
Civic engagement	−.12	−1.45	−.18	−1.91
Ethnic identity	.04	.49	−.38	−4.07***
2. Engaged	$F(3, 138) = 5.14, p = .002$, $R = .32$, adj. $R^2 = .08$		$F(2, 95) = 4.62, p = .01$, $R = .30$, adj. $R^2 = .07$	
Civic engagement	.30	3.59***	.27	2.71**
Ethnic identity	.06	.75	.13	1.33
3. Stress	$F(4, 137) = 9.76, p = .001$, $R = .47$, adj. $R^2 = .20$		$F(4,93) = 4.15, p < .01$, $R = .39$, adj. $R^2 = .12$	
Engaged	.40	5.05***	.37	3.62***
Disengaged	.01	.11	−.03	−.27
Civic engagement	.06	.77	.04	.37
Ethnic identity	−.20	−2.57*	−.02	−.15
4. Self-esteem	$F(5, 136) = 8.70, p = .001$, $R = .50$, adj. $R^2 = .22$		$F(6, 91) = 4.45, p = .001$, $R = .48$, adj. $R^2 = .18$	
Stress	−.23	−2.70**	−1.60	−3.46***
Engaged	.06	.66	−.45	−2.11*
Disengaged	−.13	−1.75	−.04	−.34
Ethnic identity	.39	4.96***	.24	2.32*
Civic engagement	.01	.02	.06	.61
Interaction	—	—	1.63	2.90**
5. Depressive symptoms	$F(5, 136) = 4.20, p < .001$ $R = .37$, adj. $R^2 = .10$		$F(5, 92) = 3.29, p < .01$ $R = .41$, adj. $R^2 = .12$	
Stress	.28	3.09**	.31	2.97**
Engaged	−.07	−.73	−.02	−.14
Disengaged	−.04	−.46	−.14	−1.32
Ethnic identity	−.21	−2.57*	−.29	−2.80**
Civic engagement	−.05	−.58	−.01	−.04

Note: * $p < .05$, ** $p < .01$, *** $p < .001$.

SB 1108 Stress

The overall models for the stress response outcome were significant for both ethnic groups, accounting for 12 percent of the variance among non-Latino whites and 12 percent for students of Mexican descent. Whites reported significantly more stress when they were engaged with SB 1108 and when they reported a lower ethnic identity. Mexican-descent students who reported being engaged with SB 1108 reported more stress.

Mental Well-Being

Multiple linear regression models were conducted to determine the effects of responses to SB 1108 (engaged, disengaged, stress) to predict self-esteem or depressive symptoms (see table 5.5). These models were run separately for non-Latino whites and for individuals of Mexican descent. In the first step, predictors included SB 1108 stress, engaged coping, and disengaged coping. In the second step, ethnic identity and civic engagement were added. In the third step, an interaction between engaged coping and stress was tested.

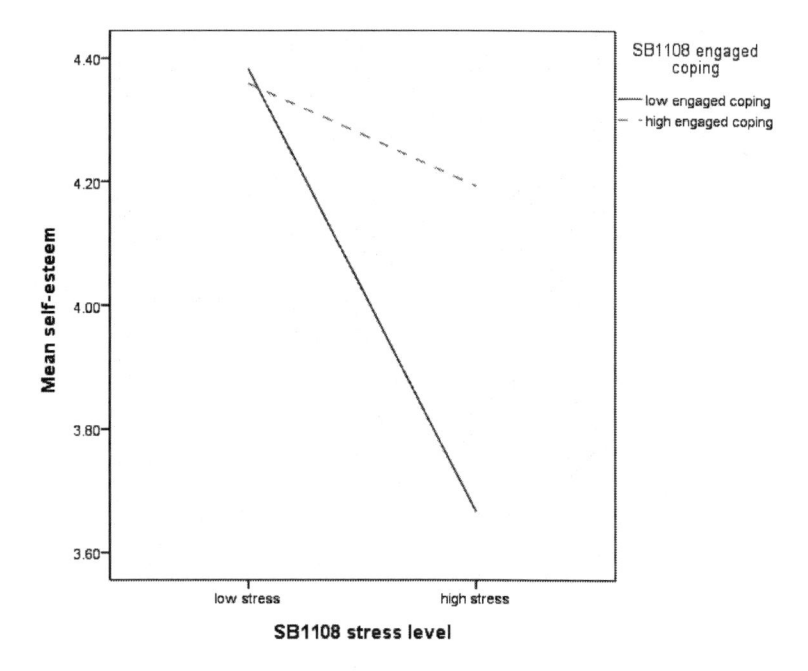

Figure 5.1. Interaction of level of stress and engaged coping with SB 1108

The overall model to predict self-esteem among students of non-Latino white descent accounted for 22 percent of the variance. Higher self-esteem was associated with less SB 1108 stress and higher ethnic identity. The model for Mexican-descent students accounted for 18 percent of the variance. Higher self-esteem was associated with less SB 1108 stress, less engaged coping, and higher ethnic identity. The interaction between stress and engaged coping was significant such that more engaged coping at higher stress levels was associated with higher self-esteem (see figure 5.1).

For depressive symptoms, the overall model accounted for 10 percent of the variance for whites and 12 percent of the variance for Mexican-descent students. For both ethnic groups a similar pattern was found; more depressive symptoms were associated with more SB 1108 stress and lower ethnic identity.

Discussion

The current study investigated students' reactions to the proposed anti–ethnic studies legislation and the impact on their mental well-being. Students did report stress due to SB 1108, and stress levels did not differ by ethnic group; however, Mexican-descent students reported more engaged coping and non-Latino white students reported more disengaged coping strategies. Our findings also indicate that mental well-being was negatively affected by SB 1108 stress in both Mexican and non-Latino white students.

Additionally, a more positive ethnic identity based on knowledge of one's history and traditions was associated with more self-esteem and fewer depressive symptoms for both white and Mexican-descent students. Both ethnic groups reported that more civic engagement in general was associated with more engagement with SB 1108; however, being more engaged also was associated with more SB 1108 stress. Ethnic identity functioned differently for white and Mexican-descent students in regard to coping responses. A more positive and developed ethnic identity was associated with fewer disengaged coping strategies for Mexican-descent students. White students who reported a higher or more "mature" ethnic identity reported more stress due to SB 1108. A take-home message from these results is that a positive ethnic identity based on knowledge of history and traditions of one's ethnic group was a significant predictor of mental well-being for both white and Mexican-descent students. This finding brings home more than ever the need to include ethnic studies classes for all students so that they have an opportunity to learn more about their origins based on history and educational knowledge.

Another important finding of this study is that when Mexican-descent students reported using engaged coping strategies (talking, praying, learning, activism) in response to legislation such as the anti–ethnic studies bills, they were more likely to retain a higher level of self-esteem at high levels of stress. This unique form of resilience is termed protective enhancing, which has a stronger impact on resilience at higher levels of stress. This is critical to understand that students' overall positive sense of self was protected by their greater engagement in response to hostile legislation. In conclusion, the truth of the experiences of those students who were running through the desert to save ethnic studies is reflected in our study here, in a broader sample of undergraduate students.

Notes

This research was funded by a seed grant from the University of Arizona Department of Mexican American Studies awarded to Dr. Romero. For all future correspondence please contact the first author at: Dr. Anna O'Leary Ochoa, Mexican American Studies, University of Arizona, 1101 E. James E. Rogers Way, César E. Chávez Building #23, Tucson, AZ 85721–0023, olearya@email.arizona.edu. Thank you to all students who assisted with this project including: J. J. Federico, Michelle Rascon, Gemma Kartes, and Rebecca Covarrubias.

References

Cervantes, R.C., A. M. Padilla, and N. Salgado de Snyder. 1990. "Reliability and Validity of the Hispanic Stress Inventory." *Hispanic Journal of Behavioral Sciences* 12(1): 76–82.

———. 1991. "The Hispanic Stress Inventory: A Culturally Relevant Approach to Psychosocial Assessment." *Psychological Assessment* 3: 438–47.

Compas, B. E., J. K. Connor-Smith, H. Saltzman, A. H. Thomsen, and M. E. Wadsworth. 2001. "Coping with Stress during Childhood and Adolescence: Problems, Progress, and Potential in Theory and Research." *Psychological Bulletin*, 127: 87–127.

Edwards, L. M., and A. J. Romero. 2008. "Coping with Discrimination among Mexican Descent Adolescents." *Hispanic Journal of Behavioral Sciences* 30: 24–39.

Flanagan, C. A., A. K. Syvertsen, and M. D. Stout. 2007. CIRCLE WORKING PAPER 55 May 2007.

Fox, Jonathan. 2005. "Unpacking 'Transnational Citizenship.'" *Annual Review in Political Science* 8:171–201.

Joiner, G.W., and S. Kashubeck. 1996. "Acculturation, Body Image, Self-esteem and Eating Disorder Symptomatology in Adolescent Mexican-American Women." *Psychology of Women Quarterly* 20(3): 419–35.
Marcelo, Karlo Barrios, Mark Hugo Lopez, and Emily Hoban Kirby. 2007. "Civic Engagement among Minority Youth." Center for Information and Research on Civic Learning and Engagement. http://www.civicyouth.org/PopUps/FactSheets/FS_07_minority_ce.pdf.
Marin, G., and R. J. Gamba. 1996. "A New Measurement of Acculturation for Hispanics: The Bidimensional Acculturation Scale for Hispanics (BAS)." *Hispanic Journal of Behavioral Sciences* 18: 297–316.
Marsiglia, F. F., S. Kullis, M. L. Hecht, and S. Sills. 2004. "Ethnicity and Ethnic Identity as Predictors of Drug Norms and Drug Use among Preadolescents in the US Southwest." *Substance Use and Misuse* 39(7): 1061–94.
McIlwain, Charlton D. 2007. "Racial Identity, Ideology and the Youth Vote: Observations from the 2004 Presidential Campaign." *American Behavioral Scientist* 50(9): 1231–38.
Montoya, Lisa J. 2002. "Gender and Citizenship in Latino Political Participation." In *Latinas/os: Remaking of America*, ed. Marcelo M. Suarez-Orozco and Mariela M. Paez, 215–35. Berkeley: University of California Press.
Muñoz, C. 1989. *Youth, Identity, Power: The Chicano Generation*. Verso.
O'Leary, Anna Ochoa, Andrea J. Romero, Nolan L. Cabrera, and Michelle Rascón. 2012. "Assault on Ethnic Studies." In *Arizona Firestorm: Global Immigration Realities, National Media and Provincial Politics*, ed. Otto Santa Ana and Celeste González de Bustamante, 97–120. Lanham, MD: Rowman and Littlefield.
Pallares, A., and N. Flores-Gonzalez. 2010. ¡*Marcha! Latino Chicago and the Immigration Rights Movement*. Urbana: University of Illinois Press.
Phinney, J. S. 1992. "The Multigroup Ethnic Identity Measure: A New Scale for Use with Diverse Groups." *Journal of Adolescent Research* 7: 156–76.
Phinney, J. S., et al. 1990–1991. "Ethnic Identity in Adolescents and Adults: Review of Research." *Psychological Bulletin* 108: 499–514.
Radloff, L. S. 1977. "The CES-D Scale: A Self-Report Depression Scale for Research in the General Population." *Applied Psychological Measurement* 1: 385–401.
Roberts, R. E., J. S. Phinney, Louise C. Masse, Y. R. Chen, C. R. Roberts, and A. J. Romero. 1999. "The Structure and Validity of Ethnic Identity among Diverse Groups of Adolescents. *Journal of Early Adolescence* 19(3): 300–322.
Romero, A. J. and R. E. Roberts. 2003. "Stress within a Bicultural Context for Adolescents of Mexican Descent." *Cultural Diversity and Ethnic Minority Psychology* 9(2): 171–84.
Rosenberg, M. 1965. *Society and the Adolescent Self-Image*. Princeton, NJ: Princeton University Press.
———. 1979. *Conceiving the Self*. New York: Basic Books.
Verba, Sid, Kay Lehman Schlozman, and Henry Brady. 1995. *Voice and Equality: Civic Voluntarism in American Politics*. Cambridge, MA: Harvard University Press.

CHAPTER SIX

The Social Justice Education Project

Youth Participatory Action Research in Schools

Julio Cammarota

Youth participatory action research (YPAR) offers great potential as a methodology for investigating and improving educational practices (Cahill 2007; Cammarota and Fine 2008; Fine et al. 2005; Kirshner 2007; McIntyre 2000; Morrell 2006; Torre 2009; Tuck 2009). Research in which young people are both the researchers and the focus of the study can provide critical insider perspectives into how schools produce success or failure. Young people are arguably the most important stakeholders of education inasmuch as their everyday school experiences provide a wealth of knowledge, ranging from the obvious to the subtlest interactions. This knowledge allows students and other stakeholders (teachers, families, and education researchers) to take action to improve various aspects of education, including teacher effectiveness, pedagogy, service learning, school counseling, school safety, student-teacher relationships, school climate, and student engagement, to name a few (Akom 2009; Berg, Coman, and Schensul 2009; Krueger 2010; Ozer, Ritterman, and Wanis 2010; Smith, Davis, and Bhowmik 2010; Schensul and Berg 2004).

However, rarely do adults listen to the recommendations and conclusions offered by youth who conduct their own original education-based research. Some have documented how adult audiences for YPAR projects often dismiss or challenge young people's research findings on the basis that juveniles are supposedly too young to generate knowledge worthy of attention (Fine et al. 2005; Torre 2009). Those adults who dismiss YPAR findings fail to understand that effective educational change requires the voices and ideas of students. The most important voices, and unfortunately the ones most often missing in the dialogue, are surely those of students who represent possibly the best critical evaluators as a result of their daily and long-term exposure to schooling. Education is one of the only institutional processes in which those most affected by it have the least say in its design and function. When it comes to school, the opposite should be true. Those who have the most at stake should be empowered to take part and lead in decision making. The empowerment of students through research is the basis of YPAR, thereby bringing young people into the fold of evaluating, analyzing, and ultimately changing education to better meet their needs.

This chapter discusses a YPAR program in Tucson, Arizona, called the Social Justice Education Project (SJEP) and students' research analysis of disparities between different educational tracks. The SJEP is a senior-year government course with a YPAR component built into the curriculum. Tucson Unified School District (TUSD) offered six of these specialized social science course at four high schools.[1] For this chapter, I focus on one SJEP course during the 2009–2010 school year that was offered at one of TUSD's high schools, Mountain High. I select Mountain High for this discussion because of its unique magnet structure that divides the campus into two separate and unequal schools. Mountain High offers the regular curriculum primarily for students of color. Scholastic High, a college prep school on the same campus, serves primarily white students. This overarching disparity of educational experiences establishes the premise for myriad other disparities that run through Mountain High's "regular" curriculum. Therefore, students' YPAR projects include an analysis not only of the differences between Mountain and Scholastic but also of the inequities within their own educational context.

Before discussing the students' research at Mountain High, I provide a brief explanation of the principles of YPAR, focusing on its potential as a research methodology. A discussion of the origins and purpose of the SJEP follows. Then the chapter reports on the students' YPAR project at Mountain High through an analysis and discussion of field notes taken by them throughout the school year. Field notes are the primary source of data for the students' research. Finally, I conclude with students' recommendations for improving their educational experiences and thus fostering greater equity in school outcomes for students of color.

YPAR Principles

Rodriguez and Brown (2009) state that YPAR has at least three important principles. The first is that YPAR projects should be situated in young people's lives so that they can understand and address the problems negatively influencing their experiences. Situating the research in young people's experiences allows for the opportunity to use findings and research products to engender qualitative improvements in their lives. In other words, YPAR projects should have a direct impact on young people by generating results that can change the institutions most responsible for youth policies and practices.

Second, YPAR projects are participatory in design, which involves taking a collaborative approach to the production of knowledge. Knowledge emerges within a collective dialogue in which young people work together to design, implement, and analyze their research. Each step of the inquiry process therefore requires consistent dialogue about the purpose, objectives, and outcomes to generate questions that provoke discussion and emergent insights. Thus, the inquiry-based dialogue adopts a democratic character in that intellectual and creative works in projects are collectively shared endeavors.

The third principle is that YPAR projects should be transformative. An ultimate goal of YPAR is to initiate changes to institutions, social structures, and communities in ways that promote and sustain social justice. Thus, YPAR projects intend to transform situations or conditions to liberate youth from any form of oppression, whether it is classism, racism, sexism, homophobia, or xenophobia. Liberation is accomplished through self-reflection and action, or what Paulo Freire (1993) calls praxis. By engaging in praxis, young people attain a consciousness that perceives the self above and beyond oppressive ideologies that attempt to limit their capabilities. Praxis also requires addressing those structures that hold people in a subordinate reality.

I believe that YPAR has a fourth principle of empowerment that complements Rodriguez and Brown's (2009) trio of situated, participatory, and transformative principles. Empowerment is perhaps the most important principle of YPAR when it comes to education-based research. Students feel empowered to take ownership of their education in ways that ultimately serve their needs and the needs of their communities. Once they gain analytical skills from YPAR projects, students understand how certain qualities of their education can be helpful while others can be detrimental. The YPAR analysis moves young people through a process of reflection and action that "results in increased agency at the individual level and group level" (Berg, Coman, and Schensul 2009, 349). It is through knowing what is right and wrong and being able to recognize the pitfalls of educational institutions that young people reach a higher level of empowerment, which enables them to bring changes to the institutions that have the most impact on their lives. They can comprehend the difference between a good and bad education.

The SJEP in Tucson, Arizona

SJEP started at Cerro High School in TUSD. The program expanded to three other high schools including Campo, Pima, and Mountain. A total of six SJEP courses were offered every year. The students who enrolled in the SJEP were mostly working-class Latinas/os from southwestern Tucson. This high concentration of Latino/a students resulted from the schools' locations in primarily Latino/a neighborhoods. Other ethnicities of students enrolled in the SJEP included white, African American, and Native American.

Students met every day for one period, usually second period, and four semesters straight. The social science program was aligned with state-mandated history and US government standards and involved students in YPAR projects. By participating in our second-period social justice program, students received social science credits for graduation and the knowledge of how to conduct original YPAR projects. The program was split between state mandates and YPAR; three periods per week were devoted to US history and government requirements while two periods per week focused on YPAR.

Their YPAR involved critical analyses of social justice problems and presentations to influential people in their community to initiate change. Students learned qualitative research methodologies for assessing and addressing the everyday injustices limiting their own and their peers' potential. They learned how to conduct observations of different sites on campus, including other classrooms, the main office, and the cafeteria. Students wrote up observations in weekly field notes. They also documented their observations through photographs. They learned how to conduct taped interviews of their peers at school.

The students chose to investigate problems and issues that affected them personally. For example, they selected research topics from poems they created expressing various problems they faced in their social worlds. To facilitate the student poetry, we provided them with examples of social justice-minded poems: "Still I Rise" by Maya Angelou or "I Am Joaquin" by Rodolfo "Corky" Gonzales. The students discussed these poems and their social justice messages before creating their own. Then they collectively identified the poignant social justice and "generative" themes throughout their poems.

Identifying generative words or themes in poetry derives from the literacy work of Paulo Freire (1993, 1998). In his adult literacy program in Brazil, Freire taught reading and writing with words that originated from his students' lived experiences. In others words, Freire would never teach literacy with words originating from outside the students' sociocultural context. Rather, students would select the themes, topics, or words for study themselves, which allowed for the creation of new meanings and knowledge grounded not in dominant ideologies but in the students' everyday experiences.

Thus, our SJEP students developed research topics from self-selected themes that they thought needed urgent attention. For instance, some students selected the topic of border and immigration policies because family members had died crossing the desert. Others addressed discrimination against Latinas because they saw how schools, workplaces, and governments unfairly treated them and the women in their families.

They spent the latter part of their second year analyzing the poems, notes, photos, and interviews, using Chicano studies concepts and critical race theory as their analytical lenses. Their analyses become written reports, presentations, and video documentation. The students presented their findings to family members, teachers, principals, district superintendents, school board members, and federal, state, and local officials—with their voices being the focal point of their action strategy. We hope that, through YPAR, students gained the confidence to challenge the social and economic conditions impeding their life opportunities.

The effect of conducting original research and presenting their results to key stakeholders, including family members, was that students attained the intent and goal of praxis as they thought deeply and critically about impediments to their own social and economic progress while building relationships to help them remove these impediments.

In this regard, students understood the difference between transformative resistance or actions and self-defeating resistance or actions. Solórzano and Delgado Bernal (2001) define transformational resistance as student behavior that demonstrates both a critique of oppression and desire for social justice. The goal of most YPAR projects is to provide pedagogical strategies that promote transformational resistance (Cammarota and Fine

2008). Self-defeating resistance, according to Solórzano and Delgado Bernal (2001), refers to students who may critique oppression but lack motivation for social justice. Examples of our students' transformative resistance and actions include exposing structural decay at their school; fighting to ensure that the SJEP be offered for them and future students; and, with SJEP alumni, organizing the takeover of TUSD's Post Unitary Plan Community Forums to fight to continue socially and culturally responsive curricula throughout the district.

This chapter focuses on the field notes of students from one course offered at Mountain High during the 2009–2010 school year. SJEP students examined the educational disparities within their own school and also between Mountain High and the college preparatory school, Scholastic High School, on the same campus, including a detailed look at racial tracking. Mountain High's student body is 64 percent students of color and 36 percent white. Meanwhile, Scholastic High is 42 percent students of color and 58 percent white. Not only do a majority of white students receive a better education at Scholastic High, but white students are also overrepresented in the higher tracks at Mountain High.

Intraschool Tracking

Although Mountain and Scholastic are tracked differently, tracking also exists internally within Mountain. An ability-grouping program at Mountain called the "housing" system is a prime example of how students have disparate educational opportunities within the same school. A senior SJEP student, Anita Diaz, wrote about her experiences being tracked at Mountain High in the housing system when she was a freshman:

> In this system, we were separated into different groups. There were four groups, which were known as the green, orange, pink and gold houses. The green house was known as the honors group since all the students had Advanced Placement classes. The rest of the houses, according to the teachers, were supposedly at the same level. But the students thought differently. They believed the houses were at different levels and placed in these different levels according to how smart the students were. When I was a freshman, students told me that the green house was the first, gold house second, pink was third, and orange fourth. At the beginning of the freshman year, we were never asked which house we wanted to be in. We were never given the choice. The green house was

mostly made up of white students but there were some exceptions. The other houses were mostly minority students. While being placed in these houses, we didn't get a chance to meet other people for almost two years except for those who were placed in the same house as you were.

I was placed in the pink house for my freshman and sophomore years. The pink house was mainly minority students. Everyone in the same house had the same group of teachers, whether it was English, math or science. In my second semester, my math teacher gave up on us. He no longer taught us anything. He would just put a power point on, sit behind his desk and talk to his teacher's aide or look at his computer. There was also my science teacher. In the beginning of the year, we would do projects but by the second semester we ended up doing only bookwork. We would get to class, open our books and read and answer questions from the text. In those two classes, I didn't really learn anything. In one class, the teacher gave up on us. In the other class, we did only bookwork.

The house system placed us into different tracks. For instance, the green house was preparing students to go to college. The rest of the houses were not preparing students to go to college, especially if you had teachers who didn't care if you received an education. One time I was given an auto shop class, which I didn't want. I tried to switch out but all the other business classes were already full. We are put into this track to lead us into a job instead of going into college.

With her observations, Anita provides a fine-tuned analysis of some of the problems of tracking. First, she describes how the students were segregated by race in ways that provided white students with better educational opportunities. Second, she states that she was prevented from actually meeting other college-bound students (white or youths of color), which according to social capital theory indicates that she was denied relationships with peers who could help her improve her academic performance. Third, the quality of teaching was inferior in her track. Some teachers were negligent, failing to provide the kind of instruction needed to learn. Fourth and last, she realized the some students, especially the white students in the green house, were receiving an education that was preparing them for college. Meanwhile, Anita felt that her education was leading her to some kind of vocational career.

Another student, Ana Federico, wrote field notes about her experience as one of the only Latinas in her Advanced Placement English class at Mountain. She states:

The change that these classes so desperately need is the presence of racial diversity. Diversity is always lacking in these classes, because all I see are Caucasian students. I hear conversations of college plans, moving out of parents' house to have their own apartment, someone's new car of the year. And not a single student is something other than Caucasian. And I can't help but wonder why that is? The answer is that everything was planned out for them since the beginning. Their families led them to a track of academic achievement; they were there for them to help in anything and putting them in extra curricular activities. Many other friends that I know could do it too I'm sure of it, but social reproduction retrains the capacity of many of them and others.

Ana sees white students who have the privilege of material wealth. They do not have to worry whether they will obtain the items or experience the conditions that make life comfortable. Their world is different than Ana's. She does have to worry about resources and whether she will have enough money to afford college. She makes an important distinction between the white students and herself by realizing that they do not have the same worries as she does and therefore can focus on their future plans without much distraction.

The SJEP course provided Ana with the theory of social reproduction to help her understand why some students have better opportunities than others. Social reproduction is the process by which economic classes reproduce themselves from one generation to the next. For instance, a white middle-class youth will receive certain advantages from his socioeconomic background, such as economic resources, educated parents, and a well-funded school system, which provide him or her a better chance at staying in the same class location or rising above his or her parents. Meanwhile, someone of lower economic status experiences a life of diminished resources and opportunities and most likely will not have the possibility to leave his or her class location. Ana realizes that people she knows have the capability to take Advanced Placement classes but were denied the opportunities that would have prepared them for such classes.

The resource differential that produces varied opportunities for young people exists not only in society but also within Mountain High. Lola Martinez talked about the difference in resources between her SJEP class and an Advanced Placement (AP) English class. She was a student aide in the AP class, which provided her with an insider's view. She states that the AP English class has "good desks and the students all have computers. They all have good books and chairs that move around." She then compares her

SJEP class with the AP class. She writes that they did not "have books, computers, good desks." The differences were apparent, making Lola realize that certain students at her school were expected to learn while others were expected to fail.

The disparity of resources translates into a hierarchy in which certain students believe they are superior and thus more entitled than others. Another SJEP student, Lisette Montoya, wrote in her field notes about a conflict between students in her English class that shows how certain students perceived that they were culturally superior, and believed that the school therefore should have a preference for their cultural orientation. The incident happened after the school announcements over the PA system, which were given in both English and Spanish—English first and then Spanish immediately after. When the Spanish announcements were completed, one student shouted, "How Ghetto!" Lisette states that one "girl yelled, 'Speak English,' while another added, 'We're in America.'" A Latina student angrily stated, "Well look around the majority at this school are Hispanics." A white student responded by saying, "I speak English so everyone else should too, we're in America." The anti-Spanish students were obviously attempting to maintain their dominance over the majority at the school. Although the school's demographics were rapidly changing, white students wanted to sustain the English dominance at the school and thus keep their advantage. Becoming a white minority does not mean that these students would lose their power and status. An apartheid structure at Mountain is a present and unfortunate reality. By maintaining English as the dominant language, these students continue to hold onto and argue for cultural superiority, even though they represent the minority.

Interschool Tracking

Mountain students are painfully aware that Scholastic students have the greater prestige and therefore the better capacity for academic advancement. Ana Federico states that Scholastic students receive an education that "prepares them for college, while Mountain students get a lower education that prepares them for work." This difference, according to Ana, makes Mountain students want to "rebel" against their school, "due to the unbalanced education."

The differences between the schools' reputations translate into differences in expectations. In the minds of SJEP students, Mountain and Scholastic students share the same academic capabilities. However, it is obvious that Scholastic students experience higher expectations, thereby making a world of difference in educational experiences. Ana Federico wrote, "Mountain and Scholastic students start the same way in having dreams, everything starts as a dream." She states that accomplishing dreams is difficult "because there has to be people who will believe in that dream and will help in following it." The primary difference between Mountain and Scholastic students, according to Ana, is that "Scholastic students are given that opportunity in which their teachers and parents believe in them. Parents and teachers are essential in this process because they have the power more than anyone to place students on the right path toward reaching their dreams."

As part of their research, SJEP students documented the rare occasion when they needed to visit Scholastic High School. On these occasions, SJEP students noticed the unique dynamics between teachers and students. One SJEP student, Geraldo Castro, had to bring a note to a teacher at Scholastic High. When he reached the classroom, he noticed:

All the students are looking forward and writing on their papers. I'm surprised that no student turns to look and see who is at the door. Not one movement, they are robots. The teacher stops abruptly and stares at me. The worst stare I have been given, my heart turned cold and my eyes felt heavy. I ask the teacher if she's the teacher whose name is on the note and she yells at me, "I was told that there wasn't going to be any interruptions during my class!" I asked her again are you this teacher? She responds, "No! She is in the computer lab three doors down! Now leave my class and let me teach these bright students."

Geraldo was not bothered by the teacher's demeaning attitude because he was a Mountain High student. Instead, he was concerned that "no student talked, no student moved while the teacher yelled at me. I felt uncomfortable knowing that many of my friends went through that. I felt that they had no life during school." Geraldo felt sorry that Scholastic students learned to behave as if they had no feelings, indicating that they had internalized passivity. They had become submissive to the teacher's authority and remained consistently silent, even in times of crisis.

Other SJEP students had the impression that Scholastic students seemed stoic and passive in their classes. Judy McDougal visited Scholastic to see how it compared with Mountain. She asked the teacher if she could observe his classroom for one period. He agreed and told Judy to sit in the back. She wrote in her field notes:

Each student filed in one by one, really no one talking to another. There was an assignment written on the board. The students made their way to their seats and started pulling out their work, no words said. The late bell rang, the door closed and let me tell you no one was late. The teacher was sitting at his desk not saying a word, not even a hello to the students. They have to review the page they read for homework (a whole chapter) and read another chapter and answer the review questions. There were no moans or groans from the students saying that it is too much work. A couple words are said from student to students here and there but no conversations.

Judy noticed that Scholastic students have higher expectations in that a greater amount of work is assigned to them, which they accept without complaint. However, the difference in workload was not what concerned Judy. She observed that there was little to no communication between the students and the teacher. The students' primary task was to sit quietly and engage with the text without any dialogue. They were learning individually, missing out on the opportunity to share and build knowledge collectively.

When the teacher finally interacted with the students, he lectured and handled the dissemination of knowledge as a one-way street from him to the students: "He stands there and lectures starting from the beginning of the sections that the students read for their homework. They automatically take out notebooks and start taking notes. These students sit here as the teacher banks the education into the students' head. He doesn't even ask for the students' perspective on the subjects he was talking about."

In the SJEP course, students learned about Paulo Freire's (1993, 1998) concept of problem-posing education, which centers on building knowledge not as the distribution of unquestionable facts, figures, and ideas, but through problems that the students address with questions facilitating the discovery of solutions. The differences between the banking and problem-posing pedagogies are vast. The former leads students to the kinds of knowledge that the teacher wants them to learn. The latter allows students to discover knowledge as the primary process of learning, which shows students how they can create and develop knowledge on their own. The problem-posing approach teaches autonomy such that students realize they can become knowledgeable without the help of an authority. Problem-posing pedagogy promotes leaders who can solve problems with their own intellectual processes. In contrast, banking education forces students to become passive learners who cannot think independently of an authority or outside expert. Outcomes for problem posing include students who think critically and pose questions to find the best solution to a particular problem.

Despite the differences in expectations between the two schools, SJEP students would rather attend Mountain given the opportunity to choose. Judy McDougal wrote, "[there are] huge differences between our two schools. These students [at Scholastic] are taught to all be the same, pretty much have no individuality. If it were left up to me, I would go to Mountain." More specifically, SJEP students felt that the problem-posing education that they received in the SJEP course was the reason for their choice.

Implications

Within Mountain High, students experience the range of consequences of tracking. In the lower tracks, expectations are minimal so students feel less motivated to achieve. There is also a difference in resources between high and low tracks, which makes higher-track students appreciate their learning opportunity while lower-track students, who realize they have been shortchanged, tend to resent their education. In addition, the educational focus seems to be different for each track. Higher tracks are geared toward college preparation, while lower tracks guide students toward vocational learning.

Moreover, students from different tracks rarely interact, which deprives lower-track students of important social capital. If they had the opportunity to interact with higher-track students (white or youth of color), then those in the lower tracks could build the type of peer relationships that could help them achieve academic success. Furthermore, separating students by "ability" often is a proxy for separating them by race and culture. This racial segregation leads to tensions between groups such that the dominant racial group will attempt to maintain dominance while the subordinate group will struggle for equal rights and treatment.

SJEP students recommend that the negative aspects of tracking be removed, including lowered expectations, limited resources, unequal preparation, and racial segregation. The students would also like to see the two schools, Mountain and Scholastic, merged to construct one college preparatory high school. They believe that all students have the same capabilities to excel but not all students have the same opportunities. If the students at Mountain and Scholastic were given the same opportunities, more students would graduate and experience academic achievement.

SJEP students would like the SJEP pedagogy of inclusion and participation to become standard throughout the school. Allowing students to participate in the construction of knowledge and have their voices and ideas matter engages young people in the learning process.

These feelings of inclusion and participation are not necessarily experienced throughout the general curriculum at Mountain High. In some Mountain High classes, students experience banking education. Ana Federico wrote about her English class, "Everyone is quietly reading and waiting for her [the teacher] to say today's assignments, which is a discussion of the chapters we were supposed to read by today. As always everyone is afraid to say his or her opinions, afraid to say anything to this woman, this figure of authority known as the teacher. We have witnessed her making faces and rolling her eyes at the opinions students make. We are afraid to express our opinions and have become silent."

Teachers who show authority by judging students in ways that make them feel ignorant tend to cast a shadow of fear over the classroom. When students feel afraid, they accept their silence and hold back their opinions and ideas. A classroom in which the teacher negatively judges students' thinking becomes a place of a singular source and ownership of knowledge. Without the space for a collective production of knowledge, the classroom will appear fiercely undemocratic and oppressive.

With YPAR, students in the SJEP course have the experience of a democratic pedagogy, and any other type of education seems oppressive in comparison. They are treated as complete human beings with thoughts and ideas and the agency to bring changes to their environment. In settings of banking education, SJEP students feel less than human, because their intellectual and emotional capacities are suppressed. Once they experience democratic pedagogy, students understand that learning in this way is naturally human—an educational situation in which all students' intellect and ability to construct knowledge are engaged. Moreover, a natural way of learning involves not only the students' understanding of history but also their recognition that they too have the agency to become history makers. This approach of empowerment is what makes democracy such a compelling structure for education. Collectively, people learn to participate in how to understand and engage their world. Collective participation in the construction of knowledge leads to a sense of equality among participants. YPAR collectives challenge "traditional social hierarchies" and encourage democratic relationships among students (Torre and Ayala 2009, 389).

Once students learn that they too can contribute to history, they become more engaged in their education. YPAR is empowering for young people, particularly young people of color, because they comprehend their places and possibilities in history. Schooling that fails to develop the historical agency of students is the reason why so many young people of color feel disconnected from education. Most often students of color attend schools that focus on social control instead of promoting pedagogical practices that increase their agency. Young people who miss the opportunity to learn how to become agents of change will lack the motivation to seek knowledge. People who feel as if they have no effect in the world will avoid engagement and participation. YPAR builds agency and the sense that they can have an effect. Students of color, through YPAR, see their place in history and thus recognize their capacity to make positive contributions.

Notes

1. As of 2012, all SJEP courses were suspended as a result of ARS 15-112 (A).

References

Akom, A. A. 2009. "Critical Hip Hop Pedagogy as a Form of Liberatory Praxis." *Equity and Excellence in Education* 42(1): 52–66.

Berg, Marlene, Emil Coman, and Jean J. Schensul. 2009. "Youth Action Research for Prevention: A Multi-level Intervention Designed to Increase Efficacy and Empowerment Among Urban Youth." *American Journal of Community Psychology* 43: 345–59.

Cahill, C. 2007. "The Personal Is Political: Developing New Subjectivities through Participatory Action Research." *Gender, Place, and Culture* 14(3): 267–92.

Cammarota, J., and M. Fine., eds. 2008. *Revolutionizing Education: Youth Participatory Action Research in Motion*. New York: Routledge.

Fine, M., J. Bloom, A. Burns, L. Chajet, M. Guishard, Y. Payne, T. Perkins-Munn, and M. Torre. 2005. "Dear Zora: A Letter to Zora Neale Hurston 50 Years after Brown." *Teachers College Record* 107: 496–528.

Freire, P. 1993. *Pedagogy of the Oppressed*. New York: Continuum.

———. 1998. *The Paulo Freire Reader*, ed. M. A. Freire and D. Macedo. New York: Continuum.

Kirshner, B. 2007. "Supporting Youth Participation in School Reform: Preliminary Notes from a University-Community Partnership." *Children, Youth and Environments* 17(2): 354–63.

Krueger, Patricia. 2010. "It's Not Just a Method! The Epistemic and Political Work of Young People's Lifeworlds at the School-Prison Nexus." *Race, Ethnicity and Education* 13(3): 383–408.

McIntyre, A. 2000. "Constructing Meaning about Violence, School, and Community: Participatory Action Research with Urban Youth." *Urban Review* 32: 123–54.

Morrell, E. 2006. "Toward a Bottom Up Accountability System in Urban Education: Students as Researchers in Urban Schools." In *Beyond Resistance: Youth, Communities, and Social Justice: Toward the Development of a National Strategy*, ed. J. Cammarota, S. Ginwright, and P. Noguera. New York: Routledge.

Ozer, Emily J., Miranda L. Ritterman, and Maggie G. Wanis. 2010. "Participatory Action Research (PAR) in Middle School: Opportunities, Constraints, and Key Processes." *American Journal of Community Psychology* 46: 152–66.
Rodriguez, Louis F., and Tara M. Brown. 2009. "From Voice to Agency: Guiding Principles for Participatory Action Research with Youth." *New Directions in Youth Development* 2009: 19–34.
Schensul, Jean J., and Marlene Berg. 2004. "Youth Participatory Action Research: A Transformative Approach to Service-Learning." *Michigan Journal of Community Service Learning* 10(3): 76–88.
Smith, Laura, Kathryn Davis, and Malika Bhowmik. 2010. "Youth Participatory Action Research Groups as School Counseling Interventions." *Professional School Counseling* 14(2): 174–82.
Solórzano, D. G., and D. Delgado Bernal. 2001. "Examining Transformational Resistance through a Critical Race and LatCrit Theory Framework: Chicana and Chicano Students in an Urban Context." *Urban Education* 36(3): 308–42.
Torre, M. E. 2009. "Participatory Action Research and Critical Race Theory: Fueling Spaces for Nos-otras to Research." *Urban Review* 41(1): 106–20.
Torre, M. E., and Jennifer Ayala. 2009. "Envisioning Participatory Action Research Entremundos." *Feminism and Psychology* 19: 387.
Tuck, E. 2009. "Re-visioning Action: Participatory Action Research and Indigenous Theories of Change." *Urban Review* 41(1): 47–65.

CHAPTER SEVEN

Encuentros with Families and Students

Cultivating Funds of Knowledge through Dialogue

Julio Cammarota and Augustine Romero

On a balmy night in Tucson, we waited anxiously for parents and family to attend our first-ever Encuentro. As University of Arizona researchers, we worked with a public high school teacher to develop a youth participatory action research (YPAR) program (Cammarota and Fine 2008) called the Social Justice Education Project (SJEP) (Cammarota 2007; Cammarota and Romero 2006) and believed that creating a forum for students to present their research and blossoming intellectualism (Romero, 2008) to parents would be a powerful demonstration of the transformations that transpired within our classroom and most importantly within our students. We based this idea, the student presentation or Encuentro, on theories of learning situated in processes of dialogue and the formative potential of tightening social bonds. We read Freire (1993), Fals-Borda (1986), and Vygotsky (1994), and now was the time to put into practice the building of knowledge through a dialogue based on the students' and the community's social experiences of marginalization and injustice.

Six o'clock came and went, and not one parent showed. We thought that this might happen. Most of the parents were working-class Latinos with plenty of reasons not to come on a Thursday evening. Many parents, as well as the students, work evening shifts and it is sometimes difficult to get off work when the family depends on their hourly wages. Some families lack additional transportation beyond the one car needed to transport someone to work. Moreover, Tucson schools generally have been somewhat hostile to Latino families, often neglecting to invite them to any events or even attempting to translate so that they might feel welcomed in their first language. Historically, the hostility extended deeper than neglect as schools—in the not too distant past—were places of outright denial that served as factories of failure or torture by beating children who spoke Spanish.

There are plenty of reasons for families to distrust schools or to believe that schools do not have their best interest in mind. One devastating reason to avoid school is the perspective that Latina/o families maintain cultural deficits that supposedly render them indifferent to education (Valencia 1997; Valencia and Black 2002). However, plenty of evidence to the contrary exists; Latina/os do value education (Cammarota 2008; Conchas 2006; Delgado-Gaitán 1991; Fine 1993; Gándara 1995; Valencia and Black 2002). Nevertheless, school officials believe that Latina/o families lack any interest in their children's education and therefore fail to integrate them into school communities. Tucson schools do not have any outreach programs to increase Latina/o family involvement in education. Rarely, if ever, do school officials formally speak to Latina/o parents to find out their needs or to solicit their input on educational policies and practices (Moll and Ruiz 2005). This failure of outreach leads to a disconnection between families and the students' learning.

In the SJEP, families are not perceived to have deficits. Rather, they are regarded as possessing valuable cultural resources, knowledge, and experiences that can enrich students' education (Romero 2008). The SJEP follows a "funds of knowledge" approach (Gonzalez 1995; Gonzalez, Moll, and Amanti 2005; Moll et al. 1992) in which families cultivate cultural practices that become necessary for their survival and advancement. These cultural practices bear sophisticated intellectual content that is applied to negotiate the various exigencies of existence in poverty. The SJEP program introduces families' funds of knowledge or "community cultural wealth" (Yosso 2005) through Encuentros, which are meetings with students, teachers, families, and community members to dialogue about the injustices facing Latinos in education. The SJEP holds several Encuentros throughout the year in which families' inherent cultural wealth mediates their children's learning.

In this chapter we discuss how the SJEP Encuentros became spaces for funds of knowledge that raised consciousness around injustices in Latina/o education. The first section reviews the concept of funds of knowledge and how it counters deficit perceptions of working-class Latino families. The second section examines the SJEP program and our involvement as both researchers and educators. Encuentros are discussed in the third section, providing evidence of how Latino families can mediate their children's learning about social injustices in education. The fourth and final section briefly explains some student outcomes of the SJEP and how integrating funds of knowledge into student learning leads to academic success.

Funds of Knowledge: Community Cultural Wealth for Working-Class Families

Vélez-Ibáñez and Greenberg (1992) first introduced funds of knowledge in relation to educational theory and practice. Their conceptualization forwarded an implicit yet important epistemological critique of Bourdieu's (1977, 1985; Bourdieu and Passerson 1977) notion of cultural capital. Since the dominant class develops most economic institutions, policies, and practices, Bourdieu asserts that culture with profound effects in the economic realm derives from this class only. However, as Vélez-Ibáñez and Greenberg (1992) indicate, working-class families also maintain cultural practices that have direct economic implications. These cultural practices, which they term "funds of knowledge," are passed down from previous generations and are critical for the household economy and family survival. Funds of knowledge may include special bartering and trading practices or informal home businesses and production among a network of households. Thus, funds of knowledge are forms of valuable capital, perhaps bearing more sophistication than the dominant culture, because working-class practices must help families survive in economic and social conditions antagonistic toward their survival. Sophistication within working-class culture implies a postmodern, critical epistemology in that valuable, worthwhile knowledge is attributed not only to dominant practices but also to those practices aimed at helping people challenge and overcome oppressive conditions.

Yosso (2005) asserts that forms of cultural capital exist that transcend the insular and ethnocentric beliefs of middle- and upper-class privileged groups. Similar to the funds of knowledge, Yosso claims that the home and community are spaces that inherently engender cultural resources, assets, and wealth. Moreover, Yosso argues that these different forms of "community cultural wealth" can be used to analyze and address injustices that marginalize communities. This concept implies that funds of knowledge are critical for communities to understand how oppression operates and how to overcome barriers maintaining marginalization.

A pedagogical application of funds of knowledge (Gonzalez 1995; Gonzalez et al. 2005; Moll et al. 1992) or community cultural wealth (Yosso 2005) offers a unique strategy for transcending the institutionalized Euro-American cultural bias and deficit perspectives of communities of color promoted in traditional schools. In the standard approach, teachers learn ethnographic research methods and then visit their students' households to document the cultural practices or funds of knowledge families utilize for everyday survival. Their knowledge may include informal trading, home-based manufacturing, or herbal remedies for illness. Once teachers observe the sophisticated cultural practices that facilitate families' survival in difficult circumstances, they understand the relationship between Latina/o culture and intellectualism. Teachers then integrate their observations into the curriculum and create lessons on such subjects as cross-border trade networks or ethnobiology. When students witness the validation of their culture within the educational process, they concatenate their identities as family members, students, and emergent intellectuals. Moreover, the cultural substance of their identities feeds and sustains an academic persona (Romero 2008). Teachers acknowledge that the students' culture contains valid and sophisticated knowledge; the students thus see themselves as creators of knowledge (Delgado-Bernal 2002; Romero 2008).

The SJEP version of the funds of knowledge involves students conducting research on how they live socially with an emphasis on using this knowledge to teach us (adults in general) how to improve their lived conditions and those within their schools and communities. SJEP students gain considerable support from adults in the community, including parents, because many realize they act in the best interest of all children. This realization results from Encuentros in which students and families dialogue at community gatherings about the students' research findings. The Encuentro dialogues produce new funds of knowledge that lead to an understanding of how injustices impede the educational progress of Latina/o students.

The teacher in the SJEP class assists the student researchers by guiding them through the development and implementation of their research projects. University researchers, including the authors, inform the teacher and students about a variety of qualitative research methodologies and the steps for producing research findings. The sites for research extend beyond the family to include neighborhoods, schools, peers, workplaces, and the larger community. The students' entire social contexts become key milieus for study and analysis, with the intention of acquiring funds to change conditions within them and influence the players that can make the needed changes.

Evaluation of the Social Justice Education Project

The authors, as university researchers, assisted the instructor of record with the implementation of the YPAR projects. Eight SJEP classes were offered at four different high schools throughout the school district. However, ARS 15-112 (A) has since shut the program down. Instructional practices were documented in weekly notes. During weekly visits, we often conversed with teachers and SJEP high school students and took field notes. Field notes were also taken after Encuentros. We also conducted interviews with SJEP students to evaluate the efficiency and effectiveness of the program. The interviews were informal, with open-ended questions pertaining to the students' academic experiences and their perspectives of school or community-based activism. Surveys completed by the students at the end of the course provided additional evaluation data. The evaluations were used to quantitatively measure the SJEP's influence on the students' commitment to social justice, critical awareness, academic performance, and college preparation. Exit interviews were conducted with students to document their own assessment of the program's effectiveness at augmenting their critical consciousness, academic performance, and willingness to attend college.

As part of the SJEP evaluation process, students' research was collected, including field notes, poetry, and photos, to assess their engagement and critical understanding. Therefore, documentation of the SJEP consists of field notes, evaluation surveys, exit interviews, and student-produced research. SJEP data illuminate how Encuentros contribute to funds of knowledge that address the injustices plaguing Latina/o education.

The First Encuentro

By seven o'clock, that night in Tucson, a handful of family members did show up: about one-quarter of the fifty parents, students, and siblings that we originally estimated. If a dozen people showed we were still ready to move ahead with our first-ever Encuentro. When the students presented their research and described injustices they experienced at school, parents started to pay attention. They focused on their children's words because what the students were saying eerily reflected their own experiences when they were students.

The following paragraphs present an example of an exchange between a parent and student during the first Encuentro, demonstrating the power of dialogue and cultivation of strong social or community relationships in the learning process. People learn about sophisticated sociological processes through mediation of their own experiences. When those experiences are shared generationally, social structures of injustice become plainly apparent through profound historical connections.

During the first Encuentro, students showed a short slide presentation of project photos; each image evoked some aspect of the students' research topics. We asked the students who took the photos to say something about the images and why they took them. A student named Kati presented the first picture, a group posed photo of the auto shop class. She explained why she took the photo—most students were Latino males, and vocational education rarely focuses on developing critical thinking skills. Kati asked, "How much academic critical thinking will you do when you are learning how to fix a car?" She proceeded to say that AP (advanced placement) classes have more content that develops students' critical thinking skills, but most students in AP classes are Anglo.

The father of an SJEP student, the first to speak up at the Encuentro, said, "Well, don't these students choose to be in the auto class?" Drawing from participant observations of her school's counseling office, she said, "Not really. You see, counselors and teachers guide these students more to the vocational education track and do not help them prepare for AP classes. This starts in middle school." The student's father said that it was astounding, but the auto shop class looked the same when he went to high school, some twenty years ago. He was in that class, and nothing has changed. After he realized the static situation of Latina/o education, he began to see that maybe something else was happening besides the student's individual choice to not advance academically; something systematic was indeed the problem.

The student's father then described how the construction company he worked for received millions of dollars for school infrastructure repairs. He said that all the schools slated for repairs were in white communities, and he did not visit one school located in a Latina/o community. At the time, it seemed odd but he did not think much about it. Yet after Kati's presentation, he put things together. Clearly, he realized that there is symbolic import to all this: whose children are expected to succeed and lead in this society and who are forgotten?

The dialogical praxis embedded in the Encuentros transforms the students' subjectivity by revealing the historical roots of the social problems under investigation. The dialogue with parents about the historicity of the students' research leads to a subjectivity of awareness in which students realize they can identify structural obstacles impeding their progress. The father who worked for the construction company was transformed in the Encuentros. He connected to a remembrance of oppressive challenges within his past, and realized—through the students' funds of knowledge— the deep entrenchment of these challenges. Forgetting pushes the entrenchment deeper, whereas remembrance brings injustice to the surface to reveal possibilities for change.

Encuentros as Funds of Knowledge

Encuentros represent true funds of knowledge such that transformation occurs in students as well as their families. Students, through their actualization as public intellectuals, see themselves as knowledgeable and thus solidify their academic identities. Family members, including parents and siblings, realize that SJEP students act on their behalf by producing new funds of knowledge that could potentially create better opportunities for them and their communities. Buy-in and support for the SJEP grew considerably over the last few years of the program because of the prevalent belief among families that the experience provided by the program (in and of itself) would improve academic and social outcomes for Tucson's Latina/os. At the last few Encuentros, more than just a handful showed up; hundreds of parents attended, making the meetings standing room only.

The following excerpt from field notes taken after a full-capacity Encuentro focuses on a conversation between an SJEP student and another student's parent and how new funds of knowledge are transmitted through engaged praxis.

> The most interesting aspect of the Encuentro was the dialogue after the presentations. Selena's mother stated that most of the time the reason students don't do well in school is because they just don't care, that teachers always put their best effort into teaching and students just don't try. Validia [an SJEP student] provided a contrary perspective from her own experiences. She stated to Selena's mother that there are some bad teachers out there who don't really care about the students or their job. She cited examples to support her argument much in the same way that

a researcher would do, convincing me that her experiences with the SJEP provided her with the skills for effective argumentation. She said teachers had told her she should become a dishwasher, teachers had told her to drop out, teachers had told her "why bother." . . . She should drop out and find a job to help her family. Selena's mom didn't respond back to Validia. She seemed shocked that teachers would say such things to students. It seemed as if she assumed all teachers had good intentions and that students were the bad ones in the formula of failure. The idea that teachers could be negligent and malicious was a new revelation to her. She may have learned something new that day. Because Validia was speaking from the truthful place of her own experiences, Selena's mother could not dispute her.

It is difficult to say with any certainty whether Selena's mother changed her perceptions about education, teachers, or students. However, the format of the Encuentro—the honesty and reciprocity of discussions—at least put her in the position of listening to Validia as an equal and accepting her ideas as a peer. She will remember what Validia had to say. Validia's funds of knowledge may not have changed Selena's mother's opinion but at minimum her words were a revelation.

Certainly, Validia was transformed. When we first met Validia, her school identified her as failing. She scored far below average on standardized tests, and although the school listed her as a junior, technically she had earned credits only equivalent to freshman status. She often contemplated dropping out.

The SJEP not only motivated Validia to stay in school but instilled in her a desire to attend college. In SJEP Encuentros, Validia publicly stated that the SJEP motivated her to work hard. She declared that she plans to study both sociology and anthropology—sociology as an undergraduate and anthropology in graduate school. She wants to further her education because she enjoys analyzing society and then imparting her knowledge about problems and change to other people. Through the Encuentros, Validia developed new funds of knowledge about herself that allowed her to understand how she could personally overcome social barriers preventing her advancement.

During an Encuentro, an SJEP student, Jaime, presented on how racism in his community foments low self-esteem and self-hatred that lead to various forms of violence. As research evidence, Jaime used his own experiences with violence by talking about how his mother was shot to death. He stated, "This poem was about my mom, I was writing up an observation. . . . It's like I was standing in front of her what was it called, 'casket,' and I was seeing her face. And this is not just me, this is about my family, too." The following fieldnote is how Jaime presented his research at the Encuentro.

> I'm standing in front of my family and tears go down their face. My brothers, cousins, uncles, aunts have come together in a sad place. We are all standing in front of the coffin gazing upon a lost life that won't be found, lost kisses, last hugs, only in my head I hear the sound, I go up on the coffin and all I see is the face of the one who got me here, the face of the one who has protected me, the face of the one who has always loved me, the face of the one who has always loved me, the face of the one I will never forget, the face of the one I will always love that face is the one who has made me who I am, my mom.

The elements of healing should be obvious in this example. Jaime was provided with an opportunity to testify about the tragedy that forever changed his life. Using his own experience as research and presenting at the Encuentro allowed Jaime to cultivate funds of knowledge that helped him process deep and troubling emotions. The community also healed by witnessing how this young man boldly faced this tragedy and offered testimony for change to prevent the violent self-hatred bred by racism.

In another standing-room-only Encuentro, students presented on discrimination against those speaking Spanish. Often a school official might tell a student that he or she was not allowed to speak in any language other than English. Although Proposition 203 rendered bilingual education improbable in Arizona, the law restricts teachers, not students, from speaking languages other than English for instruction. Thus, the law does not prohibit students from speaking Spanish or other non-English languages. Such legislation would violate the students' First Amendment right to freedom of speech.

Students skillfully presented evidence of teachers and security monitors who forbid them to speak Spanish. The students also presented on language and speech rights to demonstrate how teachers and other school personnel violated their rights on a daily basis. After hearing the students' presentation, one parent stood up and said that his boss would often tell him and his coworkers that they could not speak Spanish. However, after he heard his son explain about language rights, he told his boss that such prohibitions violated his right to speak whatever language he desired.

Building Trust in Encuentros

Encuentros represent the opportunity to participate in critical reading and engagement. This opportunity allows students to generate funds of knowledge that not only solidify academic identities among themselves but influence new possibilities of change for families and communities. The students' adoption of intellectual status promotes epiphanies among those who engage and listen to them. Their knowledge reveals the sense that they are acting in the best interest of others and could potentially lead to improved conditions in schools and communities. Trust is also a key element of success of the SJEP Encuentros. Families want their children to participate in the program not only for the academic benefits but also for the trust students initiate by producing funds of knowledge to help others "read the world" and transform it.

At the last few Encuentros, parents showed up in such great numbers that we had to reserve an entire floor of a university building to accommodate them. The high level of attendance was the result of trust. Families believed that we were serving the best interest of their children and communities. One parent shared her thoughts about how much the SJEP contributed to her daughter's and other students' intellectual growth and community involvement:

> My daughter has been involved with the SJEP program. In this time, the transformation I have witnessed is nothing short of remarkable. Malia was always a conscious, compassionate, and motivated student. She is intelligent and committed. These characteristics proved to be fertile ground for the educational team. Today I see a young woman, encouraged to be a critical thinker and confident in her quest for knowledge. I see a young woman, eyes bright, and right fist clenched in unity, with others determined to right the wrongs in our society. They raise a fist in solidarity but the fight, they know, will be won with their minds ... through grace and strength and integrity of character. I have seen presentations by these high school students that would challenge the critique of a seasoned college professor. They are expressive, sincere and brimming with knowledge. They want to represent themselves, their beloved teachers, their families and our community to the highest level—and they do! These young men and women work hard, seek out truth and create solutions on a daily basis.

Moreover, students trust us. They trust us because we help them to learn in ways that help them succeed, and in ways they want to learn.

SJEP students who failed the Arizona Instrument for Measuring Standards, the exit exam necessary for graduation, the year prior to participating in the program passed these same tests while enrolled in the SJEP at rates of 68 percent (reading), 76 percent (writing), and 54 percent (math). In contrast, non-SJEP students who also failed prior to retaking the exam passed at much lower rates: 23 percent (reading), 17 percent (writing), and 21 percent (math). Thus, the data suggest that SJEP students were three times more likely to pass the reading, four times more likely to pass the writing, and two and a half times more likely to pass the math portions than their non-SJEP peers. After graduating high school, 67 percent of SJEP students enrolled in postsecondary education. This is nearly three times the national average of 24 percent for Mexican American students.

A total of 776 students responded to evaluation surveys given out each year from 2003 to 2008. The following are key results:

- 96 percent of students agreed or strongly agreed that working on this project or taking this class has improved their writing skills.
- 97 percent of students agreed or strongly agreed that the project or the class has better prepared them for college.
- 97 percent of students agreed or strongly agreed that working on this project or taking this class has improved their reading skills.
- 95 percent of students agreed or strongly agreed that they were willing to do homework in order to keep the project moving along on time or to ensure participation in the class.
- 98 percent of students agreed or strongly agreed that working on this project or taking this class has helped them believe that they have something worthwhile to contribute to society.
- 96 percent of students agreed or strongly agreed that they talked to their parents and/or other adults about what they learned in this project or in this class.

The most significant finding from the survey results presented above is that students agreed that the SJEP increased the likelihood that they would talk to their parents about their learning. The Encuentro not only provided the space for student and family dialogue but started a process in which they communicated throughout the year. Young people often desire to discuss how their futures might be better, not only for themselves but for their families and communities.

Unfortunately, the Arizona legislature and governor passed SB 1070, a bill that effectively criminalizes undocumented individuals. Now that the

Encuentros with Families and Students · 133

bill has become law, we will become anxious once again about how many parents will show up at Encuentros when we restart the SJEP. Families will have another reason to distrust schools or institutions. One thing we can learn from Encuentros is that trust is essential for engaging Latinas/os in schools so that they become effective learners and contributors to our society.

References

Bourdieu, P. 1977. "Cultural Reproduction and Social Reproduction." In *Power and Ideology in Education*, ed. J. Karabel and A. H. Halsey, 487–511. Oxford: Oxford University Press.
———. 1985. "The Forms of Capital." In *Handbook of Theory and Research for the Sociology of Education*, ed. J. Richardson, 241–58. New York: Greenwood.
Bourdieu, P., and J. C. Passeron. 1977. *Reproduction in Education, Society and Culture.* Beverly Hills, CA: Sage.
Cammarota, J. 2007. "A Social Justice Approach to Achievement: Guiding Latina/o Students toward Educational Attainment with a Challenging, Socially Relevant Curriculum." *Equity and Excellence in Education* 40(1): 87–96.
———. 2008. *Sueños Americanos: Barrio Youth Negotiate Social and Cultural Identities.* Tucson: University of Arizona Press.
Cammarota, J., and A. Romero. 2006. "A Critically Compassionate Intellectualism for Latina/o Students: Raising Voices above the Silencing in Our Schools." *Multicultural Education* 14(2): 16–23.
Cammarota, J., and M. Fine., eds. 2008. *Revolutionizing Education: Youth Participatory Action Research in Motion.* New York: Routledge.
Conchas, G. (2006). *The Color of Success: Race and High Achieving Urban Youth.* New York: Teacher's College Press.
Delgado-Bernal, D. 2002. "Critical Race Theory, Latino Critical Theory, and Critical Raced-Gendered Epistemologies: Recognizing Students of Color as Holders and Creators of Knowledge." *Qualitative Inquiry* 8(1): 105–26.
Delgado-Gaitán, C. 1991. "Involving Parents in Schools: A Process of Empowerment." *American Journal of Education* 100(1): 20–46.
Fals-Borda, O. 1986. "The Application of Participatory Action Research in Latin America." *International Sociology* 2(4): 329–47.
Fine, M. 1993. "[Ap]parent Involvement: Reflections on Parents, Power, and Urban Public Schools." *Teachers College Record* 94(4): 682–729.
Freire, P. 1993. *Pedagogy of the Oppressed.* New York: Continuum.
Gándara, P. 1995. *Over the Ivy Walls: The Educational Mobility of Low-Income Chicanos.* Albany: State University of New York Press.
Gonzalez, N. 1995. "The Funds of Knowledge for Teaching Project." *Practicing Anthropology* 17(3): 3–6.
Gonzalez, N., L. C. Moll, and C. Amanti. 2005. "Theorizing Practices." In *Funds of Knowledge: Theorizing Practices in Households, Communities, and Classrooms*, ed.

N. Gonzalez, L. C. Moll, and C. Amanti, 1–27. Mahwah, NJ: Lawrence Erlbaum.
Moll, L., and R. Ruiz. 2005. "Educational Sovereignty for Latinos in Latino Education: An Agenda for Community Action Research." In *Latino Education: An Agenda for Community Action Research*, ed. P. Pedraza and M. Rivera, 295–320. Mahwah, NJ: Lawrence Erlbaum.
Moll, L. C., N. Gonzalez, C. Amanti, and D. Neff. 1992. "Funds of Knowledge for Teaching: A Qualitative Approach to Connect Households and Classrooms." *Theory into Practice* 31(2): 132–41.
Romero, A. 2008. "Towards a Critically Compassionate Intellectualism Model of Transformative Urban Education." PhD diss., University of Arizona.
Valencia, R. R., ed. 1997. *The Evolution of Deficit Thinking: Educational Thought and Practice*. Washington, DC: Falmer.
Valencia, R. R., and M. S. Black. 2002. "Mexican Americans Don't Value Education." *Journal of Latinos and Education* 1(2): 81–103.
Vélez-Ibáñez, C. G., and J. B. Greenberg. 1992. "Formation and Transformation of Funds of Knowledge among U.S.-Mexican Households." *Anthropology and Education Quarterly* 23(4): 313–35.
Vygotsky, L. S. 1994. *The Vygotsky Reader*, ed. René van der Veer and Jaan Valsiner. Oxford: Blackwell.
Yosso, T. J. 2005. "Whose Culture Has Capital? A Critical Race Theory Discussion of Community Cultural Wealth." *Race, Ethnicity and Education* 8(1): 69–91.

CHAPTER EIGHT

Researching the Institute for Transformative Education

Critical Multicultural Education in an Embattled State

Lara dos Passos Coggin

The Institute

The two institutes I've been to, I thought, were very healing. . . . I think racism is the elephant in the living room, in American education. . . . We don't talk about it with kids. Tucson Unified School District's been involved in some sort of court for equality since I've been a teacher. What is going on? 'Cause I've been a teacher for a very long time. Anything like the institute that opens it up may create great passion in some people, but opening it up is exactly what we need to do.[1]
—ARLENE REAGAL, HISTORY TEACHER AT A HIGH SCHOOL SERVING
TEENAGE PARENTS, JUNE 2009[2]

I initially took part in the Institute for Transformative Education (hosted every summer by Tucson Unified School District's [TUSD's] Raza Studies Department) in July 2008, as a student of critical multicultural education and as an educator (I had just finished teaching two Upward Bound high school summer courses at a local community college).[3] The week of the 2008 institute was an intense period of self-reflection, and portraits of unsuccessful pedagogy painted by institute presenters struck uncomfortably close to my recent classroom experience. I was unable to connect my theoretical understandings of liberatory teaching with the problems I had faced as an instructor; that first summer, I walked in a teacher's shoes.

It became evident that, if I were to continue teaching, I would have to take up the dual role of teacher-researcher, not only to maintain a connection to my academic career but to help me make sense of my behavior toward my students, their behavior toward me, and our respective relationships to the content between us. During this first summer of my attendance, institute presenters included Sandy Grande (a critical indigenous education scholar), Antonia Darder (a critical race scholar with a particular interest in Latino communities), Christine Sleeter (a critical multicultural education scholar), and Peter McLaren (a Marxist scholar of education whose work closely relates to Grande's).

I decided to conduct research with teachers at the Institute for Transformative Education at the invitation of a frequent contributor to its programming, Dr. Julio Cammarota, associate professor of Mexican American studies and teaching, learning, and sociocultural studies. I imagined that researching the institute would allow me to provide scholarly perspectives on a program whose association with TUSD raza studies courses made it a subject of political debate. I had no wish to perform an evaluation of the institute's effectiveness; I was more curious about how attendees saw themselves as educators and as members of social, political, and cultural communities. I predicted that, for some, their attendance at the institute would feel like a validation of those memberships, and for others it would seem more like a challenge.

To answer my own questions about what was happening at the institute, I would have to come up with a list of key ideas or tenets unifying institute programming, find out if those ideas were making their way out to attendees, and discover whether attendees felt that the four-day series of seminars and workshops had, in fact, been "transformative." And I would need to investigate the history and evolution of this annual gathering to gain a sense of where, in its development, my study would be placed.

During the 2009 and 2010 sessions, the period during which I collected data, institute staff registered 217 individuals of diverse ages, occupations, and cultural affiliations. One of the many details that could easily be lost in the media fray that has engulfed the Mexican American Studies (MAS) Department is that its summer institute has grown more, not less, diverse since its founding, both in its attendees and its speakers.

Presenters at the 2009 Institute included Tim Wise (an antiracism activist), Sonia Nieto (a multicultural education researcher), Mari Matsuda (a feminist and critical race law scholar), and Daniel Solórzano (a scholar of critical race theory in education). The following summer brought a less noticeable focus on critical race theorists, and a cultural-spiritual strand

Researching the Institute for Transformative Education · 137

featured more prominently in the presenter cohort, including a scholar of indigenous epistemology and medicine (Patrisia Gonzales), the community activist and artist Felicia Montes, the community educator and artist Olmeca, and Jerry Tello, a community cultural counselor and mentor.

Over the three years of my attendance at the institute, I distilled a number of central principles from the keynote presentations I attended:

- Culturally relevant, critical, action-oriented pedagogy is effective in serving low-income students and students of color.
- Race is a fulcrum of oppressive social structures in the United States and critical pedagogy must address this centrality.
- Educators from any racial, cultural, and socioeconomic background can be effective critical pedagogues, through processes of critical self-reflection, study, and apprenticeship with master educators.
- Colonialism is a historical and a contemporary force in control of educational and social resources, both symbolic and material.
- Students' cultural heritage must not be used as an excuse for low achievement or to cover up inequitable power relations.

Throughout the summers of 2008–2010, the format of the institute was consistent. The following sample schedule offers a condensed version of the first day of the 2009 institute program:

8:00–8:30 a.m.	Ceremonia: Kalpulli Teocalli, Jesus "Chucho" Ruiz
8:30–8:45 a.m.	Welcome: Hon. Richard Elías, Chairman, Pima County Board of Supervisors
8:45–9:45 a.m.	Keynote: Social Justice Education Project
9:55–10:55 a.m.	Keynote: Julio Cammarota, PhD, Diversity and Dissent in Democratic Education
11:05 a.m.–12:05 p.m.	Keynote: Daniel Solórzano, PhD, Racial Microaggressions and Education
12:05–12:50 p.m.	Lunch
12:55–1:55 p.m.	Keynote: Tim Wise, Writer and Activist
2:05–3:05 p.m.	Concurrent Breakout A: Social Justice Education Project, Dialogue and Reflection Concurrent Breakout B: Julio Cammarota, PhD, Dialogue and Reflection Concurrent Breakout C: Daniel Solórzano, PhD, Dialogue and Reflection

3:10–4:10 p.m.   Concurrent Breakouts A, B, C
4:20–5:20 p.m.   Concurrent Breakouts A, B, C
5:20–5:30 p.m.   Evaluation

As noted above, each day typically began with an opening ceremony recognizing the earth and its four cardinal directions (as well as the sky and the earth), performed by the Aztec group Kalpulli Teocalli. Following announcements, three keynote speakers would present to the full group of over one hundred attendees in the College of Education auditorium before lunch, with perhaps one speaker after the break, and each afternoon attendees would disperse to three hours of breakout sessions. The morning keynotes allowed scholars, educators, and activists to report on their work in schools and communities, with limited interaction from attendees in the form of question-and-answer periods between presentations. In contrast, afternoon sessions were designed to accommodate more interaction between presenters and attendees, in a smaller classroom setting. While this format remained consistent over the 2008–2010 program years, other aspects of the institute have changed with time.

In addition to undergoing changes in theme, presenters, demographics, and title, the institute has retooled its theoretical model and incentive structure, and changed location. Not all of these changes have been reactive; as Augustine Romero, the institute's organizer and founder, narrates, there were several important cultural and community-driven factors in its evolution. Before there could be a summer training event for teachers of Chicana/o studies, there had to be an MAS Department:

> In 1997, [TUSD] created a community board.... The first time that the district took a vote on the creation of the MAS/Raza Studies department... it was voted down.... The community came back and wouldn't let the issue die, so then the superintendent at the time... said, okay, we'll pull together a committee of people from the community to study this... and they'll make a recommendation in June of '97. And the main recommendation was for the creation of a department. And... a seminar for teachers interested in teaching Chicano studies. (A. Romero, 2010. Personal communication. Tucson, Arizona)

The first summer institute had a fiesta atmosphere, where a predominantly Chicana/o and Latina/o group of educators celebrated the fact that they had "actually got this thing." Romero describes his desire to widen the institute's appeal, both to stabilize attendance and to reflect the organizers' ideas about diversity:

In 2003, we went beyond just having Latino-based speakers to having a cultural diversity of speakers and . . . perspective[s]. I thought that was incredibly healthy for the district because . . . despite the [fact] that the district . . . was starting to become majority Latino, I still thought we needed to address the needs of those who had been historically underserved. . . . We need to ensure that we actually meet . . . each child where they're at, and . . . recognize . . . that the child walks into the class as a historical being, not ahistorical, and as a cultural being, not a-cultural. . . . Those became sort of the platforms of the Institute.

Romero and the Institute for Transformative Education's co-organizers have a strong sense of the institute's guiding principles and have articulated some of them in published work relating to the MAS department's school-based programs (see Cammarota and Romero 2006). Romero outlines the major influences behind the institute's current form:

From what the Indigenous people tell us, we need to understand . . . that we represent seven generations past, and so . . . Paulo Freire talks about the connection between the social moment and the historical moment, [which] allows us to more deeply contextualize this moment. . . . And . . . we represent seven generations forward. Paulo talks about . . . tri-dimensionalizing our understanding, [so] we have to [know] what our social condition is now, we connect that to historical social conditions, and then understand what we've learned from . . . those pieces of history, and then that becomes our reflection. And the most important thing is what do we do with [this new understanding] in the future, which becomes our action, which takes us into practice.[4]

After reading comments made by participants in this study, I noted how influential the various elements of the organizers' theoretical viewpoints were in shaping the content and atmosphere of the institute, and the kind of socially mediated communication and learning that went on there. Romero articulates a strong link between the programmatic goals of the school-based MAS courses and the institute:

I have [a PowerPoint] slide where it talks about identity, purpose, and hope. On the bottom of [the slide, you see] the human measures, and . . . the state measures. In the state [educational bureaucracy], what most [educators and administrators] will start their conversations with in terms of creating [a program is] what it's going to accomplish, how will it improve test scores, how will it improve graduation rates, decrease dropout rates, decrease suspension and referrals. Our conversation [in MAS] wasn't about that. And if you listen to our [institute] speakers over time, the vast majority of [presenters] don't even go there in their conversations. What we talked about . . . is [trying] to instill a sense of identity, purpose, and hope in our students. So if we offer that to our students, shouldn't we then offer it to . . . colleagues or teachers, offer them a deeper sense of identity, a deeper sense of purpose, a deeper sense of hope?

Romero and the representatives of the MAS Department are aware of recurrent trends in measurement of educational outcomes, and consciously avoid replicating those patterns in their work with students and teachers. It was therefore no surprise to me, when I asked participants in this study whether the institute resembled what they had previously thought of as teacher professional development, that they felt it was entirely new in form and content, and that its differences from traditional district offerings attracted them.

Something personal is at stake for teachers, counselors, and other school personnel when they embark upon an experience like the institute, more so than if they were engaged in professional development in their content area or in technical training. In the consciousness-raising environment of the institute, teachers are encouraged to look through new lenses.

The participants in this study confronted at the institute, some for the first time, the idea that we are all involved in what schools have become. The organizers of the institute propose that, instead of grasping at attractive but superficial solutions, we admit race, class, gender, language, culture, and history onto our mental stage. Some teachers in my study eagerly welcomed the arrival of these players, and recognized in the institute an affirmation of the complex issues they dealt with in their everyday practice. But it was the variety of participant responses and their cognitive, emotional, and professional understandings that attracted me to the topic.

Identity in teacher education is not well understood, especially as it pertains to the roles teachers ascribe to themselves in their practice, and how their personal, cultural, and emotional identities intersect with their professional development. The main reason for this, according to scholars who have analyzed policy reaching back to the inception of the US government's role in education, is the evaluative, quantitative lens often applied to teacher education (Apple 1988). Understandably, federal agencies want to assure taxpayers that their monies go to effective professional development programs. But in the desire to assuage fears about misspent funds, policymakers, legislators, and state and local administrators lose sight of teachers' complexities and the ways that teacher self-conceptions can morph in the context of teacher educational programs. How teachers see themselves is a principle indicator of how and what they choose to teach; even under duress, many Arizona teachers have made a commitment to teach in ways consistent with their identities (Loughran 2006).

Content knowledge, undergraduate course work, compliance with state standards, and other officially sanctioned forms of training and regulation are what teachers, administrators, and policymakers list as principal indicators of teaching quality. Because it did not focus on any of those areas, the institute was a compelling site in which to study teacher learning and discourse on race, class, and culture.

The institute belongs to a sector of teacher professional development that can be described as critical multicultural teacher education. Most studies analyzing and evaluating multicultural teacher education concern course work offered in graduate teacher preparation programs, such as Ensign's (2009) study categorizing four teacher education programs as either replicating inequality or facilitating transformation. Therefore it is difficult to estimate the scope and impact of the institute in relation to other similar programs, since it targets educators who have, in most cases, long since finished their preparation course work. If we look at a typology of perspective, we may be able to better place the institute within its genre.

To do this, we will need to situate the institute along a spectrum of teacher professional development, from the less critically oriented content area or training programs to more critically oriented multicultural teacher education programs. At the less critically oriented (though not necessarily less rigorous) end, we observe programs whose goals are raising educator skills in their content area, such as the seminar "National Geographic Alliance on Primary Sources," which David Foster, a middle school teacher and participant in this study, referred to as an enriching past experience with professional development.

This type of program also includes training designed to help educators deliver content in a particular way, such as reading through phonics or cooperative learning, the topic of another influential seminar David attended. These types of teacher professional development may be consistently funded and widely delivered by school districts at mandatory weekly in-service meetings at teachers' school sites, although large-scale studies to support such observational evidence is difficult to find. For example, one national study examined only math- and science-focused district-supported teacher professional development as part of the Eisenhower Professional

Development Program (Desimone et al. 2007). Such a study focused on multicultural teacher education remains to be done.

With the growth of interest in and awareness of multicultural issues in public education, a number of other types of professional development opportunities have become available, wherein educators gain exposure to the cultural, linguistic, racial, and socioeconomic diversity of their students' communities. These kinds of programs may also be funded and delivered by school districts, as they provide a nonthreatening, sometimes celebratory way to address diversity without encouraging educators to ask more difficult questions about equity in schools (Jennings and Smith 2002).

These programs may claim to be infusing their content with diverse perspectives, in an effort to fulfill guidelines set by their accrediting organizations, but in reality they provide incomplete and overly simplified information to educators (Ensign 2009). Cochran-Smith critiques this trend: "the 'new multicultural education' envisioned by theorists does not seem to be in place, at least if we judge by the research about the practice of teacher education." She finds that "teacher education programs report they have integrated multicultural perspectives," whereas "external reviews conclude little has changed" (2003, 21).

Finally, at the critical edge of the spectrum, critical multicultural teacher professional development goes beyond content area skills, and beyond recognizing diversity in schools. Critical multicultural programming pushes teachers to interrogate race, class, culture, gender, undocumented and/or refugee status, ableism, and many other issues that cut across students' lives as they receive and resist schooling.

Christine Sleeter's work as an educational and epistemological scholar brings teacher education to the fore and illuminates the process of teacher education curriculum design. She generalizes about what kinds of results we can expect from teacher education programs, based on how they prioritize teacher learning and reflection about US multicultural history and its possibilities for a more equitable educational future. Sleeter (2000) contends that teachers will need to survive an encounter with epistemological questions if they are to fully commit to learning about race, class, and culture in their classrooms. These programs seem far less common among district-funded offerings and do not appear to enjoy institutionalization in the form of weekly in-service meetings.

Rather, they tend to be either preservice courses (Milner 2006) or intense, one-time seminars for in-service teachers held once a year, which describes TUSD's Institute for Transformative Education. In the future, the literature relating to this genre of multicultural professional development will need to address program longevity and the reasons for attrition when such programs end. The Institute for Transformative Education was in a struggle to prove its legitimacy and maintain its district funding after the summer of 2011.

The institute, though funded by a local district, originated in a partnership between district and nondistrict stakeholders: the University of Arizona College of Education, Pima Community College, the TUSD MAS Department, and the Mexican American Studies Community Advisory Board. This partnership evinces a high degree of involvement from communities (low-income families, Mexican and Mexican American families) whose histories and ways of knowing have been excluded from nation-state schooling. The spaces of inquiry it creates are therefore not entirely grounded in any institution or district, but are temporary and elective, and serve only a small subset of the in-service educators reached by district-mandated programs.

The Context of the Institute

When I first got your email [asking me to participate in this study], I thought you were a Tom Horne flunkie.
DAVID FOSTER, MIDDLE SCHOOL SOCIAL STUDIES TEACHER, JUNE 2009

David Foster was not the only one of my study participants to question my motives, but he was the only one to openly associate my research with the office of then-superintendent of public instruction Tom Horne. Other teachers participating in my study shared accounts of threats made against their teaching materials, site-based research, or pedagogy. It would be difficult to overestimate the effect on this research of Arizona's highly public disputes between Horne and supporters of ethnic studies programs. After serving as superintendent, Horne was elected as Arizona attorney general, and was replaced as superintendent by John Huppenthal, also a Republican, who has expressed an interest in keeping raza studies under a public microscope.

At the time of this study, Horne and Deputy Superintendent Margaret Dugan were calling on TUSD to videotape MAS classes, and threatening to cut funding to those schools where either teachers refused to be recorded or their curriculum was found to be objectionable (Horne 2010). A group of eleven raza studies teachers responded with a lawsuit challenging the constitutionality of HB 2281, legislation passed with the clear purpose of terminating Mexican American/raza studies classes in TUSD.

The analytical tools provided by discourse analysis, scholarship on language ideologies, and critical theories helped me to sample the spoken and written texts surrounding raza studies educational programs for disingenuous or manipulative symbols, such as the willful conflation of "raza" with "race" (Schieffelin, Woolard, and Kroskrity 1998). This particular equation had an electrifying effect on public perceptions of the MAS Department, such that organizer Augustine Romero recalls being asked by district officials to change the institute's name: "I think . . . the concern was to take raza out of it. . . . Part of it was political. . . . The reason we didn't fight the political recommendation was because we had already been thinking about changing the name. So the district response [was that they offered] what they believed to be a compromise, that [they hoped might] help alleviate some of the future attacks, which didn't help."

Multiple issues were involved in changing the name of the institute; the negative political reception of the former title, Raza Studies Institute, is inseparable from its status as a legitimate expression of Spanish in a public space.[5] First, then, the term itself: "raza," in the context of the institute, refers to diverse Latino, Chicano, and Mexican American communities. Urrieta writes, "Raza, contrary to most whitestream analyses of the term, does not mean 'race' in the literal sense of what race means in the U.S. white supremacist context. Raza connotes a people with a similar social, cultural, and historical experience with oppression" (2007, 139).

There is an unofficial linguistic and ideological resistance, not particular to Arizona but certainly of recent relevance here, to Spanish taking on the status of a professional language on par with English. Urciuoli documented socially allowed spaces for Spanish usage in her thirteen-year study of Puerto Rican families in New York City: "The range of situations in which people use Spanish is ordinarily limited to the intimate, familiar, and equal, although there are exceptions: bilingual classrooms, Spanish-speaking churches, some public media, some workplaces" (1996, 6). The institute, as an educational event hosted by a state-funded university, falls undeniably into Urciuoli's exception category.

It is doubtful that then-state superintendent Horne or the district officials who urged Dr. Romero to opt for a less objectionable name have noticed in themselves or would admit to any linguistic prejudice, since most Americans' experiences with English dominance probably began too early to remember. Urciuoli locates the development of these ideologies in school cultures: "English-dominant students come to see Spanish-language elements (like accents) as signs of contamination, internalizing Anglo teachers' perceptions of their non-standard English as deviant" (1996, 7).

The change from a Spanish/English-titled institute to monolingual English also illustrates the danger of mixed codes, or Spanish and English use within close linguistic proximity, in the public, state-sponsored setting of the district. This mixing is a characteristic of Tucson, southern Arizona, border communities, and many of the communities TUSD serves.

As I continued to decode the symbols associated with the institute and its sponsor, TUSD's MAS program, I found articles such as "'Raza Studies' Defy American Values: Some Public Schools Teach Program That Divides Students by Ethnicities" (Julian 2008) and "Radical Education" (2008). Engaging with the institute has allowed me to perceive, at close range, some of the psychological effects that institute organizers experience as a result of repeatedly speaking out on what feels like the wrong side of political divides on the public education scene. The institute, and the district's MAS program, are affected by the same emotionally heated discourse as the regulation of Arizona's troubled international border.

Southern Arizona experiences socially divisive rhetoric in ways that are common to other southwestern states, and also particular to this place. Here, discussions of race are not primarily black and white (though passage of SB 1070 galvanized support from the NAACP and concerned African Americans who recognized that a blow to the civil liberties of Mexican and Mexican American residents of the US is of interest to various racially, politically, and economically oppressed populations). Instead, southern Arizona's consciousness of race is white and brown (Arizona counts 30.1 percent of its population as Hispanic or Latino, and 4.2 percent as black), and ideas about language, in conjunction with skin color, create opportunity gaps between public school students, whose districts have dramatically different visions of their potential.[6] For example, Orozco (2009) discusses school district mission statement language that separates and devalues (primarily Mexican, Mexican American, and Native American) minority students.

This study took place in a climate where "the immigration debate" (which is how popular discourse frames the social, economic, linguistic, political, ecological, historical, and racial dynamics of the porous border) finds its way into nearly every nightly newscast. Local news stations do little to problematize or enrich the discourse of immigration (for example, by explaining the role of NAFTA in destroying small farm economies or presenting retrospective views of the US government's Mexican guest worker policies). Print and broadcast journalists consistently associate immigration with threats to national security, smuggling of humans and drugs, and rising health care costs in border hospitals, rather than global labor flows, Arizona's status as a right-to-work state, or other relevant background issues. Increased media attention in 2010 and 2011 has brought Arizona national recognition, mainly for Governor Brewer's stance against federal regulation of the state's immigration policy.

Meanwhile, Arizona's teachers face negative public perceptions at both the state and national levels. It has become a common, though seldom critically examined, refrain that US public schools lack instructional rigor, a sentiment clearly expressed nearly three decades ago by leaders with a heavy stake in US global economic dominance, in *A Nation at Risk: The Imperative for Educational Reform* (National Commission on Excellence in Education 1983). But no wide consensus exists as to which content is least rigorous or how the solutions to low-quality instruction should look. Those concerned about the future of education seem to have a sense that improving teachers is a crucial part of the puzzle of school reform (Apple 1988). In practice, attempts at improving teacher performance may take the shape of privately operated, for-profit teacher professional development workshops, in-service training days, or summer institutes, all with varying degrees (and measurements) of success.

At the Institute for Transformative Education, teachers entered a space of questions, criticism, and unorthodox ideas, one that editorial writers, bloggers, and self-appointed outside experts have negatively evaluated (especially when that critical environment is re-created in middle and high school classrooms). For this reason, raza studies secondary school programs would likely be more contested sites for study than the institute (which proceeded almost unnoticed by the media for twelve summers).

When they collaborated on legislation to eliminate raza studies secondary school programs, Horne, State Senator Russell Pearce, and their supporters likely felt confident that they knew how raza/MAS courses help or hurt Arizona's students, but little documentation has analyzed what their professional equivalent, the institute, does for teachers. A group of high school students attending the 2010 institute wrote letters to then-superintendent Horne about the impact of their experiences there; suddenly the visibility of the institute was raised (this time, as an inappropriate influence on minors). Dr. Romero remembers a time when the MAS Department, and its summer institute, sought public recognition:

[The Institute] was [formed in] a situation where the [MAS] department had its own autonomy; there wasn't the same level of scrutiny that exists now, and [the Institute] was well attended, people spoke well of it, different leadership people would come [and] make statements there. . . . We were always trying to give it more attention, and to gain it more interest throughout the district, but . . . the manner in which we have the attention now is not what we were looking for. . . . So it wasn't . . . the idea . . . you hear [radio host] Jon Justice talking about [that] we were under this veil, we were trying to keep things secret. It was quite the contrary. . . . We were constantly trying to get our stuff out there.

Meanwhile, Arizona's students, teachers, and families are struggling to acquire the skills necessary for social and economic mobility in a state ranked fifty-first in the nation for per-pupil K–12 education funding (Arizona Education Association 2010). Behind official state discourse about failing schools and community-based resistance to that discourse, there is an opportunity for researchers, educators, legislators, and concerned civic actors to learn about critical multicultural teacher education through the activities of the institute. In Arizona, as in the rest of the country, a fault line runs through any argument on teacher education. On one side are those who think that teachers and students are broken, and on the other are those who believe our schools are a pressurized environment in which some of the most dangerous and unhealthy dynamics of our national soul develop.

The authors of a 2009 report issued by Arizona State University's Center for Competitiveness and Prosperity Research judged the state's consistently decreasing funding for primary through higher education to be in violation of Arizona's own constitutional requirement to "insure the proper maintenance of all state educational institutions."[7] We might wonder why, if many Arizona-based corporations express willingness to pay higher taxes rather than see education harmed, the state government seems dedicated to continuing its current strategy of reductions in funding and programs (Kossan 2009).

I wondered if the ideological divide between the state government and the students, professors, and researchers of the state's three public universities might have to do with differences in educational background; up to one-third of the legislature's current members may not have any experience with Arizona's institutions of higher education (twenty-six of ninety currently serving Arizona state legislators choose not to share information about their educational background on their member pages).[8] Yet several currently serving Latino and Latina legislators, lacking four-year degrees, consistently sponsor legislation supporting equity for immigrants and funding for public education, whereas State Senator Russell Pearce and legislators who have voted to defund higher education and criminalize immigration hold advanced degrees. There is, in short, no clearly credential-linked index for legislative behavior toward ethnic studies curricula and higher education.

Republican Jan Brewer became Arizona's governor in early 2009 as an unelected replacement for Democrat Janet Napolitano, who left to assume the directorship of the Department of Homeland Security. In November, Brewer won the general election against former Arizona Attorney General Terry Goddard, a Democrat. Soon after taking office, Governor Brewer signed SB 1070 and HB 2281, designed to empower local police to investigate immigration status and to abolish ethnic studies (though the language specifically targets raza studies rather than ethnic studies classes in general) in Arizona schools, respectively. Brewer is a former attendee (but not graduate) of a community college and does not list any educational information in her biography (http://governor.state.az.us/), yet her earliest legislative actions (SB 1070 and HB 2281) directly impacted schools and students' families, and came in the wake of 2009 proposals to cut funding for Arizona's three public universities by $600 million (Cruz 2009). Because educational researchers, who depend on state funding for higher education, are particularly well-positioned to help demystify the public debate about ethnic studies' legitimacy, it is difficult not to see the legislative agendas on ethnic studies and higher education as connected.

Multiple constituencies are affected by the negative educational climate in the state legislature. For example, having come to Tucson to study critical multicultural teacher education from indigenous perspectives, I was dismayed to observe that students from Arizona's tribal communities tend to be seen as culturally marginal or as low achievers rather than as valuable contributors to schools. In fact, despite a relatively large population of native students in Arizona schools (4.9 percent of Arizona's last census respondents were American Indian and Alaska Native, compared to 1.0 percent nationally), their political and educational status could be described as almost invisible (Brayboy 2003 addresses the dilemma of visibility for Native students).[9] Meg Chambers, an African American history and special education high school teacher and participant in my study, described her impressions of this lack of political voice, upon moving south after completing a master's degree at Northern Arizona University: "It's strange coming from Flagstaff, where we had a very strong and very vocal . . . Native American community, and coming here, it's . . . as far as I can tell, silenced. At least in my little bubble. . . . And I'm not used to that; . . . it's like taking a step back in time. . . . What went wrong?"

A facet of Tucson's cultural dynamics that seldom arises in Arizona's teacher education programs (except at the institute) is the link between

Chicana/o and Latina/o identity, and the indigenous peoples of the Southwest. Enrique, an interdisciplinary studies graduate and substitute teacher who spoke to me as part of the study, explained his view of those historical and cultural links:

> If you use some of the oldest buildings in Tucson, let's say San Xavier, built, in what, the 18th century . . . the Anglos didn't know anything about what was going on in the Southwest. And by that time, the Spaniards were already in the Southwest for . . . almost 200 years. . . . For sure, if the Spaniards didn't bring their women, they had offspring with the natives, Mestizos, and here we are, the Chicanos, the Mexican Americans, and we're still here, and we still go to the church [San Xavier]. So, our identity is in the land, our identity is in this area.[10]

Complicating the picture further, native students with Spanish surnames sometimes find it difficult to be recognized as culturally and linguistically distinct from southern Arizona's large Mexican and Mexican American student population, and recent legislative measures limiting or eliminating bilingual education in the state have almost completely ignored the protected status of tribal language and culture programs in schools. Similarly, media outlets and public discourse fail to distinguish between various ethnic studies programs in Arizona, where African American studies, Native American studies, and Mexican American studies programs serve students with a variety of academic, social, and cultural support systems. The diversity of TUSD's student body connects to the early establishment of Tucson.

Though mainstream media coverage tends to focus on the volume of recent Mexican arrivals to the state, Mexican and Mexican American families range, in the depth of their Tucson roots, from first generation back to the city's first families.[11] According to Lydia Otero, a historian who has documented conflicts over space, access to economic advancement, and social status in Tucson, by 1856 "no other U.S. city [had] remained under Mexican control longer than Tucson, where Anglo Americans represented only a minority of settlers" (2010, 2). Reviewing her accounts of *la calle* (the street), a strand of vibrant and racially diverse commercial and residential neighborhoods running north-south along the Santa Cruz River, it is hard to conceive of the magnitude of the reversal that has taken place in the Tucson valley with the influx of Anglo settlement over the past 150 years.

Through a series of heavy-handed legal and political maneuvers, Anglo business owners and politicians not only razed the heart of *la calle*'s Mexican American neighborhoods during the 1967 Pueblo Center Redevelopment

Project ("Arizona's first major urban renewal project"), but they managed to recast Tucson as an Anglo city for the future, and retroactively, by rewriting its history of diversity (Otero 2010). Mindful of this historiography, it is primarily the cultural, political, economic, and racial status of Mexican and Mexican American students that the institute illuminates.

This history is not commonly known to newly arrived Tucsonans (including several of the teachers who participated in my study) and is largely absent from the Internet and television images of Tucson projected to a national audience. Indeed, Marie Peale, a math and language arts teacher at a Tucson charter high school, commented during our interview, "It's interesting 'cause my family lives out East, mostly in New Jersey, and the way things are depicted on the national news and everything . . . they think that there are border crossers . . . walking down the street, and just everywhere, and they don't understand the dynamic."[12] Marie's position, as an educator in Tucson schools, a recipient of popular media images of the border, and a source of information on local conditions to her East Coast family, highlights the mutually constitutive nature of Arizona's educational issues and those of the nation. While investigating market discourse in local debates over math pedagogy, Lisa Rosen wrote, "translocal struggles do not simply determine local conflicts; rather, local people appropriate them for their own purposes, and local conflicts partially shape translocal struggles" (2003, 240). Participants in this study contribute, on one hand, to the nation's political dynamics in their interactions with Tucson students, families, and colleagues, and feel the impact, on the other hand, of the nation's view of Arizona's policies.

In her study of Tucson's urban renewal, Otero gives historical context to the institute's programming, offering portraits of the cultural significance of Tucson's American Indian, Mexican, and Mexican American buildings. One example of the process whereby physical structures acquired distinctively Tucsonan identity is the construction, in 1868, of the Church of San Agustín, Tucson's patron saint. The edifice (destroyed in 1936) was, in all respects, a symbol of community cooperation:

> Wealthier *tucsonenses* [longtime Tucsonans of Mexican American heritage] provided the funds for construction materials, but the faithful of all classes provided the labor needed to build the new church. "After each morning's religious services the community made the adobes," Ana María Comadurán Coenen remembers. "The entire church was built by the people of the parish." "The men made the adobes," Atanacia Santa Cruz adds, "and the women carried water in ollas on their heads for the

mixing of the adobe mud. The finished adobes were also carried by women, who fashioned a ring of cloth and placing it on their heads, placed the adobes on it and carried it to the men building the walls." (Otero 2010, 30–31)

These powerful, concrete connections to Tucson's physical landscape and history permeate Mexican and Mexican American understandings of space, place, and cultural continuity in Tucson, and particularly in TUSD, where the MAS courses and the Institute for Transformative Education originated. This study took place in an environment where native Tucsonan connections to history collide with Anglo historiography; the institute, over its ten-year history, has tried to chart other destinies, new patterns of social relations, for teachers and students in Tucson's schools.

The legislature and the state's raza studies programs continue to exchange volleys, and I have deepened my experience working in Tucson schools. With the passage of time, I am learning to see my doctoral research as a strategic act, one in which I strengthened my own abilities to make informed decisions about the future of this community.

Study Findings

Perhaps because the institute presenters are grounded in epistemological and critical theoretical pedagogy, and because these are not common subjects for in-service teacher professional development, several participants in this study diverged widely from the central ideas of the institute in their conversations with me. Whether they spoke with me before or after their first attendance at the institute, or after having attended for several years, these participants interpreted race, class, and culture in relation to their teaching practice very differently than presenters at the institute. They clearly observed and attended to these categories in the context of their classrooms, their students' neighborhoods, and the policies of the state of Arizona. However, their tools for interpreting these experiences and insights often came from popular ideologies and, consequently, some participants used the opportunity of our conversations to reexamine their analyses.

Study participants did describe the transformative aspects of the institute, narrating moments of constructive discomfort, of being inspired, and of being part of a community of learners. But participants also mourned the short duration of the conversation started by the institute and questioned whether transformative learning could continue outside the stimulating space it provided. One participant, Jane Reichlin, asked if TUSD's MAS Department could continue a program called Redemptive Remembering, in which educators could meet with an institute organizer one evening per month to keep alive the discussions that had begun at the institute.

During my discussions with institute founder Dr. Romero, I learned that despite his beliefs that it should continue, the Redemptive Remembering group had ended because of the enormous time commitment required of MAS educators involved in the lawsuit against HB 2281 (legislation attacking the legitimacy of MAS courses in TUSD schools). One perspective on HB 2281 echoed by institute organizers and observers is that this legislation attacks MAS courses because they are clearly transformative for TUSD students (as documented in Romero 2008), and because the activism they manifest as part of this transformative process is threatening to various state authorities.

At times, looking over my data, I wondered if the MAS secondary programs might be more effective at transformation than the institutes. One key difference between the school-based programs and the institute is that the MAS secondary programs involve contact between MAS educators and students throughout the academic year, several times per week, and sometimes secondary students enroll in MAS courses for two consecutive years. Contrast this high level of interaction between educators and students with the short, intensive, four-day institute, during which participants spend most of their time listening to and watching presenters. If sustained interactions and meaningful relationships are key components of transformative learning in the MAS secondary program, then it is no mystery why transformative learning is so hampered for participants in the institutes. The one condition that is necessary for those interactions and relationships to develop is time, and time is a resource the institute's organizers cannot negotiate (at least not without appropriate funding, which was reduced in 2011).

This research has challenged my ideas about the connectedness of scholarly production to the political sphere. I have observed a lack of interest in the state of Arizona in general, and in TUSD administrators in particular, in the complex ideas and copious data needed to understand what is happening at these annual gatherings of teachers and scholars. In this atmosphere, it would be easy to fall below the expectations for accurate representation of scholarly work to the public, at the same time disappointing MAS educators, whose work could be legitimized by strong scholarly support.

Internally inconsistent ideas participants expressed in their interviews did not seem to correspond to white or nonwhite identity, nor gender identity, but how much exposure to critical learning environments they had gained during their undergraduate and graduate course work, and through their professional development experiences. This correlation seems to echo the idea (expressed in different ways by Pierre Bourdieu and Paulo Freire) that raw social experiences do not make one a social analyst (any more than having been a student enables one to analyze educational systems). According to Bourdieu and Freire, insight and transformation come about only through reflecting upon and analyzing experiences, questioning the "normal" behaviors of one's family, neighbors, and superiors, so that the normal is no longer normalized but interrogated. Freire (1998) writes that action without reflection is mere practice, but action that is reflected on and altered becomes an enriching cycle called praxis. Several study participants were rich in social observations and in teaching experience, but relatively new to the essential reflection and analysis step recommended by Freire and Bourdieu. The way to address this gap in educators' analytical skills is more, not less, sustained support for intellectually stimulating critical multicultural teacher education.

Reflections on the Institute

The institute presented educators with an opportunity to view their schools and their practices critically, one which they concurred was not offered by other district-sanctioned professional development programs. But the institute has imparted another quality to its participants, which is not often discussed in studies on critical multicultural teacher education, and that quality is an understanding of the teacher education program's contested history of place. The geographical place in which student learning and teacher education occur is a largely silent partner in those processes, except at the institute. To explore this unusual aspect of the institute among critical multicultural professional development programs, it may be useful to step back and consider what it means to conduct teacher education in Tucson, a city with deep roots. Tucson's current geography and demography overlie a long record of human interventions:

> Even in the early 1860's, when [the journalist J. Ross] Browne passed through Arizona, the Santa Cruz was not a perennial river. Instead it, like so many other drainages in the Sonoran Desert, was an intermittent

stream, much of its sandy passage to the Gila dry except during floods. Water trickled past Tubac only to sink into the alluvial sand a few miles to the north. Luckily for Tucson, though, surface flow reappeared at a place called Punta de Agua about two-and-a-half miles south of San Xavier. . . . Wherever it reached the light of day, oases of human settlement occurred—Hohokam, Piman, Sonoran, and finally Anglo. (Sheridan 1986, 10–11)

The institute's physical environs are far more than incidental to its content. The participants at the institute are marked by the degree to which they endorse a particular collective image of Tucson's history, its present composition, and its likely futures. Their shared imaginations are a little like the meandering Santa Cruz, now visible on the surface, now sunk into the sand. At the institute, the dispersed waters rise again, and certain neglected elements of community, of cooperative purpose, become visible once more. The anthropologist Virginia Nazarea draws memory as a network including experience, mind, and behavior, emphasizing the proactive nature of nurturing memories across the passage of time with the term "memory work" (2006, 9).

Participants in this study embarked on memory work during the four days of the institute, an activity that brought their social and professional practices together. At the institute, these fields were interlocking and interacting sectors of consciousness. But suggesting that these sectors are linked can prompt educators to deny that relationship, on the grounds that it implies some irrationality in their behaviors or responses to contemporary events.

Recognizing that memory is essential to planning thoughtful future action is not the same thing as enshrining memory in a mantle of legitimacy or equating it with history. Nazarea writes, "Memory is not history; to expect it to possess the same virtues is to underrate seriously its potential to deliver more insights but of a different kind" (2006, 9). After talking with study participants, listening to their accounts of their relationships with students and of those students' relationships with each other, I am convinced that knowledge of a place, over time, must be an explicit part of educators' moving toward their own potential as critical multiculturalists, toward their learning.

There is no easy solution that involves privileging the knowledge of self-professed local actors over any other. Nevertheless, there is some sense, in the data I gathered for this study, that local knowledge of Tucson is necessary to avoid repeating certain of the more egregious injustices of colonial history. My field notes from introductory remarks of the 2009 and 2010 institutes indicate, through the comments (edited for content) of a frequent speaker there, Pima County Supervisor Richard Elías, that a struggle to reclaim Tucson's memory is taking place at these gatherings:

FIELD NOTES: DAY 1 OF INSTITUTE, JULY 14, 2009

Richard Elías, chairman, Pima County Board of Supervisors
There is an amnesia among [our] elected officials. . . . The legislature said we can spend again on education in Arizona but didn't provide the revenue. . . . History should be taught, but Latinos should forget their own. This is really about voting rights and civil rights.

FIELD NOTES: DAY 2 OF INSTITUTE, WEDNESDAY, JULY 14, 2010

Richard Elías, Pima County supervisor
My family has been in Tucson for five generations, in Arizona for seven. We welcome new immigrants here. . . . The Pima County courthouse was built on top of a Tucson cemetery, and money was spent to respectfully exhume the graves and repatriate the remains to tribes, in contrast to the courthouse built in Manhattan on top of slave graves, where no attempt was made to treat them respectfully. We cannot allow history to be covered up like that here, in the denial of our right to teach Ethnic Studies.

In these excerpts, amnesia, forgetting, and covering up are examples of the kind of memory work (because forgetting is also a form of memory work) that the institute prompted.

In contrast to the multigenerational roots and memory Elías claimed, a young study participant (and relatively new arrival to Tucson), Karen Malden, admitted her lack of connection to the place in which she teaches: "I like to joke that Tucson's one of those places that people come to when they get stuck. It's not really a joke, 'cause it's not funny. But yeah, they come and they get stuck and then, never really find a way to get out." Elías and Malden inhabit distant ends of the spectrum of local knowledge, and the space between them presages a new era of conflicts over Tucson's public education system. The institute was a space they both entered willingly, knowing they were likely to encounter challenges to their respective relationships to Tucson. At the time of this research, the institute occupies a tenuous position in TUSD; current district superintendent John Pedicone has not expressed support for either the institute or for MAS secondary programs. The 2011 institute operated under a reduced schedule; if it is to continue, the Tucson community will need to vocally recognize the institute's value as a public forum and as a space for the forging of new collective understandings.

Notes

1. By "court for equality," Arlene refers to desegregation orders for Tucson schools, in effect until a Post-Unitary Status Plan was submitted to a US district judge in 2009.
2. This is a pseudonym, as are all participant names.
3. From here on, I refer to the professional development institute hosted by TUSD as "the institute," for brevity, and because the program has undergone a name change (from the Raza Studies Summer Institute to the Institute for Transformative Education).
4. Brazilian philosopher Paulo Freire's (1921–1997) pedagogical and political ideas continue to influence education scholars and educators concerned with equity in public schools.
5. I am indebted to Dr. Norma González for this observation.
6. For these US Census data, see "State and County QuickFacts: Arizona," United States Census Bureau, http://quickfacts.census.gov/qfd/states/04000.html.
7. Based on expenditures per $1,000 of personal income, spending per student adjusted for inflation, and spending per student per $1,000 of per capita personal income.
8. See Arizona state legislator member pages, Arizona State Legislature, http://www.azleg.gov/memberRoster.asp?Body=H.
9. See "State and County QuickFacts: Massachusetts," United States Census Bureau, http://quickfacts.census.gov/qfd/states/25000.html, for these census data.
10. San Xavier is a Spanish-era mission church located on Tohono O'odham land, southwest of the Tucson city center.
11. See Dobyns (1976) for an explanation of Tucson's earliest residents and the mestizo migration of the 1770s.
12. Contemporary scholarship features both historical examinations of media discourse on immigration (Flores 2003) and more recent snapshots of coverage (Cisneros 2008).

References

Apple, M. 1988. *Teachers and Texts: A Political Economy of Class and Gender Relations in Education.* New York: Routledge.
Arizona Education Association. 2010. http://www.arizonaea.org/.
Brayboy, B. J. 2003. "Visibility as a Trap: American Indian Representation in Schools." In *Invisible Children in the Society and Its Schools,* ed. S. Brooks, 32–52. Mahwah, NJ: Lawrence Erlbaum.

Researching the Institute for Transformative Education · 157

Cammarota, J., and A. Romero. 2006. "A Critically Compassionate Pedagogy for Latino Youth." *Latino Studies* 4: 305–12.
Cisneros, J. D. 2008. "Contaminated Communities: The Metaphor of 'Immigrant as Pollutant' in Media Representations of Immigration." *Rhetoric and Public Affairs* 11(4): 569–602.
Cochran-Smith, M. 2003. "The Multiple Meanings of Multicultural Teacher Education: A Conceptual Framework." *Teacher Education Quarterly* 30(2): 7–26.
Cruz, Johnny. 2009. "Shelton, Hay Respond to Massive Higher Education Budget Cuts." UANews, February 2. http://uanews.org/node/23822.
Desimone, L., A. Porter, B. F. Birman, M. S. Garet, and K. Suk Yoon. 2007. "How Do Management and Implementation Strategies Relate to the Quality of the Professional Development that Districts Provide to Teachers?" *Teachers College Record* 104(7): 1265–1312.
Dobyns, Henry F. 1976. "Population Dynamics at the Tucson Military Post, 1776–1797." In *Spanish Colonial Tucson: A Demographic History*, 142–48. Tucson: University of Arizona Press.
Ensign, J. 2009. "Multiculturalism in Four Teacher Education Programs: For Replication or Transformation." *Multicultural Perspectives* 11(3): 169–173.
Flores, L. A. 2003. "Constructing Rhetorical Borders, Peons, Illegal Aliens, and Competing Narratives of Immigration." *Critical Studies in Media Education* 20: 362–87.
Freire, P., and D. Macedo, eds. 1998. *The Paulo Freire Reader*. New York: Continuum.
Frohne, Andrea E. 2002. "The African Burial Ground in New York City: Manifesting and Representing Spirituality of Space." PhD diss., State University of New York at Binghamton.
Grande, S. 2004. *Red Pedagogy: Native American Social and Political Thought*. Lanham, MD: Rowman and Littlefield.
Horne, T. 2010. Arizona Department of Education. Accessed August 3. http://www.azcentral.com/arizonarepublic/ works; please provide title of press release and updated URL.
Jennings, L., C. P. Smith. 2002. "Examining the Role of Critical Inquiry for Transformative Practices: Two Joint Case Studies of Multicultural Teacher Education." *Teachers College Record* 104(3): 465–81.
Julian, L. 2008. "'Raza Studies' Defy American Values: Some Public Schools Teach Program That Divides Students by Ethnicities." National Review Online, July 2. http://www.cbsnews.com/stories/2008/07/02/opinion/main4227721.shtml.
Kossan, P. 2009. "Proposal to Cut $600 Mil Draws Record Crowds to Regents Meeting." *Arizona Republic*, January 23. http://www.azcentral.com/arizonarepublic/news/articles/2009/01/23/20090123reents0123.html
Loughran, J. 2006. *Developing a Pedagogy of Teacher Education: Understanding Teaching and Learning about Teaching*. New York: Routledge.
Milner, H. R. 2006. "Preservice Teachers' Learning about Cultural and Racial Diversity: Implications for Urban Education." *Urban Education* 41: 343–75.
National Commission on Excellence in Education. 1983. *A Nation at Risk: The Imperative for Educational Reform*. Washington, DC: Department of Education.
Nazarea, V. D. 2006. "Local Knowledge and Memory in Biodiversity Conservation." *Annual Review of Anthropology* 35: 317–35.

Orozco, R. A. 2009. "Framing Hostilities: Comparative Critical Discourse Analyses of Mission Statements from Predominantly Mexican American and White School Districts and High Schools." PhD diss., Oregon State University,
Otero, L. 2010. *La Calle: Spatial Conflicts and Urban Renewal in a Southwest City.* Tucson: University of Arizona Press.
"Radical Education." 2008. Opinions, *Arizona Republic*, July 14. http://www.azcentral .com/arizonarepublic/opinions/articles/2008/07/14/20080714mon1-14.html.
Romero, A. 2008. "Towards a Critically Compassionate Intellectualism Model of Transformative Urban Education." PhD diss., University of Arizona.
Rosen, L. 2003. "The Politics of Identity and the Marketization of U.S. Schools: How Local Meanings Mediate Global Struggles." In *Local Meanings, Global Schooling: Anthropology and World Culture Theory*, ed. K. M. Anderson-Levitt, 161–83. New York: Palgrave.
Schieffelin, B., K. Woolard, and P. Kroskrity, eds. 1998. *Language Ideologies: Practice and Theory.* New York: Oxford University Press.
Sheridan, T. E. 1986. *Los Tucsonenses: The Mexican Community in Tucson 1854–1941.* Tucson: University of Arizona Press.
Sleeter, C. 2000. "Epistemological Diversity in Research on Preservice Teacher Preparation for Historically Underserved Children." *Review of Research in Education* 25: 209–50.
Urciuoli, B. 1996. *Exposing Prejudice: Puerto Rican Experiences of Language, Race, and Class.* Boulder, CO: Westview.
Urrieta, L. 2007. "Identity Production in Figured Worlds: How Some Mexican Americans Become Chicana/o Activist Educators." *The Urban Review* 38: 117–44.

CHAPTER NINE

Deconstructing the Doublethink Aimed at Dismantling Ethnic Studies in Tucson

Jeff Duncan-Andrade

Anyone that spends time in schools serving the children of working-class and poor people knows how rare it is to find classrooms where students are genuinely engaged in what they are learning. Year after year, school districts all over the country rack their brains and spend billions of tax payers' dollars trying to figure out how to improve these classroom experiences. At the end of the day, that is what most parents want for their children. It should also be what our society wants for all children, as the benefits of engaging classrooms echo across communities for multiple generations.

This is what makes the state of Arizona's decision to kill the Mexican-American Studies (MAS) program in the Tucson Unified School District so baffling. In those classrooms, levels of student engagement were remarkably high. Of course, there was also the elevated achievement that comes along with greater engagement in rich and meaningful academic work. Had there actually been rigorous evaluations of all classes in those schools, there may very well indeed have been cause for outcry about the education students are receiving in Tucson's public schools. However, I doubt seriously that any evaluators that recognize good teaching would have had cause for concern with the ethnic studies classes because they would have encountered the very conditions that we claim to want for all our students. Instead, the outrage would have been directed at many of the other classes where hour after hour these same students experienced social, emotional, and intellectual disconnection. There should be a state-level investigation into Tucson's public schools, and every public school district in the country for that matter, where the failure of large percentages of children has gone unaddressed for decades. There should be policies outlawing certain types of classes and teaching; places where drill-and-kill test-driven curricula slip creative young minds into borderline comatose relationships to learning, crushing their intellectual engagement in school. The widespread nature of these conditions is cause for alarm, and it is indeed a threat to national security that warrants a House bill outlawing it.

Sadly, this sort of inquiry into school failure did not happen in Arizona. That is not shocking since it has not happened anywhere else in the country and there is no real state of national commitment to radically rethinking how we educate poor and working-class children or children of color. What makes the Arizona situation so utterly absurd is not that they failed to outlaw bad teaching, but that they actually outlawed good teaching. They actually passed a law that put an end to a program that was working for large numbers of students; the same students, by the way, that the state and the district admit they are not serving effectively.

What has gone on in Arizona is doublethink at its finest. In George Orwell's dystopian novel, *1984*, he coins the term "doublethink," which he describes as "the power of holding two contradictory beliefs in one's mind simultaneously, and accepting both of them. The [participant] . . . knows that he is playing tricks with reality; but by the exercise of doublethink he also satisfies himself that reality is not violated. The process has to be conscious, or it would not be carried out with sufficient precision, but it also has to be unconscious, or it would bring with it a feeling of falsity and hence of guilt" (Orwell 2003, 220). Doublethink is not just lying. It is self-deception that requires people to fool themselves. Orwell's insight, then, is that to tranquilize such blatant cognitive dissonance requires not only ideology but also a kind of self-hypnosis.

One need not be a particularly keen observer to see the layers of doublethink used to justify Arizona's House Bill 2281. It is a worthwhile exercise, however, to continue to call attention to the strategies used by white supremacists and others looking to maintain elements of the status quo that do documentable harm to members of our society.

In this vein, this chapter illuminates three examples of doublethink used to justify the elimination of effective teaching in Tucson's public schools: teaching about oppression is bad; achievement is irrelevant; government should obstruct community choice. The first example comes from the contradictory arguments used to suggest that teaching students (of color) from the lens of their own cultural history is inappropriate and harmful. The second example of doublethink comes from duplicitous conversations about accountability for achievement results. The third example comes from the political Right, whose position is one of minimal government intervention and market-driven decision making, but who decided that heavy-handed governance was required because they know better than the community what their children need in school.

Teaching about Oppression Is Bad (for People of Color)

The curriculum used in US public schools continues to be, to a large extent, centered in an Anglo-Eurocentric worldview. This fact is rarely discussed with any vigor in policy and practice circles, despite the fact that even conservative estimates suggest that people of color will be the majority of the US population by 2040, and we all know that people of color are far and away the global majority. Indeed, in the United States in 2011, more nonwhite babies were born than white babies. In the Tucson Unified schools, over 60 percent of the students are of Mexican descent, whether they are US born or recent immigrants. The massive disconnect between who is being taught, what they are being taught, and who is doing the teaching is particularly problematic in schools where very large percentages of the students are not of Anglo-European descent. But it is also a problem in predominantly white schools given that this country continues to have major issues with racism while becoming an increasingly multiracial and multiethnic society.

Research has repeatedly shown that the Anglo-Eurocentric nature of the US curriculum and teacher workforce is increasingly out of sync with the growing nonwhite population in the country. This is not to say that students of color cannot learn effectively from white teachers, or that they are disinterested in learning European-US history. What the research suggests is that the curriculum and teachers are overwhelmingly white, and that this has a negative impact on students of color over time. There is sufficient research to make a decisive argument that the standard curriculum's treatment of people of color is shallow at best, and deliberately racist and exclusionary at worst, and that this needs to change if we are going to prepare students for life in the twenty-first century.

Research is also clear about the importance of students understanding the history of their own cultural heritage. Some have argued that this responsibility should rest entirely with the family. This is an interesting argument in that the sentiment seems to be applied only to nonwhite groups. When curriculum and instruction lean heavily toward an Anglo-Eurocentric worldview, delivered by an overwhelmingly white teacher workforce, there is no threat to the well-being of children or national security. It is deemed acceptable to use a curriculum that numerous scholars have shown to be exclusionary, incomplete, or even categorically false in its representation of African, indigenous, Asian, and Latin and South American peoples because there is not enough room in the curriculum to cover them.[1]

Here is our first example of doublethink in this debate about the value of ethnic studies in schools: one of the central figures in the dismantling of the MARS program was Tom Horne, Arizona's state superintendent of schools at the time of his campaign against ethnic studies.[2] One of Horne's primary arguments against ethnic studies was that it was creating an unnecessary psychological burden on the students. His sense was that instruction and curricula that studied the perspectives of people of color (Latinas/os in this case) would lead to conversations about oppression. These conversations about oppression would, in turn, make kids depressed.[3]

Again, the research does not bear this out at all, but rather indicates that an important facilitator of human development and healing, and a critical protective factor for recurring trauma, is having access to a community where people are able to talk about their struggles and connect to others with similar experiences. If people focus on struggles that they have been through as individuals or as a group, what the focus actually reveals is their resiliency. It makes them feel hopeful. It makes them feel empowered.

I would be deeply troubled if I thought that the top-ranking education official in Arizona could be so profoundly misinformed and then make policy based on that ignorance. But the truth is that I know he's not. Doublethink is a conscious act. We can be assured of this point because Horne has always supported Arizona schools teaching children the narrative of struggles to overcome oppression. A story of oppression is at the center of the dominant narrative about the founding of this nation: an account of a group of English commoners that freed themselves from the oppressive conditions levied upon them by the British monarchy. This tale is repeated to us over and over again in school. It is at the core of our national identity. Why doesn't this make students of British descent become depressed? On the contrary, it makes them feel empowered. Why does it make them feel empowered? Because they realize in the telling and the retelling of that history that they have agency, that when they feel that conditions are unfair, they can respond. That seems to be the American way; if things are wrong, we should speak up. Thomas Jefferson himself said that every generation should have its own revolution. But according to Horne and some members of the Arizona legislature, by engaging this same narrative through the lens of the Mexican in America, the MARS program was breeding revolutionaries on the road to sedition.

Orwell would remind us that this is how doublethink works. One must hold two contradictory beliefs in one's mind simultaneously, accepting both of them. My eighty-two-year-old mother would just shake her head and say, "You can't have your cake and eat it too." Well, we cannot on the one hand pride ourselves as a nation on our ability to engage in revolutionary action, celebrating and lauding the principal actors in those events, insisting that all members of our society revere them, and then at the same time say that those principles are only intended for white students and can only be taught through an Anglo-Eurocentric frame. That's doublethink.

Achievement Is Irrelevant

Nearly everyone is calling for accountability for schools. For approximately the past ten years, despite widespread criticism, that accountability has remained heavily centered on statewide standardized testing. The students in the MARS program were outperforming their peers on those tests. But those tests do not measure Mexican American or raza history. Students in MARS classes also improved their math scores, a subject that was not even taught by the program. In fact, the results for young people in the MARS program were astounding, across a broad spectrum of achievement outcomes. For people that have actually engaged in successful practice with students of color, or that have kept up with the research on effective practices with youth of color over the last one hundred years, the link between the pedagogical strategies used in MARS and the improved student outcomes was not surprising or perplexing.

What the data from the MARS program reaffirm is what we have known in the research and practice communities for quite some time. The stronger the sense that young people have that their lives matter, that their culture matters, that their language matters, and that the history of their people matters, the better they will do across all subjects; indeed, the better they will do in our society writ large. From educational research to health research to basic common sense, it is clear that programs like Tucson's MARS are not a threat to national security; quite to the contrary, they are actually essential to it.

What I find particularly interesting about the so-called debate surrounding the MARS program is that it came after a decade-long national frenzy about educational accountability. Entire states have been allocated or denied federal funding based on their alignment with national priorities for test score improvement strategies. Teachers and school districts find themselves under constant attack from local and national policy wonks and lobbyists that sling around hyperbolic rhetoric about prioritizing kids and families over bad teachers and failing schools. Amid all this, we had a program that was actually accountable to these results and to the families and communities of students that schools have failed from time immemorial, and it was dismantled. This beggars belief. I thought school districts like Tucson Unified were under the accountability microscope and that it was high time that they started raising achievement for their students of color. When confronted with the MARS program's achievement results, proponents of HB 2281 failed to discredit the results and effectively took up the position that the move to close down ethnic studies was not about achievement.[4] If Arizona's schools are not about achievement, what are they about?

Doublethink was alive and well at the highest levels of Arizona's educational leadership. The MARS program was not sound practice (even though it worked); it was sedition. This is how doublethink works. You must hold two contradictory positions simultaneously, all while attempting to convince yourself (and national audiences in "debates" televised on major networks) that there is no contradiction in your position. Orwell's predictive powers astound.

Government Should Obstruct Community Choice

Horne, his successor John Huppenthal, and the horde of political conservatives around the country that supported the dismantling of the MARS program are the very same conservatives that relentlessly argue for less government intervention. They insist that we must let the market correct itself. Wait... what? Public schools are intended to serve young people and families, which means those young people and families are the market. Following their political ideology, then, they must have conducted an examination of the market position on the MARS program and diligently reviewed the existing market evaluations of the program. From these evaluations, they must have discovered clear and decisive evidence that the majority of students and families were demanding that ethnic studies be shut down.

Indeed, these public servants, so deeply committed to uphold their democratically conservative beliefs that the market must decide, examined reviews of the MARS program. They even commissioned an external evaluator of their choosing to conduct a full program evaluation. One of the evaluations they reviewed was conducted by an external, national evaluation team, of which I was a member. In 2007, a colleague from Chicago and I reviewed the entire ethnic studies program in Tucson Unified. As part of this study, we randomly selected focus groups out of the MARS classes. What we found, to a person, was that these were the classes where students were most likely to feel loved and cared for, and where they felt like their lives and opinions mattered. Students and parents alike told us that the MARS program had revived their love for knowledge and provided inspiration to excel in other classes. Our review also found that the MARS program was far and away the most successful of all the ethnic studies programs in the district. In our recommendations, we encouraged the district to use MARS as its model for the entire ethnic studies program and for any other instructional programming that was attempting to serve students of color and historically underserved groups.[5]

Despite our evaluation being based on the widely accepted research practice of data triangulation, it would not surprise me if our report was discarded as biased. Then Huppenthal somehow managed to cobble together the financial resources, despite Arizona's fiscal crisis in education, to hire the Cambium Learning Group to evaluate the MARS program. He chose this external evaluation team. Having read Cambium's report in its entirety, it is difficult for me to write this section of this chapter because it moves me away from using the term "doublethink." Doublethink strikes me as an irrational way of acting that is driven by political motivations. But the thoroughness of Cambium's evaluation of the MARS program and their subsequent unequivocating conclusions of the complete absence of evidence that the program violates any portion of Arizona's HB 2281 forces me to make a different conclusion about the intentions of people that supported the dismantling of ethnic studies. The decision to close the MARS program was a deliberate act of racial hatred. There is simply no way around this conclusion. Huppenthal's own evaluation team was completely decisive in their position that the MARS program was a positive good for the schools, the city, and the nation. There should be no quarter for such acts of vile racism, especially when the offices of elected power have been used to carry them out.

I do not make these comments lightly. If one were to read the broad spectrum of my writings, you would find that I have never taken up such a strong position of indictment and consequences on any single issue. I encourage anyone engaged with this chapter to read the evaluation and come to their own conclusions (Cambium 2011). I am certain that even those that came out against ethnic studies will find that there is simply nothing in the report that warranted the destruction of the program.

The evaluators found that "no evidence exists in any format" that the program was in violation of any of the provisions of the House bill used as justification for its closure. Cambium interviewed eight different focus groups, including businesspeople and nonparticipating parents, principals, students, teachers, and elected officials, and found that the program had incredibly widespread support. Frankly, there is almost nothing on the planet that all these groups would agree upon for our schools, and yet all were in favor of the work of the MARS program in Tucson. To find even the slightest discontent with the program in Cambium's evaluation requires a fine-toothed comb, and even then the criticism is minor.

Neither our group's review nor Cambium's were ever discredited or even challenged. They were, however, summarily ignored. This ability to abandon your most profound ideological beliefs and deny that you are doing so is at the heart of doublethink. As Orwell explains, to engage in doublethink requires one to

> tell deliberate lies while genuinely believing in them, to forget any fact that has become inconvenient, and then, when it becomes necessary again, to draw it back from oblivion for just so long as it is needed, to deny the existence of objective reality and all the while to take account of the reality which one denies—all this is indispensably necessary.... For by using [doublethink] one admits that one is tampering with reality; by a fresh act of doublethink one erases this knowledge; and so on indefinitely, with the lie always one leap ahead of the truth. (2003, 220)

The subsequent use of Arizona's HB 2281 to effectively outlaw ethnic studies in Tucson's public schools was the definition of heavy-handed government intervention in public life. Political conservatives should be outraged that members of their party could be so cavalier with their most tightly held belief about how to govern. That is doublethink for you.

Reality Check

The banning of ethnic studies is criminal. However, the greater crime lies in the fact that we still need ethnic studies programs. It suggests that we have made virtually no progress in the nearly fifty years since the student strikes at San Francisco State University that fought for classes teaching the history of people of color. Indeed, the case in Arizona suggests that we are going backward in our commitment to serving students of color in our public schools. Given that schools are a social mirror, this reflects poorly on our society's commitment to becoming the multiracial, pluralistic democracy it has promised to become and that it touts itself as all around the world.

In a society as ethnically diverse as ours, there is simply no reason that every course that students take should be anything less than an ethnic studies course. Let me also point out that people of various European descents have ethnic cultures, many of which are taught matter-of-factly every day in schools as a normal part of the curriculum—they don't call it ethnic studies, but it is. The fact that students and families whose origins fall outside of Europe are forced to ask for separate courses so that they can learn about their ancestors and the ways in which they have shaped the history of the United States and the world is absurd—and also racist. The need for ethnic studies courses puts us in a legal time warp, running us all the way back to the Supreme Court's 1896 *Plessy v. Ferguson* decision that separate and equal was acceptable.[6]

As a nation, we cannot even meet a pathetically low social standard from the nineteenth century. Instead, every day in schools and communities all over this nation, we maintain a de facto position of separate and unequal. Despite the Supreme Court's 1954 promise of "all deliberate speed" to create racially integrated and equitable schools and institutional resources, it was clear that mainstream schooling institutions were not interested in a speedy pursuit of equity.[7] So people committed to racial equity pursued ethnic studies in the 1960s, seeking some modicum of control over their education.

The fact that students of European descent have never been required to learn the histories that are taught in ethnic studies, while students of color are mandated to learn Anglo-European histories is nothing short of a hegemonic project of cultural supremacy.[8] The fact is that the curriculum and assessments used in the overwhelming majority of US public schools are not reflective of the student population, the broader society, or the world. Behind all the rhetoric of a global market economy and training students for the twenty-first-century workplace, very little is happening in schools that suggests there is any intention to do this for the majority of students. Rhetorically speaking, this is "un-American" in every way, shape, and form. In reality, it is quintessentially "American" because there has never been a time in this country's history when it provided a high-quality education to all its citizens.[9]

Forward, How?

A few weeks before starting this chapter, and just two days before my parents' sixty-second wedding anniversary, my father was killed in a car crash outside my parents' home.[10]

"What now?" I asked my eighty-two-year-old mother.

"I just have to remake myself, son. I will take each day as it comes and focus on what needs to be done. My glass is still half full," she replied.

She was simply repeating a lesson she taught me as a child when she ordered me to the kitchen table and placed a half-filled glass of water between us. Pointing at the glass, she asked, "Half full or half empty?" I refused the bait and stared blankly at the glass.

"Son," she continued, "how you choose to answer that question is how you will live your life. Your glass will always be both half full and half empty. If you choose to see your life as half empty, focusing on the things you don't have, then you will never fill your cup. But if you learn to see your life as half full, seeing all the things that you do have, then you will fill your cup. It will overflow, and you can share that with others."

The education of poor and working-class people in this country has often been treated as a glass half empty. For generations, we have rationalized why we have not, why we will not, and why we cannot serve "these" families. But, as my mother's lesson suggests, this is a choice that we make. It is not inevitable. We could, if we so desired, choose to see all children for their potential and invest in them accordingly. Were our nation to become serious about such an effort in education, we would, as my mother suggests, need to remake ourselves.

This remaking would begin with an honest accounting of the fact that the status quo approach to educating our children is failing miserably. We are not even close to meeting the needs of our student population. If not ethnic studies, then what? What is it that anti–ethnic studies factions think we should do in schools? Their methods have failed for decades. All we hear is that we should keep it the way it is. Well, the way it is does not work for the vast majority of working-class and poor children, regardless of their ethnicity. Everyone knows this to be true.

Simply put, if you are not going to get down in the dirt with some new and creative ideas, then step aside. The same people that toiled and labored to build this country will be the ones that save it from itself, and on that path they will humanize and value all people, regardless of their ethnic origins. That is not doublethink. That's ethnic studies.

Notes

1. See the work of James Loewen (1995) and Howard Zinn (1995) for a list of half-truths and lies regularly taught in US curricula. They are both white historians, by the way. You can also see the work of Rudolfo Acuña (1995) and Antonia Darder (2012)—if they are not banned where you live. I am not just talking about history classes either. This happens across the curriculum at all grade levels.
2. Horne is now the Arizona attorney general.
3. Horne's contention implies that these now "depressed" youth would otherwise have been happy to be "American" if they were taught the mainstream curriculum.
4. Quoting a 2007 article in the *Arizona Daily Star* titled "Horne Seeks Info on Ethnic Studies Programs in TUSD": "Horne said his inquiry is not based on a question of academics or education, but 'values.'"
5. It should be noted that in our review of the program, we found that there were non-Latina/o students enrolled in MARS classes and that their satisfaction levels, and that of their families, was equally as high as Latina/o students and families.
6. *Plessy v. Ferguson*, 163 US 537 (1896).
7. *Brown v. Board of Education*, 347 US 483 (1954). Very little has changed since. In honor of the fifty-year anniversary of the *Brown* decision, the Harvard Civil Rights Project (now the UCLA Civil Rights Project) released "*Brown* at 50" (2004) evaluating the nation's progress. Their data revealed that schools in all regions outside of the South are more racially segregated now than before the *Brown* decision. Nationally, Latinos and African Americans are more segregated now than they were in 1968.
8. The implementation of ninth grade ethnic studies classes in San Francisco Unified Schools may change this fact in at least one city.
9. I put the word "American" in quotation marks because, as part of this project of white supremacy, the United States has claimed the title of America, even though we are one of several countries that make up the Americas. So, in fact, Canadians, Mexicans, and every other group from North and South America are actually Americans.
10. My closing thoughts in this chapter borrow heavily from the introduction of a longer piece about the direction I propose for improving education (Duncan-Andrade, 2012). For the full essay, see http://bankstreet.edu/occasionalpapers/op27/part-iii/glass-half-full/.

References

Acuña, R. 1995. *Occupied America*. New York: HarperCollins.
Cambium Learning. 2011. *Curriculum Audit of the Mexican American Studies Department, Tucson Unified School District*. Miami Lakes, FL: Cambium Learning. http://saveethnicstudies.org/assets/docs/state_audit/Cambium_Audit.pdf.
Darder, A. 2012. *Culture and Power in the Classroom*. Boulder, CO: Paradigm Publishers.
Duncan-Andrade, J. 2012. "A Glass Half Full." New York: Bank Street College.
Loewen, J. 1995. *Lies My Teacher Told Me*. New York: Simon & Schuster.

Orfield, G. and C. Lee. 2004. *Brown at 50: King's Dream or Plessy's Nightmare.* Cambridge, MA: Harvard University Civil Rights Project.
Orwell, G. 2003. *1984.* New York: Penguin.
Sanchez, G. 2007. "Horne seeks info on ethnic studies programs in TUSD." *Arizona Daily Star*, November 15, 2007.
Zinn, H. 1995. *A People's History of the United States.* New York: HarperCollins.

CHAPTER TEN

Expanding on Freire

Enriching Critical Pedagogy with Indigenous Theory toward a Pedagogy of Humanization

Chiara Cannella

If you don't have strong roots, the wind will blow you.
EMILIO GUERRERA, 2008

Political controversy has surrounded Tucson Unified School District's (TUSD's) Mexican American Studies (MAS) program for years. But when the school board voted in 2012 to halt all MAS classes, controversy turned to turmoil, and educators and scholars across the country became outraged that such an effective program was targeted for ideological reasons. Accompanying this outrage was increasing interest in the day-to-day pedagogy of the program. As increasing numbers of former MAS program students have become vocal and active in efforts to reinstate the program, activists and educators have sought to understand how MAS increased achievement across subject areas, as well as fostering increased social agency and civic engagement among program participants. This chapter draws on a two-year ethnographic case study of the Social Justice Education Project (SJEP), one component of the MAS program. Data collection included participant observation in SJEP classes, SJEP advisory board meetings, parent Encuentros, school board meetings, and community events; document review of student assignments, program curriculum, and planning; and participant observation in the SJEP summer research internship program. I examined the classroom curriculum and pedagogy, as well as their effects on students. Findings indicate that the program

171

impacts vary depending on students' initial academic and ethnic identities. Across these variables, however, the SJEP prompts shifts in students' academic identities and social agency. Increasing identification with school subject matter fosters intellectual empowerment that often extends beyond the context of school to affect broader social identities. Findings detail the ways that participants can come to see their actions as socially and historically grounded, eventually coming to think of themselves as social actors.

It became clear that the MAS model is unique—and effective—because of its explicit acknowledgment of the sociohistorical context of schools and their students; the SJEP typifies this. The motivation for the creation of the SJEP was to take the culturally relevant pedagogy of ethnic studies classes and augment it with more focused attention to critical pedagogy, institutional racism, and participatory action research, all in an effort to foster students' increasing "critical consciousness" (Freire 1993) and social action (introduction of this volume; see also Romero 2008). The goals of the program for students include not only learning about their culture and history, but also developing social agency. As a result, students' critical transformation is a major element of the SJEP, a process that codirector Augustine Romero describes as aiming to help youth "nurture their critical consciousness, [help] youth find their voice in this consciousness, and then [find] a way to help these youth . . . take this thing and place it into action" (A. Romero, personal communication, July 11, 2007).

Critical Pedagogy in the SJEP

The program rests on the philosophy of teaching—and of life—that all people's actions and identities are shaped by their sociohistorical context and political positionality. All students of color are marginalized in a racialized society, facing discrimination on a daily basis; white students are also dehumanized by the dominant ideology, which fails to teach people to recognize and respect the humanity in all people. In addition, because of the specific history of Arizona and the ongoing political assault against the rights of people identified as Mexican, as well as the expression of Mexicanness, many SJEP students in Tucson have learned to feel ashamed of their Mexican identities. Students from a very young age may refuse to learn or speak Spanish, disassociate from peers who have more recently immigrated from Mexico, and seek to project a more assimilated identity (see also Valenzuela 1999). This is described, in the context of the SJEP, as symptoms of students' "internalized racism," which contributes to their own "dehumanization."

These beliefs shape both the pedagogy and curriculum of SJEP courses, which seek to disrupt these patterns by engendering Freirean "critical literacy" and "critical consciousness" (Freire 1973, 1993; Freire and Macedo 1987; see also introduction of this volume).[1] The concept of critical literacy grows from literacy scholarship but extends the notion of reading and writing beyond decoding or inscribing written texts (Freire and Macedo 1987; Gee 1997; Hull 1993; Morrell 2002). Freire describes coming to "see the world not as a static reality, but as a reality in progress" and to see society as "the object of transforming action by men and women" as crucial steps (1993, 86). Instead of seeing the world as natural and fixed, the critically literate are able to see that reality is the effect of choices and actions taken by people and that social conditions can indeed be affected by those willing to take action. Morrell and Duncan-Andrade argue that teaching youth to "read the world" enables them to "name [their] environment . . . to begin to understand the political nature of the limits and possibilities of life within larger society" (2004, 249). This allows one's understanding of society to move beyond the superficial explanations for what is real and what is possible, to see the world as socially constructed—and as subjective and vulnerable to change. It is this view of reality as vulnerable to human efforts for change that can promote increased social agency. Through attaining critical literacy, students may construct for themselves "authentic liberation," which, for Freire, constitutes "the process of humanization" (1993, 79).

These are precisely the activities in which the SJEP attempts to engage participants. Critical pedagogy offers a crucial way for SJEP students to learn to view the world in its political and sociohistorical context, which is fundamental to the program's goals. And program instructors emphasize the need for students to develop and act on solutions to the problems they identify around them; it is not enough to critique. One must also take positive action.

Based on their experience with students, SJEP staff also have found that Freirean critical pedagogy alone does not articulate a way for marginalized students to reconcile the impact of institutionalized racism and internalized oppression on themselves and their families from a personal perspective. Before students can take positive social action, they must have a more detailed framework for understanding whether those actions are constructive or if they maintain a cycle of racism and prejudice. One SJEP teacher, Emilio Guerrera, stated, "What Freire proposes is beautiful except I don't think he gives us the tools to accomplish that, to address those historical and psychological and social trauma that we've endured in our lives, our short life span" (Guererra, interview, 2008).[2]

But for students to envision themselves as capable of taking positive social action, an additional tool is needed. Freire's concepts of magical, naive, and critical consciousness, for example, often do change the way students view the world. However, the steps between viewing the world differently and envisioning ways to act that humanize others can be a big leap for high school students; they need smaller steps and more scaffolding through that process.

In an effort to address that gap in the critical pedagogy model, SJEP instructors add a component of indigenous theory to the class, mainly the Nahui Ollin, a framework that helps students reconcile some of the social and historical trauma they experience, facilitating the process of humanization. This framework walks students through processes of reflection, action, reconciliation, and transformation that are consistent with the concept of praxis. But it adds layers to the idea of critical pedagogy, outlining a link between identifying injustice and forgiveness; between reconciliation and transformative action. In addition, the fact that this framework is indigenous provides those students with conflicted ethnic identities—usually manifesting in the form of working to erase their own Mexicanness—a framework for constructing a strong ethnic identity outside of the context of being Mexican in the United States.

This is possible because of the distinctive and responsive SJEP pedagogy. I describe this pedagogy in more detail below, and then discuss some of the most notable patterns of effects on students. The majority of data collection for this study occurred in the classroom of one SJEP teacher, Emilio Guerrera. Because of the very personal nature of teaching style and pedagogy, these data cannot be generalized as consistent across all SJEP classrooms; however, the content and overarching pedagogical approach are present in all SJEP classes, as evidenced by my own and others' studies with other SJEP teachers (see, e.g., Romero 2008; Cammarota and Romero 2006; Stauber 2012).

Indigenous Theory: Fostering Resilience in a Hostile Environment

If you don't know who you are, society will tell you, and then you are lost.
EMILIO GUERRERA, 2007

Program staff view their responsibility as setting their students on a path toward humanization, which they can best accomplish by teaching students more constructive ways to view the world, as well as a lens to analyze their own actions—and therefore role—in the world. The program accomplishes this using two main tools: (1) indigenous theory, detailed below; and (2) the social, political, and historical contextualization of students' lives. As teachers outline the broader context of students' lives—aspects of history, politics, and social theory—students come to understand that their own circumstances and opportunities are shaped not only by the choices and actions of individual people. Rather, they come to see broad patterns that shape their lives and families' decisions, patterns that span education, employment, and public institutions. This pedagogy of humanization uses additional tools to accomplish "conscientization," but at its core, is concerned with the "authentic liberation" of students.

Guerrera's indigenous philosophies shape how he presents all aspects of course material. He argues that American society places certain people at a disadvantage because of race, ethnicity, and socioeconomics, causing social and historical trauma in marginalized communities.[3] Schools exacerbate rather than mitigate that struggle for Latina/o students, largely because of the history and accepted purpose of public education. Indigenous theory can help students navigate those realities and develop resiliency as well as critical consciousness. Guerrera believes his role as a teacher is not confined to academic subject matter:

> The institution of education . . . goes back to the industrial age, and it is just mass producing [people who] are all similar, and when you try to interject something that is human and you try to create critical thinkers—and kids who are doing things not because of a grade but because it's about who they are and who they're becoming—it's tough for them and the curriculum doesn't lend itself to that. But at some point . . . I think as a professional, as a human being, it's our responsibility, whether they are being tested on this or not, to interject and provide them this way of seeing the world. (interview, 2008)

For Guerrera, indigenous theory can provide students with the framework they need to engage in that process because of its potential for providing them with strategies to address and overcome that marginalization and trauma.

The framework of indigenous studies Guerrera adds to the SJEP curriculum is based on the Aztec calendar and associated deities who represent various forces in the world, generally referred to as the Nahui Ollin. As he explains to students, these forces carry with them principles that people can choose to live their lives by, which can help people to live in ways that humanize themselves and others; this entails "being a positive human being," embodying respect for all peoples' identities and life experiences, and refusing to promote—even through silence—attitudes that dehumanize other people. This framework, described by Mr. Guerrera as "the four *campañeros*" or "the four Tezcatlipocas," includes the following:

- Quetzalcoatl: intelligence and self-reflection; includes understanding of history and identity
- Huitzilopochtli: "beautiful knowledge," acquired by being conscious; complements
- Freire's theory of praxis
- Xipe Totec: associated with rejuvenation and springtime; change and transformation
- Tezcatlipoca: reflection and reconciliation; the embodiment of change through conflict

In addition, the term *panche bé* describes the act of "getting to the root of the truth" through critical analysis. This parallels the idea of critical consciousness, in the context of the SJEP. These four campañeros entail "a code for personal and community transformation," which Guerrera shares with students as guidelines that people can aspire to live by. In his view, this model contains all the elements of learning, thought, and action that young people of color need in American society: "That's the beautiful thing about the Nahui Ollin, because it has the reflection and reconciliation, and then the action component, and the transformation in there, and it is all something that has been here in the Americas forever. And it is something that is theirs that they can reflect on" (Guerrera, interview, 2008). He is explicit with students that he is not only teaching them this model, but that it is something he uses in his own efforts to "be a good human being": he tries to live by those guidelines, explaining their importance to him and their potential benefit for all people.

Early in the year, Guerrera presents these lessons as a way of helping students reflect on their lives and make decisions that are responsible and humanizing. Each of the four elements is a crucial step in the process of positive action, first for personal and then community or social change. Guerrera explains these elements in terms of how students can use them in their own lives. The process of Quetzalcoatl focuses on reflection as a tool for understanding of one's self, one's identity, and others; Guerrera emphasizes the importance of understanding history and equipping oneself with relevant information. Huitzilopochtli entails an understanding of the underlying causes of phenomena, as well as consciousness about how they can be changed. This parallels closely the concept of critical consciousness, understanding that reality is a result of human actions, and that students can also take action to have an impact. Xipe Totec is the process of acting for constructive change, in alignment with one's reflections and consciousness. Tezcatlipoca is the recognition that conflict bears potential to instigate constructive change, in Guerrera's description, challenging Western epistemology in its assumption that conflict is necessarily negative.

In the class, these ideas are woven throughout conversation all year, identified by Guerrera as relating to various other ideas in the class, including humanization, critical analysis, and checking oneself. These are useful tools in helping students understand both the personal and institutional forms of discrimination and bias, which he considers the first step toward critical consciousness. Perhaps more importantly, according to Guerrera, this framework does a great deal to address the social and historical trauma that he argues all people of color experience and need to overcome: "We talk about Tezcatlipoca. We talk about reconciliation, and you know, giving them visuals, exercises to look at their historical trauma. So it's a continuous process" (Guerrera, interview, 2008). For example, Tezcatlipoca provides a model for students to reflect on the causes of violence or injustice, especially domestic violence. They can come to recognize the root social or economic causes for that violence or injustice, and then become able to forgive individual actions, which is a key to the ability to reconcile their past and move forward in constructive action. Guerrera describes the four campañeros as "the foundation of the class," which helps him meet his goal "for them to begin to wrestle and struggle with that rehumanization process and getting them to love who they are and be affirmative people."

This thread throughout the class gives students the chance to reflect on these concepts and integrate them as guidelines for their own thinking and actions. Guerrera explicitly tells students that the most important thing for them to learn in his class is how to be "a good human being." This means treating all people with respect no matter what they do or say, and taking care not to say or do things that dehumanize any other person. He tells students that the four campañeros can help them make decisions that reflect their values, including study and work ethics, the importance of education, and acting on these principles in all situations. He reminds them of how important it is not only to listen to what is being discussed in the SJEP and agree with it in class, but to enact social justice through their actions outside of class, exhorting them, "Practice what you preach. Make the world a better place," by treating people with respect. He asks them, "If you see a student who is being bullied, do you walk by? Because if you walk by, then you are saying that that is okay with you. Or do you step in and say, 'That is not okay with me'?" Through these lectures and discussions, Guerrera works to instill in students the principles they should live by and to reinforce the importance of acting on those principles in every context.

In combination with the concept of critical consciousness, the four campañeros provide a useful tool to students. During a presentation to parents of SJEP students, Gloria exemplified how students have come to understand these concepts in her description to the audience:

> We study the four campañeros every day. We learn how to use them as our problem solving. Mr. Guerrera teaches us never to forget bad times but always to forgive those who wronged you because this is the only way you can learn how to love yourself.
>
> The four Tezcatlipocas are Huitzilopochtli, Tezcatlipoca, Xipe Totec, and Quetzalcoatl.
>
> Quetzalcoatl: we acquire this knowledge through the study of history and our own identity.
>
> If you know yourself, you accept and forgive in yourself and in others.
>
> Tezcatlipoca: reflection and reconciliation.
>
> Huitzilopochtli: action or will of people to take action; it's important for us to know we can take action; it's important that we do it in a positive way because that way we can make the lives of those who come after better.
>
> Xipe Totec: teaches you to accept the past and allows you to move on.
>
> You can see how . . . together they represent a positive influence in our lives. (field notes, October 2007)

For Guerrera, teaching these ideas can help equip students with tools to overcome the difficulties in their lives, and to counteract the effects of the marginalization they experience. He tells parents, "If we don't know who we are, *estámos perdido* [we are lost]." He teaches his students indigenous theory to help them become able to locate themselves.

While this indigenous theory could be taught in a way that leaves out students from some ethnic backgrounds, the SJEP use of the Nahui Ollin articulates it as being applicable to everyone. Guerrera repeatedly reinforces to students that the term "indigenous" to America simply refers to people who lived in the Americas before contact with Europeans, so that all "Mexicana/os are indigenous" because "everyone who is of Mexican descent has some Indian blood in them." He also points out that white and African American people whose ancestors have been in the United States for a long time very likely have some indigenous American blood. But most importantly, he reminds students repeatedly that all people, regardless of their race or ethnicity, can choose to incorporate these principles into their way of living; the important parts of the Nahui Ollin are not about a particular ethnicity or cultural heritage but provide all people with a model to reflect on their lives and make their actions constructive:

> Mechicayo is what it's called, the essence of being human, you know, and that's what I tell the kids. At some point we are all indigenous. . . . And that's beautiful, and you get different kids and it's about finding yourself. . . . But you know, [for] kids [who are white or African American], it's not about being Mexican; it's about being human. And that's the beautiful thing and that's what attracts me so much to the Aztec *calendario*, you know, and the *mechicayo*, the essence of being human. (Guerrera, interview, 2008)

The purpose of teaching the Nahui Ollin is to provide students with an additional tool to humanize others—and thus, themselves—through reflection on the effects of their actions.

The foundation of these principles is that students have a strong belief in who they are so they are able to recognize and stand up to counterproductive patterns in society, which is particularly difficult for people of color. Guerrera tells students, "We don't think about who we are; that comes from reflection. If you don't know who you are, society tells you and then you are lost."

Sociohistorical Contextualization

Another crucial element of the SJEP pedagogy is the consistent focus on locating students' life experiences in a sociohistorical context. The SJEP course is designed to teach students a critical understanding of American government, with special focus on how history and current events affect Latina/o communities in the United States. Because of program teachers' discussions of history and politics and how they reverberate through students' lives, students come to recognize the ways that larger social patterns do, in fact, have direct effects on the opportunities and limitations they are subject to. Class discussions invite students to describe their own experiences in school, with law enforcement, and with media, as well as what they have witnessed among family and friends. These experiences are then linked to aspects of history, economics, and the actions of individual people and institutions. Instead of remaining abstract, the topics of American government class are examined for their impact on everyday people's lives. The students in Guerrera's class reflect on and share how these academic topics relate to what has happened to them personally, or their cousins or neighbors. As a result, they begin to see that they are subject to sociohistorical dynamics, a first step in coming to view themselves as sociohistorical actors as well.

For example, Guerrera discusses with his classes patterns in many Mexican American communities—as well as African American, Native American, and other low-income and marginalized communities—that are a source of trauma and conflict for students. SJEP teachers discuss these issues explicitly and explain how they can affect young people, including their academic success and ethnic identities. Guerrera teaches students that such broad patterns of destructive behavior demonstrate that they are not cultural deficiencies but are symptoms of social, economic, and political injustice. As he explains that such symptoms are consistent across racially and economically marginalized communities and not a product of any particular racial or ethnic heritage, students may see their families differently.

This includes the history of the experiences and accomplishments of their ancestors, which teaches many students that they too can accomplish great things. Luciana said, "The way [Mr. Guerrera] talks about certain things, the history, he gets our history as Latino/as involved" (interview, 2007). This has a distinct impact on many students. Angelica explains, "When you hear [that] your ancestors, people of your own race, [have] done things," it changes the way that she and other students see their own abilities (interview, 2007).

Before studying history "from a Chicano perspective," Angelica did not think of herself as capable of getting good grades and doing well in school. She says, "I used to hear that Mexicans are dumb or don't care about education, so I started to believe that" (interview, 2008). After studying the history of Mexican and Mexican American people in multicultural studies classes and the group Movement of Chicano Students of Aztlán, however, she learned about her ancestors' accomplishments and how smart they were. This began to change how she thought of her own educational and intellectual potential. Angelica saw their accomplishments as evidence that she could be one of them, that she "could be smart, too." When asked what fostered this shift in her academic identity, she said, "[learning this history allowed me] just to know that I can do something . . . to know that I can be smart, and do something for myself." Linked to this is a sense of ethnic pride that comes from understanding a nondominant version of history and having this history socially and institutionally validated. This requires studying the historical and contemporary experiences of Mexican Americans, including migration, immigration, colonization, indigenous ancestry, and being a person of color in racialized American society.

A significant feature of the SJEP class curriculum is that it includes political and social theory, poetry, and books by and about Mexican or Mexican American people. Students read the poems "I Am Joaquin" by Rodolfo Corky Gonzales and "Seekin' the Cause" by Miguel Piñero; readings by Daniel Solórzano and Tara Yosso on critical race theory; Paulo Freire's *Pedagogy of the Oppressed*; and sections of Howard Zinn's *Declarations of Independence*, including those on American ideology and law and justice. Through teaching personal stories (through poetry, literature, and music) alongside political critique and political theory, teachers work hard to illustrate for students how personal stories are political. For some students, reading Mexican and border-region history has a greater impact on them; for others, it is literature about Mexican-heritage people in the United States that allows them to "see themselves" (Luciana, interview, 2007) in their class work for the first time. In both cases, school subject matter that students identify as being about them, their families, and their communities' history allows students to engage elements of their ethnic and cultural identity that are generally disregarded in school.

Distinctive elements of Guerrera's classes are his incorporation of frank discussions about cultural traits in Mexican American communities both as generalization and that many students can see directly in their families and communities. For example, he said, "Traditionally, Mexican people are conservative people [in that] we respect authority and respect tradition. . . . We are taught not to ask too many questions and to follow the rules of government and religion" (field notes, December 2008). Discussions about Mexican-heritage conservatism help students to understand decisions made in their families and communities; when students describe how their own parents are conservative, they are able to recognize the advantages and disadvantages of those traditions. Many students come to recognize patterns of chauvinism and sexism in their own families, for example, and ultimately to connect those patterns to opportunities they experience themselves.

Guerrera also discusses the economic marginalization that Latina/o people have experienced in the United States. He identifies it as growing out of racist discrimination and as contributing to destructive patterns in Latina/o neighborhoods, including drug use, gangs, and domestic violence. Class discussions and assignments demonstrate to students that these patterns are symptoms of economic marginalization that span all racial and ethnic categories, countering stereotypes that they are characteristic of Latina/o people. This concept is pivotal for many students, who admit that they often came to believe that issues of domestic violence, racism, chauvinism, and complications with law enforcement are characteristic of Mexican-heritage people rather than of the economic marginalization they so often experience.

He explains how the anti-Mexican climate in Arizona affects how young Latinas/os see themselves and their communities and how he tries to help students understand this situation through the class:

> You have to reconcile some ugly things, some ugly things that have happened in our life, or things that you don't like about yourself. And that's part of that social or historical trauma. Especially here [in the Southwest] Mexican kids need to rehumanize themselves with all the psychological violence that's directed toward them with the "speak English only" mentality, the idea that because we border Mexico that that is ugly and this is good. . . . That just permeates society here, and people breathe it and they act in that way. So I think it's very important for people to wrestle with that rehumanization process, that struggle. (Guerrera, interview, 2008)

He talks with students about what it means to be Mexican and how Mexican families and communities have coped with the social and historical trauma they face. This includes positive and negative things; he talks about Mexican people being more family oriented and also about patterns of domestic violence. He talks about the sacrifices parents and adults make for children, and also the sexism that women and girls face inside their own homes. He wants them to understand that they have the power to change these patterns, to humanize themselves and other people through their own everyday actions.

Humanization and Reconciliation among Students

Diego de la Garza was a senior at Tierra High who embraced the SJEP class because it addressed many conflicts in his life. Diego struggled to understand his own and others' counterproductive actions that led to involvement in the corrections system. As he struggled to identify constructive ways of understanding his difficult social conditions, Diego found that his SJEP class addressed these realities head on. Diego described how his SJEP teacher distinguished himself by demonstrating genuine care for his students: "You're never going to find a teacher that'll give you their house number, their cell phone number. 'Hey this is where I live. Come over for barbecue or if you ever need some help.' Like I got in trouble and I was thinking about calling Mr. Guerrera because I had no one else to talk to. I had no one else to call. So you never . . . you'll never ever see that, ever, in different places" (interview, 2007).

For students who, like Diego, have faced struggles outside of school, the support and respect they find in SJEP classrooms has an especially strong impact. Diego had difficult experiences in his family, encounters with law enforcement, and some drug use that troubled him. As a young child in Arizona, Diego had primarily spoken Spanish and was proud of his Mexican heritage. As he spent more time in school, however, he learned that being Mexican was something to be ashamed of. He stopped speaking Spanish, changed his clothing style, and stopped hanging out with kids identified as "too Mexican." He became increasingly alienated in school and says that, as a result, he never read a book before senior year in his SJEP class.

For Diego, the SJEP curriculum on the historical and economic experiences of Mexican people had a profound impact on his view of his own life and family: "Guerrera, the way he teaches, he makes it very [relevant] and you could relate to it a lot. . . . And learning about your parents' struggles, you never hear about that, ever.[4] So it was like a newfound respect that I had for my family and my culture. And in other classes you won't talk about your history and go deep into Mexican American history because I would like to know where my mom came from and not what happened in Spain at a certain year" (interview, 2007).

Diego has also experienced a great deal of conflict about his racial and ethnic heritage. He described himself as having "hostility" for many years toward being Mexican and speaking Spanish. He reported, "When I started school, I tried very hard to lose my accent, to not make friends who speak Spanish, to speak perfectly in English." He sought to distance himself from his own Mexicanness.

The class curriculum helped Diego to reconcile aspects of his life and family that had previously caused him grief. He was particularly affected by the topic of "self-hate," which Guerrera discussed with the class as occurring when marginalized people come to internalize negative social perceptions about their own group and subsequently seek to minimize their affiliation with that group. While participating in a summer internship, Diego insisted on studying self-hate, in spite of being asked to change topics so that another student would not have to work alone. Without going into detail about his reasons, he insisted that self-hate was what he should study.

Students who feel conflicted about their background gain a great deal from understanding elements of their ethnic heritage. Diego described how such realizations can affect students who have previously struggled with these experiences:

> I think . . . the program was really successful . . . because of just relating to the students, and how they live and the struggle they go through like every single day. 'Cause there's no book in history in American history or anything that talks about like why you got beat when you were little, or . . . like why you decided to get into drugs. Or things like that . . . and the things we see or the things we become victims of. And then in juvi they teach you to blame yourself and "Why did you get there?" When it's really not yourself, it had nothing to do with what you did. It's just the way you were put there and the plan that someone already had made out for you. (interview, 2007)

This does not mean that Diego does not accept social responsibility for his own actions, as evidenced by his commitment to identifying a career that will help other young people he describes as "younger kids in trouble or some kind of need of help." But the SJEP class gave Diego and other students the chance to see the actions of their families and themselves as not simply the bad decisions of individuals; instead, they studied the historical factors associated with people—of all races and ethnicities—engaging in detrimental actions.

Humanization as Respect and Tolerance

Students in SJEP classes also demonstrate some significant shifts in what they think it means to respect people and treat others well. They often describe this as being "conscious," recognizing the common humanity in all people and beginning with an assumption of respect toward other people. This is slightly different, in students' discourse, from the notion of critical consciousness and its main concern with institutional patterns. But it is because of students' increasing understanding of institutional racism and critical consciousness—augmented by indigenous theory—that they think of all people as deserving respect. This exemplifies the way that indigenous theory and a Freirean notion of humanization complement other aspects of the class in affecting students' perspectives.

Alejandro described the SJEP class as helping him to gain a stronger understanding of how dehumanizing language and stereotypes pervade the words and actions of even people who think of themselves as resisting destructive social stereotypes. He said, "These classes enlighten us and encourage us to fight for our rights and against what seems unjust in a peaceful way." When I interviewed him about his experience in the class, he said that the language Guerrera used helped him to understand how he unknowingly participated in dehumanizing acts:

CC: Do you think about stereotypes of people based on their race? Did you think about that before this class?

ALEJANDRO: Well, stereotypes [are], like, things you automatically think about even if you don't believe in them, even if it is just as a joke. Or even if you don't want to think about it, since you hear them so much, you are forced to not necessarily believe them but just think of them. Like when you're saying I'm Mexican, if you say, "Describe him," "Oh, he's lazy or oh, he's illegal." You don't necessarily believe them, but they just come to your mind.

CC: Like, you think about that as a generalization, but when you actually meet an individual person, do you think that you still have those stereotypes?

ALEJANDRO: Like, for me, I don't consider [that] I stereotype people but I think of stereotypes all the time because a lot of my friends are always saying stuff. I'm always telling them, like, "Stop," but it still stays with me. When I see someone describing it, it just comes to your mind.

CC: We all do that, but as Mr. Guerrera says, you just check yourself.

ALEJANDRO: Yeah, that is what I try to do.

CC: Do you think that the SJEP class has helped you think about that differently?

ALEJANDRO: Yeah. Like, I try not to think about it and now I try to see the better things in a person instead of the bad things. (interview, 2008)

Alejandro is demonstrating the type of thinking Guerrera most cares about instilling in students: compassion and consciousness toward others, in thought and action. This is not necessarily a demonstration of critical consciousness; Alejandro talks about racism, sexism, and privilege without making explicit connections to institutions. Yet he articulates the SJEP classroom discourse about viewing people in humanizing ways, which he attributes to Mr. Guerrera's teaching.

The journey toward humanization can be difficult, since students are often surrounded by friends and family who do not subscribe to these "enlightened" views about people of different races and ethnicities. Guerrera repeatedly reminds students that they must never treat anyone with disrespect regardless of their views, especially their parents. But he also acknowledges that many people may not understand ideas about humanization since they have not participated in the SJEP: "What we have to do is be very humble.... Like your parents; your parents aren't privy to what we study here" so must not be judged for making statements that do not reflect SJEP principles of justice.

Javier provided a thoughtful description of both the process of learning to "be a good human being" and also navigating this transition alongside his parents, who have conservative and sometimes problematic views:

> Before I went to this class, I didn't even know what conservative or liberal was, so I basically was conservative. And now that I learned all that, and I see a person doing something, I know that it is conservative. Maybe if it is wrong, I tell them to change. Let's say my parents—they say a lot of conservative stuff. I used to not know nothing about that, so I would just keep listening, you know. They would say stuff about "yeah, gringos" and stuff like that. And now, like, I talk to them. Tell them what I learned here and tell them why it is wrong. (interview, 2008)

He reports that his parents are receptive when he points out that their statements are disrespectful, and that they are able to discuss the ideas he learns in class in a respectful and constructive way.

Cristina: How Mexican?

Cristina is third generation, but identifies as Mexican American. She does not, however, speak Spanish, a difficult situation for a Mexican person in Arizona. During the class, a classmate may say something in Spanish and no translation is given. Cristina is visibly self-conscious about not understanding, often looking exasperated. She wants to be a part of the class and is frustrated at her inability to understand, even more than non-Spanish-speaking students or guests in the room.

Cristina's conflict about her Mexican identity is also illustrated in one of her field notes. She described Mexican people speaking to her in Spanish at work. When she told them she does not speak Spanish, their incredulity caused her great pain, which she wrote about with candor and insight:

> It was on a Sunday morning at work. I was helping some customers find their shoe sizes that they needed when a Mexican man walked up to me. He looks much older. When he approached me he started speaking to me in Spanish and I said, "I'm sorry. I don't speak Spanish." Then in English he said, "Aren't you Mexican![?]" And he said it very rude. I just shrugged and kind of gave him a smirk. When I started to think about it I thought to myself, "Just because I'm Mexican doesn't mean I have to speak Spanish!" The rest of that day I felt very upset and rebellious, like I was mad at every Spanish-speaking person that would come in. I'm not sure why it would make me so upset. . . . But now every time a customer asks me if I speak Spanish I say, "No!" And I do say it kind of rude. Yeah, I feel bad but my emotions take over. (field note, 2008)

This reflective field note documents her understanding of her own sensitivity to the accusation that she is failing to fulfill what it means to be Mexican by being a monolingual English speaker, which places in question her Mexican identity.

Guerrera explicitly discussed this issue in class, including the degree to which identity is not about the languages one speaks, one's surname, or how one looks. He provided students with information about immigration and the social climate many immigrants faced upon arrival in the United States as affecting how families assimilated and maintained ties to their traditions. He detailed vast differences in how immigrants elected to or were able to pass on elements of Mexican culture to their children and grandchildren. Cristina was able to see the story of her family in this history; she saw how Mexican people who came here at a particular phase in history were less likely to speak Spanish in their homes. This connection between history, politics, and her own story helped her make the statement "Just because I am Mexican doesn't mean I have to speak Spanish!" even as she struggled with defensiveness about this circumstance.

Ultimately, Cristina began to reconcile this conflict about her identity. At the end of the school year, she described how she could envision herself in solidarity with other people of color:

> CC: I know we talk a lot about being Mexican and Mexican heritage; do you think differently about your heritage after taking this class?
>
> CRISTINA: Um, I don't. I feel . . . I probably feel . . . stronger. Basically, like I keep saying, just speak myself, 'cause there's so many other people out there that are minorities that don't speak. So if somebody does, it makes a whole difference. I don't think it's changed really.
>
> CC: So you think if you have one person who speaks up for everyone else who's of that minority, then . . .
>
> CRISTINA: Then they'll get courage, somehow. To speak up for themselves. (interview, 2008)

She has begun to reframe how she understands her Mexican identity, from something she must demonstrate as a status marker to an instrument for unity and connection with other people. This unity is fostered not by "cultural traits" such as speaking a common language, but by the solidarity that can be forged, and the courage that she can foster in other people through her actions.[5] This is possible because the curriculum provides multiple ways for students to engage in processes of humanization.

Conclusion: Countering Alienation through Strategies for Resilience

For the program designers as well as the teachers, SJEP students' historical, social, and political study places them at a disadvantage (Romero, interview, 2007; Cammarota, interview, 2008; Guererra, interview, 2008).

The purpose of the class is to equip them with strategies and knowledge to increase their resiliency in an unjust world. A crucial aspect of this resiliency is to come to see themselves not as passive objects of natural or impervious social realities. Rather, the class curriculum and pedagogy endeavor to arm students with a sense of themselves as sociohistorical actors oriented toward recognizing the underlying political, economic, and social forces that shape their lives, and cognizant of their own capacity to have an effect on their society in turn.

Critical pedagogy provides a foundation. For students with a stable ethnic identity (most often more recent immigrants who speak Spanish and articulate their Mexican identity more clearly), this concept is eye-opening. For students who begin the program with a conflicted ethnic identity, developing a critical consciousness can lead to frustration. They learn to see the world differently but may not have a way of understanding their place in the world differently. They can see injustice but do not always see a clear path toward action. Freire and the SJEP argue that seeing a way to make change is crucial, but alienation and internalized oppression may inhibit the emerging social agency of students with a conflicted ethnic identity.

Through the additional component of indigenous theory, students gain a framework for envisioning concrete ways they can take positive action in the world every day, as well as for constructing an ethnic identity that minimizes the effects of anti-Mexican ideology. Diego and Cristina are not only learning to view the world in a political and sociohistorical context; they are also learning to understand their own identities as the products of history and ongoing political ideology. Only after understanding this are they able to respect and affirm all the facets of their own identities—as well as those of other people.

As students learn about and apply a critical eye to the history of their families and communities, they may reconcile and strengthen their ethnic identities. As they understand the institutionalized patterns of marginalization in schools and society, they may achieve in those contexts in spite of the disadvantages imposed on them. And as they recognize the effects of individual and collective action in shaping opportunities and advantages for themselves and their families, they may come to view themselves as powerful social actors. It is only when students have the opportunity to frame their lives in a historical and political context that they can come to see themselves as capable of affecting change as well.

Notes

1. Many aspects of the SJEP described here were also part of the Mexican American Raza Studies program in TUSD more generally. See Acosta, 2007; Cabrera et al., 2013; Cambium Learning, Inc., 2011; and National Education Association, 2011 for more information on that broader program.
2. Pseudonyms are used for all teachers and students involved in the program.
3. Guerrera also discusses other forms of marginalization and discrimination, including sexism, homophobia, and discrimination based on religious beliefs; race and economics are the most relevant for this discussion.
4. The direct quote from this interview is "he makes it very . . . relative," with hesitation before the word "relative"; however, I believe he meant "relevant," because of this hesitation and because he mentioned being able to "relate" to the class no fewer than eight times during this interview. So I have substituted "relevant" here, in brackets, for clarity of meaning.
5. Common "cultural traits" are difficult to identify and subject to many considerations (Cammarota and Fine 2008, 10). I put this term in quotation marks to indicate awareness of the tensions surrounding this concept.

References

Acosta, C. 2007. "Developing Critical Consciousness: Resistance Literature in a Chicano Literature Class." *English Journal* 97(2): 36–42.
Cabrera, N., E. Meza, A. Romero, and R. Rodriguez. 2013. "'If There Is No Struggle, There Is No Progress': Transformative Youth Activism and the School of Ethnic Studies." *Urban Review: Issues and Ideas in Public Education* 45(1): 7–22.
Cambium Learning, Inc. 2011. Curriculum Audit of the Mexican American Studies Department, Tucson Unified School District. Miami Lakes, FL: T. Casteel, G. Gilsean, and G. Faulkner.
Cammarota, J., and A. Romero. 2006. "A Critically Compassionate Pedagogy for Latino Youth." *Latino Studies* 4(3): 305–12.
Cammarota, J., and M. Fine. 2008. "Youth Participatory Action Research: A Pedagogy for Transformational Resistance." In *Revolutionizing Education*, ed. J. Cammarota and M. Fine, 1–11. New York: Routledge.
Freire, P. 1973. *Education for Critical Consciousness*. New York: Continuum.
———. 1993. *Pedagogy of the Oppressed*, trans. M. B. Ramos. New York: Continuum.
Freire, P., and D. Macedo. 1987. *Literacy: Reading the Word and the World*. New York: Bergin and Garvey.
Gee, J. P. 1997. Foreword. In *Changing Literacies*, ed. C. Lankshear. Philadelphia: Open University Press.
Hull, G. 1993. "Critical Literacy and Beyond: Lessons Learned from Students and Workers in a Vocational Program and on the Job." *Anthropology and Education Quarterly* 24(4): 373–96.

Morrell, E. 2002. "Toward a Critical Pedagogy of Popular Culture: Literacy Development among Urban Youth." *Journal of Adolescent and Adult Literacy* 46(1): 72–77.

Morrell, E., and J. Duncan-Andrade. 2004. "What They Do Learn in School: Hip-Hop as a Bridge to Canonical Poetry." In *What They Don't Learn in School: Literacy in the Lives of Urban Youth*, ed. J. Mahiri, 247–68. New York: Peter Lang.

National Education Association. (2011). The Academic and Social Value of Ethnic Studies: A Research Review. Washington, DC: C. Sleeter.

Romero, A. 2008. "Towards a Critically Compassionate Intellectualism Model of Transformative Urban Education." PhD diss., University of Arizona.

Stauber, L. 2012. "Chicanismo in the New Generation: 'Youth, Identity, Power' in the 21st Century Borderlands." PhD diss., University of Arizona.

Valenzuela, A. 1999. *Subtractive Schooling: U.S.-Mexican Youth and the Politics of Caring*. Albany: State University of New York Press.

Contributors

Nolan L. Cabrera, PhD, is an assistant professor in the Center for the Study of Higher Education at the University of Arizona. His scholarship focuses on whiteness formation, Latina/o college students, and racism in higher education. Dr. Cabrera's articles have appeared in the *Review of Higher Education, Journal of Latinos and Education, Journal of Higher Education, Research in Higher Education, Phi Delta Kappan,* and the *Hispanic Journal of Behavioral Sciences.* He is also coauthor of the monograph, *Advancing in Higher Education: A Portrait of Latino College Students Entering Four Year Institutions, 1975–2006.*

Julio Cammarota is an associate professor of Mexican American studies at the University of Arizona. His research focuses on participatory action research with Latina/o youth, institutional factors in academic achievement, and liberatory pedagogy. He has published articles on family, work, and education among Latinas/os and on the relationship between culture and academic achievement. He is the coeditor of two volumes in the Critical Youth Studies series published by Routledge/Falmer Press: *Beyond Resistance! Youth Activism and Community Change: New Democratic Possibilities for Practice and Policy for America's Youth* (2006) and *Revolutionizing Education: Youth Participatory Action Research in Motion* (2008). Dr. Cammarota has published an ethnography of Latina/o youth, *Sueños Americanos: Barrio Youth Negotiate Social and Cultural Identities* (University of Arizona Press, 2008). His work has been instrumental in advancing social justice in education and youth development. Currently, he is the codirector of the Social Justice Education Project in Tucson, Arizona.

Chiara Cannella, PhD, is an assistant professor of teacher education at Fort Lewis College. Her work focuses on cultural diversity in education as well as sociocultural perspectives on education. Her research addresses education for marginalized students, and she has done participatory and community-based action research in schools, engaging students' civic and social activism in disenfranchised communities.

Mary Carol Combs is a professor of practice in the Department of Teaching, Learning, and Sociocultural Studies, University of Arizona. She teaches graduate and undergraduate courses in bilingual and ESL education, sheltered content instruction and ESL methods, indigenous language revitalization, and language policy and planning. Her research interests include bilingual education policy and law, sociocultural theory, indigenous language revitalization and development, immigration and education, and bilingual and English language learner teacher preparation. She is the coauthor, with Carlos Ovando, of *Bilingual and ESL Classroom*, 5th ed. (McGraw-Hill, 2012) and has authored numerous articles and book chapters on Arizona's language policies.

Lara dos Passos Coggin, PhD, joined the Focused Inquiry faculty in the fall of 2012. She conducted her doctoral course work and research in the Department of Teaching, Learning, and Sociocultural Studies, part of the University of Arizona's College of Education. Her mixed-methods study on the 2009 and 2010 Institutes for Transformative Education explored participants' ideas about race, class, and culture in education, and the ways in which the institute fostered transformative learning for them. Created by Tucson Unified School District's Mexican American Studies Department, the institutes have been discontinued, under immense pressure from the state of Arizona. Dr. Coggin also holds a master's degree in Native American linguistics with an emphasis on Navajo grammar, a master's degree in American Indian studies, and a bachelor's degree in anthropology.

Jeff Duncan-Andrade, PhD, is associate professor of raza studies and education at San Francisco State University and director of the Educational Equity Initiative at the Institute for Sustainable Economic, Educational, and Environmental Design. In addition to these duties, he continues as a high school teacher in East Oakland, where for the past twenty years he has practiced and studied the use of critical pedagogy in urban schools (see www.rosesinconcrete.org). Duncan-Andrade has lectured around the world about the elements of effective teaching in schools serving poor and working-class children. He has authored two books and numerous journal articles and book chapters on the conditions of urban education, urban teacher support and development, and effective pedagogy in urban settings.

Anna Ochoa O'Leary, PhD, is an assistant professor in Mexican American studies at the University of Arizona, and codirector of the Binational Migration Institute at the University of Arizona. She is a 2006 Garcia-Robles Fulbright scholar for research on repatriated and deported migrant women on the US-Mexico border, and author of numerous journal articles on the topic of immigrant women and Latina/o education. She has developed a textbook, *Chicano Studies: The Discipline and the Journey* (Kendall-Hunt, 2007), and is editing a two-volume work, *Undocumented Immigrants in the United States Today: An Encyclopedia of Their Experience* (ABC-CLIO, forthcoming in 2014), and coediting a book on border research methods and ethics, *Unchartered Terrain: New Directions in Border Research Method and Ethics* (University of Arizona Press, 2013).

Andrea J. Romero, PhD, is an associate professor with joint appointments in family studies and human development and Mexican American studies at the University of Arizona. She has affiliated positions in the psychology department, Latin American studies, gender and women's studies, and public health. She received her doctorate in social psychology from the University of Houston in 1997 with a minor in quantitative methods. Dr. Romero's research has made a significant contribution to the theoretical and empirical measurement of the resilience of teens faced with bicultural, family, policy, and neighborhood stress. Her work is inspired by current social issues of adolescent health (including high rates of depression, suicide attempts, and bullying, and the political climate). Her research demonstrates that although discrimination can increase stress and has a negative impact on adolescent mental health and risky behaviors, adolescents with a strong ethnic identity and strong civic engagement seem to fare better. Dr. Romero has also found that stronger family values are associated with more parental monitoring and fewer risky behaviors among Latino adolescents. A central element of Dr. Romero's research approach to ending health disparities is participatory action research, which is done in dialogue and collaboration with community members. Dr. Romero has received federally funded grants to conduct research on substance use and HIV prevention programs for middle school–age Latino adolescents. She is currently associate editor for the *Journal of Latino/a Psychology*.

Augustine Romero, PhD, is Tucson Unified School District's director of student equity, cofounder of the Social Justice Education Project, and the architect and founder of TUSD's Mexican American studies program. Dr. Romero created the critically compassionate intellectualism model of transformative education, which has led to greatly increased academic achievement, graduation rates, and college matriculation rates for its students. It has been recognized internationally as a model of effective transformative education.

David Stovall, PhD, is associate professor of educational policy studies and African American studies at the University of Illinois at Chicago. His scholarship investigates four areas: (1) critical race theory, (2) concepts of social justice in education, (3) the relationship between housing and education, and (4) the relationship between schools and community stakeholders. In the attempt to transform theory into action, he has spent the last ten years working with community organizations and schools to develop curricula that address issues of social justice. This work has led him to become a member of the Greater Lawndale/Little Village School of Social Justice High School design team, which opened in the fall of 2005. Furthering his work with communities, students, and teachers, Stovall is involved with youth-centered community organizations in Chicago, New York, and the Bay Area. He also serves as a volunteer social studies teacher at the Greater Lawndale/Little Village School of Social Justice.

Index

ability tracking: racial and educational disparities and, 112–13
Advanced Placement (AP) courses: class size and level of teacher professional training in, 47; entrance requirements for, 48–49
Allen, Sylvia: Arizona state senator, 66–67
Alvarez v. Lemon Grove (1931), 54
A Nation at Risk: The Imperative for Educational Reform, 146
Angelou, Maya, 111
anti-ethnic studies legislation, 53
Arizona Citizenship Bill: as a challenge to US Constitution, 66
Arizona Department of Education (ADE), 68
Arizona Education Association, 76
Arizona English Language Learner Assessment (AZELLA), 68–69; manipulation of scores and, 83
Arizona Instrument to Measure Standards (AIMS): exit exam for state's high school students, 42; achievement gap AIMS between MAS and non-MAS students; between very low, medium and high income students, 43; rates of improvement between MAS and non-MAS students, 44–45; positive effect of SJEP participation on Mexican American students passing test, 132
Arizona official state gun, 64
Arizona Senate Concurrent Resolution 1010: prohibiting courts from considering international law, 67

Arizona state legislature: political and generational makeup of, 80; racial and gender makeup of, 80–81
ARS (Arizona Revised Statute) 15-112(A): and suspension of SJEP classes, 120n1, 126
Aztec calendar, 175

Baja Arizona, 67
Baldenegro, Salomón, 54, 58
banking education: concept of Paulo Freire, 117
barrio pedagogy, 28
Brewer, Jan: Arizona governor, 56; signing of HB 2281 by, 61; stance against federal regulation of the state's immigration policy, 146
Brown v. Board of Education US Supreme Court decision (1954), 54; overturning separate but equal education regarding race, 167; "*Brown* at 50" 2004 publication of UCLA Civil Rights Project, 169n7

Calpulli Teoxicalli, 60
Cambium Learning Incorporated: audit of TUSD's MAS program by, 57
Castillo, Guadalupe (Lupe), 54, 58
Center for Epidemiologic Studies–Depression Scale (CES-D), 98
Chicana/o movement: and civic engagement and ethnic identity, 94
Chicana/o studies: fortieth anniversary of, 94

197

Chicano movement and demand for Chicano studies, 54
Church of San Agustín: as symbol of community cooperation in Tucson's Mexican American community in nineteenth century, 150
Civil Rights Project: UCLA project critical of Arizona's ELD program, 86n13
conscientization and authentic liberation through pedagogy, 175
counternarratives and counterstories: defined, 16
critical consciousness building exercises, 20
critical literacy: defined, 6; Freirean concept of, 173
critically compassionate intellectualism (CCI), 15–36; model of transformative education, 18 table 1.1; tridimensionalized model of, 19
critical multicultural education, 142
critical race theory (CRT), 15; and Chicano studies as analytical lenses, 111
cultural capital, 22
"cultural deficits" theory and Latina/o families: SJEP rejection of, 123
cultural generation gap: ideological divide, 80; relation to age and ethnicity, 80; US Metropolitan areas with largest gap, 80 table 4.5

Discrete Skills Inventory (DSI), 71; designed as "sequential series of English language skills," 74–76
Dominguez, Kim, xx, 38
Dugan, Margaret: Arizona Deputy Superintendent of Public Instruction, 143
Dupnik, Clarence: Pima County Sheriff, 65; refusal to enforce SB 1070 (racial profiling law), 65

educational funding in Arizona: low rank of, 147; as a violation of state constitution, 147

Eisenhower Professional Development Program, 141–42
Elías, Richard: Pima County Supervisor, 137; as presenter at Institute for Transformative Education, 155
Encuentros: tightening social bonds through, 122; forums for student research presentations to parents, teachers and community members, 122–24; as "funds of knowledge," 128; building trust through, 131; student academic identities and, 131
engaged and disengaged coping: between ethnic groups, 101; ethnic identity and, 101–5
English Language Development program (ELD): also known as "Language Star," 69, 69 fig. 4.1, 71; four-hour daily block of, 72; explicit time allocations of, 73
English Language Learners (ELLs): education of; public discourse on, 63; political concerns about, 64; Arizona education policies on as a reaction to demographic shifts, 64, 68; under-identification of, 83
English Language Learner Task Force, 82; and defense of four-hour ELD block, 84; listing of members of, 87n18
ethnic group differences: regarding stress, coping responses, self esteem and civic engagement, 99–105
Euro-American cultural bias, 125

Flores v. Arizona: and Equal Educational Opportunity Act, 82
"Four Tables" exercise, 23
Freire, Paulo: theory of Critically Compassionate Intellectualism (CCI), xviii; author of *Pedagogy of the Oppressed*, 3; background and theories of, 4–8; Freirean approaches, 11; generative works and themes methodology, 111; banking education theory of vs. problem-posing pedagogy of, 117–18

funds of knowledge: use of with SJEP Encuentros, 122–34; theory and practice of, 124

Giffords, Gabrielle, 64
Goddard, Terry: former state attorney general and Arizona gubernatorial candidate, 148
Gonzales, Rodolfo "Corky": Chicano activist and author of poem *Yo Soy Joaquín*, 111
Grijalva, Adelita, xx
Grijalva, Raúl, 54
Guevara, Che, 3, 10

HB 2064: law requiring students to learn English in one year, 71; public discourse and, 85
HB 2177: bill to require presidential candidates on Arizona ballots to produce proof of US citizenship, 66
HB 2281: Arizona legislative bill abolishing TUSD's MAS program that became law as Arizona Revised Statute (ARS) 15–112, 52; major points of law, 57; constitutionality challenged in court by raza studies teachers, 143
Hernandez, Liz, 38
Horne, Tom: Arizona attorney general and former superintendent of public instruction, 55; testimony before Arizona Senate's Education Committee, 55; views on bilingual education, 76; threatens to cut TUSD's MAS funding, 143; view that ethnic studies would lead to depression in students, 162
Huitzilopochtli: indigenous framework defined, 30
humanization and reconciliation among students, 183–84
Huppenthal, John: Arizona superintendent of public instruction, 3, 56–57

"I Am" poems exercise, 23–24
indigenous theory in the SJEP, 174

Individual Language Learner Plan (ILLP): described, 72
Institute for Transformative Education: hosted by TUSD's Raza Studies department, 135; increase in diversity of attendees and presenters at, 136; 2008 and 2009 presenters noted, 136–37; central principles of, 137; sample daily schedule of, 137; differences between traditional teacher professional development programs and, 140; struggle to prove legitimacy and maintain funding after 2011, 143; as "inappropriate influence" on minors, 146
institutional racism, 172, 185
internalized racism, 172
interschool tracking, 115–18
intraschool tracking: and student reaction to, 112–15

Jefferson, Thomas, 162

Kalpulli Teocalli: Aztec group, 137
King, Martin Luther Jr, 17

Likert Scale: use of with civic engagement questionnaire, 96

Maricopa and Pima counties (Arizona): size of populations in, 80; strength of Democratic and Republican parties in, 81
Marx, Karl, 3, 10
Mendez v. Westminster (1947), 54
Mexican American Studies (MAS) in TUSD: banning of through state legislation, 3; summer Institute for Transformative Education and, 136; TUSD school board vote on halting of, 171
Mexican-descent students: as majority in TUSD, 162
Montes, Felicia, 137
Movimiento Estudiantil Chicano de Aztlán (Movement of Chicano Students of Aztlán or MEChA):

Movimiento Estudiantil (*Continued*)
prohibiting of by Arizona SB 1069,
91–92; historic Denver conference and
origin of Chicana/o studies, 93
multicultural Education. *See* Critical
Multicultural Education
Multigroup Ethnic Identity Measure,
97–98

Nahui Ollin, 175; names and meanings
of, 176
Napolitano, Janet: former Arizona
governor, 59; and Latino Advisory
Board, 59; becomes director of
US Department of Homeland
Security, 148
National Geographic Alliance on
Primary Sources: teacher professional
development seminar, 141
Native American students in Arizona
schools: large population of, 148;
invisible status of, 148

Obama, Barack, 66
Olivas, Eduardo, 54
Olmeca: community educator and
artist, 137
organic intellectualism: as aspect of
Critically Compassionate
Intellectualism, 19–34
Orwell, George: author of the
novel *1984*, origin of the term
"doublethink," 160
Otero, Lydia, author of history on
Tucson's barrios and urban renewal,
149–50

panche bé: meaning of, 176
Pearce, Russell, Republican lawmaker,
65; anti-immigrant stance of, 94;
voting record on education and
immigration, 147–48
Pedicone, John: TUSD Superintendent,
155
Piñero, Miguel, 181
Plessy v. Ferguson: US Supreme Court
1896 decision affirming "separate but
equal" educational policy with regard
to race, 167
Plyer v. Doe: US Supreme Court
decision, 79, 87n14
praxis: defined, 6; achieving intent and
goal of, 111
problematization, 28; process and four
phases of, 30
problem-posing pedagogy: and student
preference for, 117–18
"Procrustean bed" metaphor, 68
Proposition 203: 2000 ballot initiative
replacing bilingual education with
English immersion teaching method,
82; public discourse and, 85
protective enhancing: as unique form of
resilience, 105

Quetzalcoatl, x, 176, 178

racist movements of the right, 21
Ramirez, Grecia, 38
Redemptive Remembering, 152
resistance theory, 22
Roll, John, 64
Romero, Augustine: founder and
organizer of Institute for
Transformative Education, quoted,
138–39
Rubio-Goldsmith, Raquel, 58
Ruiz, Jesus "Chucho," 60

Save Ethnic Studies: pro-MAS group, 61;
filing of lawsuit challenging
constitutionality of AZ HB 2281, 61;
protests by, 79
SB 1069: Arizona legislative bill
prohibiting classes promoting
ethnic solidarity, 56; language of,
56; and prohibiting of student group
MEChA, 91–92; as earlier version of
SB 1108, 93
SB 1070: Arizona law allowing the
apprehension of individuals on the
basis of "reasonable suspicion" that the
individual is undocumented, 65; racial
profiling and, 78; parts of declared

unconstitutional, 78; *Arizona Republic* poll of registered voters and, 81; criminalization of the undocumented and, 132
SB 1108: Arizona State Senate bill, 3; prohibiting use of any curriculum centered on race, 55; Latina/o student stress due to, 92, 96; later version of SB 1069, 93; threatens Chicana/o studies on its fortieth anniversary, 94; and US Homeland Security, 94; student coping strategies for, 97; differences in responses to by non-Latino whites and Mexican-descent students, 101
SB 1433: Nullification of federal law bill, 66–67
Sleeter, Christine, 142
social capital, 23; theory of, 113
Social Justice Education Project (SJEP), 15; SJEP model, 33; creation and primary intent of, 34; social science program of and alignment with state-mandated standards, 110; Chicano studies concepts in, 111; and Encuentros, 122; evaluation of its Youth Participatory Research (YPAR) projects, 126; SJEP students as public intellectuals, 128; student evaluation of, 132; two-year ethnographic case study of, 171; as one component of MAS program; critical pedagogy in, 172
social reproduction theory, 22, 112
Socioeconomic status (SES): academic performance and, 42
sociohistorical contextualization: locating students life experiences within, 179–82
standardized test scores: correlation of high scores and affluence, race, 40; as a measure of race and class, 40; misunderstanding of, 40; MARS students' improved performance and, 163
Stegeman, Mark: as TUSD governing board member, 57; belief that MAS courses should be electives, 57

Structured English Immersion (SEI): as designed by the Arizona Department of Education (ADE), 68; "time on task" or "maximum exposure" principle of learning and, 84
Survey Monkey.com, 95

Tashima, A. Wallace, 61
Tea party, 21; purging of moderate Republicans by, 60; racist politics of, 60
Tello, Jerry, 137
Tezcatlipoca: Chicano epistemological practice of, 22
The Advocate: Arizona Education Association publication, 76
Tucson-Phoenix Equality and Justice Run, 60
Tucson Unified School District (TUSD): Mexican American studies (MAS) department in, 3; primary arguments in favor of, 40; creation of, 54; positive achievement results for students and, 164; seen as sedition by opponents, 164
TUSD 1969 school walkouts, 54, 61n1
TUSD 2010 graduating cohort, 46–47; graduation rate differences between MAS and non-MAS students; effect of Advanced Placement (AP) courses on, 47–48
TUSD's Post Unitary Plan community forums, 112; student takeover of, 112

UNIDOS: student group, 61; take over of TUSD board meeting, 61

Valdez, Luis, 38
"Variables Used to Determine Engaged Coping and Disengagement," 98 table 5.2

xinachtli: meaning of, 19
xipe totec: meaning of, 176

Yoeme and Akimel O'odham Nations: involvement in Tucson-Phoenix Equality and Justice Run, 60 youth participatory action research (YPAR): empowerment of students through, 107–10; participatory nature of, 109; principles of, 109; and critical analysis of social justice problems, 110; as challenge to "traditional social hierarchies," 119; and Encuentros, 122

Zinn, Howard, 169n1, 181